The Truest Heart

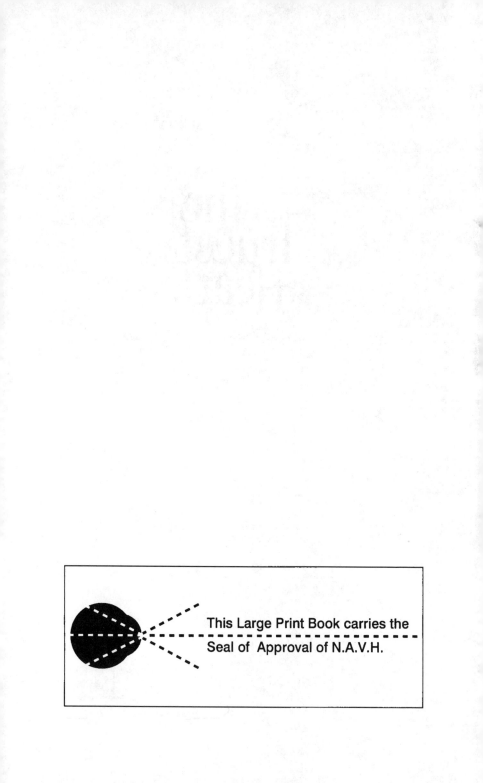

This Large Print Book carries the
Seal of Approval of N.A.V.H.

The Truest Heart

Samantha James

Thorndike Press • Waterville, Maine

Published in 2001 by arrangement with Avon Books,
an imprint of HarperCollins Publishers, Inc.

Thorndike Press Large Print Basic Series.

The tree indicium is a trademark of Thorndike Press.

The text of this Large Print edition is unabridged.
Other aspects of the book may vary from the original edition.

Set in 16 pt. Plantin by Myrna S. Raven.

Printed in the United States on permanent paper.

Library of Congress Cataloging-in-Publication Data

James, Samantha.
    The truest heart / Samantha James.
      p. cm.
    ISBN 0-7862-3700-7 (lg. print : hc : alk. paper)
    1. Great Britain — History — John, 1199–1216 —
Fiction. 2. Cornwall (England : County) — Fiction.
  3. Large type books. I. Title.
PS3560.A395 T78 2001
  813'.54—dc21
                                    2001047348

FICTION

3/02

The
Truest
Heart

Prologue

England
Early October, 1215

"Tell me. What news is there of Ellis of Westerbrook?"

The imperious command came from John, king of England, the youngest of the Devil's brood, as Henry II's rebellious sons had come to be known, for they had been ever and always at odds with their father . . . and with each other.

Gilbert of Lincoln crushed his cap in his hands and stared up into the black-bearded face of his king. Like so many of England's people, he, too, was weary of the king's greed; the grumble of discontent was heard throughout the land. Many of John's barons were outraged by his ceaseless demands to replenish his treasury — that and the call to arms that John might continue his fight to regain his lands across the Channel in Normandy and the Angevin provinces. John had signed the Great Charter in early summer, yet still refused to be humbled. The discord with his barons continued to fester. Indeed, several were so incensed — and so intent upon his demise — that they had hatched a plot to kill him.

'Twas a plot gone sorely awry.

For the arrow loosed upon King John, who had been lured away from his hunting party, had missed its mark when, at the last instant, the king's mount had reared. Instead the arrow hit one of the king's guards who had given chase to seek his errant king. The perpetrator had escaped into the woods, for the forest had been especially dense. It was several weeks later before he was eventually caught and imprisoned. . . .

It was Ellis, lord of Westerbrook.

But there was another, too . . . the wounded guard, afore he breathed his last, had gasped that there were two assailants.

The king's men had immediately taken John far, far away lest there be another attempt. And so 'twas because of this attempted slaying of the king that Gilbert of Lincoln had taken to horse and ridden madcap through the forest and the mud and the dark for nearly two days to reach his king. He was sodden to the skin by the never-ending drizzle, drenched to the very center of his being. His cloak dripped puddles on the rushes strewn beneath his booted feet. Gilbert did not relish the news he was about to impart, for he very much feared the king's mood would soon be as foul as the weather without.

"Aye, sire. I bring news of-of Ellis."

John leaned forward. Ellis, the rogue, had been caught near the Scottish border; John had ordered him taken to Rockwell, his castle nearby. But he had grown impatient with Ellis's refusal to divulge the identity of the other man responsible for the attempt on his life, though Ellis had freely admitted his own guilt.

It had posed a dilemma . . . but not for long. 'Twas plain to see that Ellis was a proud, honorable man, a man of principle. But every man had his weakness, John had reasoned, and even the stoutest back would break before the right persuasion. He'd heard how deeply Ellis loved his children — for that very reason he'd dispatched his men to Westerbrook to seize Ellis's daughter, Gillian, and his young son, Clifton. The king had surmised Ellis would sing like the veriest nightingale when his daughter and son were brought before him with a blade at their throats.

"Well, out with it then! Tell me, for I would know, and I would know now! Ellis has confessed the name of the rogue with whom he conspired to kill me, hasn't he? Who is it then? Who is the other black-guard?"

Gilbert had gone pale. He stole a glance at the other occupants of the room, the king's men Geoffrey Covington and Roger Seymour. Also present was the lord of Sommerfield, for it was at his castle that John had decided to take shelter for the night.

Gilbert locked his knees to still their quavering. If he feared for his life, he could not help it. It was well known indeed that John possessed a vindictive streak. If the king so pleased, he might order his eyes burned out or his nose slit . . . or worse. Many a soul had no doubt that John had done away with his own nephew, Arthur of Brittany, who had disputed John's right to the English throne. Ah, little wonder that Gilbert had not been eager to be the bearer of such news that he would give this night.

The king's questioning left Gilbert damp of palm and sweating at the brow. "I-I do not know, sire," he stammered. "Ellis . . . he confessed nothing of the other man."

John's smile vanished. Thick, bejeweled

fingers drummed against the tabletop, for the king was fond of excess and indulged in many. He scowled his impatience. "By God's teeth! Have I naught but imbeciles to serve me? Why the devil do you come to me, then? Has he escaped?"

"Nay, sire."

"What then?"

Gilbert swallowed. He knew full well that torture had not compelled Ellis to confess. In truth, he shuddered to think what Ellis had endured, for never would he have been so steadfast and unwavering. If all accounts were to be believed, Ellis of Westerbrook had not cried out, not even once. . . .

"He is dead, sire. Ellis is dead."

For one awful moment John said nothing. Then he leaped to his feet, his eyes ablaze.

"Dead? How can that be?"

The king gave Gilbert no chance to respond. "I gave orders that he was to be kept alive," John roared, "alive until his daughter and son were brought to Rockwell and I had returned! By God, who did this? What fool dared disobey me? I vow I will have his head —"

Gilbert spoke up before he lost his own. "You misunderstand, sire. Ellis was not killed, by your men or any other. He died by his own hand. He hung himself in his cell."

11

The king had gone white about the mouth. "What of his son and daughter?" he demanded.

Gilbert's knees had begun to shake anew, for he was aware of John's reputation of cruelty and ruthlessness. "Westerbrook was deserted, sire. Ellis's daughter and son were gone. It seems they fled in the middle of the night . . . along with many of his men."

For the space of a heartbeat the king stared at Gilbert with frightening intensity. He made not a move, nary a sound. Yet his countenance was such that Gilbert felt every drop of blood drain from his face. It spun through his mind that the king in a rage was not a pretty sight. Nay, there was nothing majestic about this man who called himself king of England. His lips drew back over his teeth in a snarl. His dark features were contorted with rage. Although John did not possess the Plantagenet coloring, the fair handsomeness of his brother Richard, Coeur de Lion, upon whose death Henry's last remaining son had come the throne of England, 'twould seem that he did indeed possess the famed Plantagenet temper of his forebears. . . .

Gilbert's mouth opened in a soundless scream. He was convinced that at any moment the king's fiery gaze would surely bore

12

through him, burning him to cinders in the very spot where he stood.

Then all at once John whirled. He stalked from one end of the hearth back to the other. Broad, leather-shod feet kicked the remains of his meal, for about his chair bones were strewn, along with heads of fish and crusts of bread. All the while black curses spewed from his mouth. The blaze of his anger seemed to vibrate and leap from the lofty rafters that spanned the width of the great hall of Sommerfield.

"By God, who does he think he is? No. I'll not be duped by him, by that traitor Ellis!"

The king's men, Lord Geoffrey Covington and Lord Roger Seymour, exchanged troubled glances. It was Geoffrey Covington who slipped from his chair and laid a hand on Gilbert's shoulder. Nodding toward the door, Covington spoke in a low tone. Gilbert was wise enough to bow to Covington's request; quickly he took to his heels, anxious to escape the hall . . . and the king's fury.

Geoffrey Covington remained where he was, one slim leg angled away from the other. The broad sweep of his brow furrowed, as if in consideration. The elder of the king's confidants, Roger Seymour, brushed a hand across his balding pate, then placed his hands on the broad plane of his knees, his expression one of decided consternation. He lowered his gaze, clearly reluctant to interrupt the king's fit of petulance. Covington's gaze had turned keenly observant, his eyes the same rich brown as his hair. Though he was a man of slender proportions, he was nonetheless a man fashioned with wiry strength and fluid, agile movement. As he looped his hands behind his back, the sword strapped to his side caught the light from the fire. He was a man of quiet demeanor, as evidenced by his words to Gilbert and the way he waited patiently for his king's wrath to expire.

At length he cleared his throat. "Sire," he said.

John paid no heed but continued his pacing. "By God, that wretch, Ellis! He thought to best me, to rob me of my revenge. I should have slit his nose. Burned out his eyes. Carved off his ear and sent it to his daughter. Then he would have talked!"

"Sire," Covington said more loudly.

"By God's teeth, he shall not deprive me of my satisfaction! Do you hear, he shall not!"

"Sire, you must calm yourself."

"Calm myself! How the devil can I?" John stormed. "I want it burned. I want

Westerbrook burned to the ground. Seymour, see to it."

Seymour inclined his head. "As you wish, sire."

"He will pay. By God, Ellis will pay. By the robes of Christ, he thought to cheat me, the king of England, of his death — of discovering the identity of the other man who would see me dead. He will not. I tell you, he will not. Ellis of Westerbrook will not cheat me! His treason must be punished."

Covington frowned. "But how, sire? He is already dead. Is that not punishment enough?"

"Nay, not for him!" John ground to a halt. "His children," he pronounced flatly. "They must die."

Covington and Seymour exchanged glances. "But, sire," Seymour said slowly, "the eldest is but a woman, scarcely out of girlhood. The other is but a boy of twelve. Surely they can do you no further harm —"

"It matters not. Ellis's seed will be wiped out. I will do what must be done. She cannot be allowed to bring forth her father's blood. Neither can her brother. Aye, Ellis's seed must be wiped from this earth . . . forever. Only then will I be avenged."

Seymour had gone pale. Even Covington appeared uncomfortable. It was Seymour who spoke. "Sire," he ventured faintly. "You cannot mean to murder them."

"And why not? Did you not hear, Seymour? I want them dead, both of them!"

Seymour placed his hands on the table. He glanced at Covington, then back to John. This time it was Covington who raised a hand.

"Sire, I pray you do not misunderstand me. I . . . we . . . do not question your judgment." Carefully he chose his words. "There are those who still believe you may be responsible for the death of your nephew Arthur, which was deplored by the world. I know — *we* know," he hastened to add, "that you have no knowledge of Arthur's disappearance. But to do away with Ellis's daughter and son would be to risk further condemnation."

By now John had lowered himself into his chair. "Then none will know but those present in this room," John declared.

Seymour broke out in a cold sweat. "But, sire," he ventured tentatively, "I must ask who . . . who would you have carry out such an onerous task?"

For the longest time King John said nothing. His gaze alighted on the dark-haired man at the far end of the table, a man whose watchful green eyes surveyed all but

16

said nothing — the man in whose castle he'd chanced to reside for the night.

John stroked his beard, thinking on all Covington and Seymour had said, for in truth, he was well aware of his own faults. He was not a trusting man — nor was he a man to be trusted. The question of who would kill a maid and a boy was a very good question indeed, he mused . . .

'Twas not a task for one of his mercenaries. Nor could it be given to a man who might lie or cheat or betray him. But it was rumored that the man opposite him, the lord of Sommerfield, had grown harsh and bitter by the death of his beloved wife early in the year. Immersed in grief, to John's knowledge, this man had not been among the army of barons at Running-Mead, those wretches who had forced him to sign the Great Charter. Oh, how he'd chortled when he learned that Pope Innocent had ruled in his favor. The pontiff had cast aside that foolish document and ordered the barons to lay down their arms or risk excommunication.

The threat had done little to dispell the barons' rumblings. But John was still king, and this time he was determined to crush them. His spies told him how they had gone back to their old ways and quarreled among themselves as bitterly as ever. No matter. They had joined together once, and John would not allow it to happen again. Nay, he would not be brought to his knees yet again.

But this man . . . this man had not been held in any particular favor by the Crown, yet neither was he in disfavor. Better yet, he was not a man given to failure; his prowess and success in tournaments was exceeded only by the likes of William Marshal — it had gained him many ransoms and prizes. Besides, John reasoned quickly, if this fellow were thus engaged in finding Ellis's daughter and son, he could not join the ranks of the other barons in plotting against him.

Ah, but lands and riches would not persuade this man to do such a foul deed as murder to a maid and boy, for he was already well endowed. Yet if he were to hold this man's young son as hostage to completion of the deed . . . that was another matter entirely.

By turn, the eyes of Covington and Seymour came to follow those of the king, fixing on the man at the far end of the table — the man whose handsome visage had taken on a cast of dark grimness.

John smiled. He spoke softly — those who knew him well knew this was a sign that he

18

was at his most dangerous. "Who better than one already at hand?" he said smoothly. "And I shall be generous, sir, for I promise I shall safeguard your son until your return. . . ."

'Twas a threat implicit . . . a threat unspoken. Perchance the king of England knew that this man now despaired the fates that had brought the king to his castle for the night; that now turned him onto a path he had no choice but to follow. Oh, but he'd thought himself so clever not to ally himself rashly with the other nobles, to steer clear of the king. For though he had championed many a battle, he was not a man without mercy or compassion. But even he could not fight the king, not when his son's life was at stake. . . .

"Ah, yes," John said slyly. "Who better than Gareth, lord of Sommerfield . . . ?"

1

There was no sleep for Lady Gillian of Westerbrook this night.

Her heart thundered as loudly as the thunder that boomed without. 'Twas said to be the most savage coast in all the land, here where the fist of Cornwall thrust into the treacherous waters of the sea. Indeed, Gillian could well believe it.

The wind howled through the crevices, an eerie sound strangely like a keening wail. The cottage was stout and sturdily built of stone; tucked into a fold of the hillside that squatted above, it was shielded from the full force of the gale and thus kept her safe. Yet the fear that the very walls about her would be lifted and flung verily into the raging tempest without was a fear that refused to be banished, try though she might. 'Twas as if a mighty hand from aloft vented his wrath upon sea and shore. As if the gale roared down from the heavens to every corner of the earth. . . .

A shiver shook Gillian's form. Indeed, the very walls seemed to shiver and shake with the force of the wind. Yea, but this was a harsh, unforgiving place, this far-flung corner of Britain. It would show no mercy to those who had not the strength to withstand its rigors.

For it was in the midst of just such a raging storm that her father, Ellis of Westerbrook, had come to her chamber. Aye, the storm reminded her piercingly of that night — the night she'd been wrenched from her home, from all she'd ever known. Her brother. Her sweet, younger brother Clifton. Nay, but it was not the first such storm that she had endured in the weeks since she had come here . . . if only it would be the last!

A wave of bleakness swept over her, as endless as the dark gray seas that stretched beyond the shore. Her heart cried out, for each day was an eternity. November had drawn to a close, and she was still here . . . How long must she remain here? Forever, she feared. How was she to bear it? *How?*

Refuge. She reminded herself it was that which Brother Baldric had sought by bringing her here to the place where he had

21

been born. He'd said that to continue to move about was to risk discovery. That they must hide here until the furor died down. Ah, but would there ever come a time when she felt safe again?

Nay, she thought with a sinking flutter of dread. Not as long as King John was alive. How could she feel safe when she felt like an outcast? Tainted.

This was not the life she'd dreamed of, not the life she had ever thought to find. Memories of the past rose up to mingle with a wistful yearning. Papa had always been one to keep his children close to him. Papa had chosen not to have Clifton foster with another family, but to begin his training at Westerbrook. The winter that her mother had died from a stomach ailment had been a difficult one for all of them. Gillian had been sixteen, and Clifton but ten.

Perhaps, after her mother's death, Papa had wanted to keep his children close to him. Papa teased her occasionally that he must find a husband for her, but in truth there had been no haste. Gillian never doubted that someday she would marry, but she knew Papa would never foist a husband on her that she did not love, a husband who did not return her love in the very same measure.

Someday, she trusted, that man would come for her. A man she would love above all others . . .

Sometimes she dreamed of him, of a man strong and valiant, and ever so dashingly handsome! And oh, his kiss — that very first kiss! He'd steal her very breath and make her tingle to the tips of her toes, with arms both tender and strong, and warm, compelling lips. Her life would be one of laughter and love and joy. She would watch in wonder and contentment while her babes toddled about, for she had already decided there would be many. A girl she could rock and tell tales of days gone by. A boy as sturdy and handsome as his father, who would teach him of honor and truth.

But now a shadow had been cast over all her hopes and dreams. A shadow that might well last a lifetime.

But what was this? Pulling the soft wool coverlet more tightly about her shoulders, she scolded herself soundly. She was foolish to feel sorry for herself, for what of her brother Clifton? She was a woman full grown, she reminded herself. And for all that Clifton staunchly proclaimed that he was a man, he was but a boy of twelve.

Not until dawn's pale light crept along the misty hills to the east was Gillian able to

23

drift away in slumber.

Yet despite the wildness of the gale that night, when Gillian tugged open the door the next morning, sunlight poured down from the sky, as pure and golden as any she'd seen in the northern shires of Westerbrook. Such was the way of it here along the coast of Cornwall. No sweet, fragrant fields and rolling hillsides here, not like Westerbrook. Tall grasses fringed the stretch of beach beyond the cottage. To the north and west, white-gray cliffs towered over the tiny inlet. She stood for a moment, gazing out. In truth, Gillian could not deny there was a raw, stark beauty to this land . . .

Her throat closed painfully. She didn't mind fending for herself. She wouldn't have minded living in this tiny, derelict cottage at all, if not for the ever-present fear . . . and the storms.

Oh, it wasn't for herself that she feared. She worried about Clifton, so young, deprived of his family. She worried about Brother Baldric, whose age made the journey here a difficult one, though he never complained.

He had come to Westerbrook as a young man; he'd once been a tenant on Westerbrook lands, even when her grandfather had been lord. But it was when her father, Ellis, was a youth that tragedy struck. Early one morn, Baldric's cottage had caught fire after he'd left for the fields.

His wife and four children had perished.

In time, Baldric had decided to dedicate his life to the Church. Perhaps it was despair that had brought him to the Church, but it was surely faith that kept him there. Of that, Gillian had no doubt. Sometimes, though, she had wondered if it was the memory of his wife and children that had kept him from taking Holy Orders.

Aye, she'd known him since she was a child. There was not a time that she could not remember him.

But she missed Westerbrook, she thought yearningly. Most of all, she missed her father and Clifton.

Darkness bled through her. One she would never see again . . . as for the other, she could only pray the day would come soon.

It was then she spied the slight figure of a man coming toward her, weaving down the path. Scarcely taller than she, he was spare and thin, his pate shaved and exposed to the wind; the set of his shoulders between his robe was bony and frail. At times she marveled that he had been able to make the journey here to the place where he had been born — that he had revealed much of his character and determination.

" 'Twas quite a storm we had last night."

The breath she drew was faintly unsteady, but somehow she managed a faltering smile. "It was," she agreed.

Brother Baldric peered at her. "I am sorry I did not come yesterday."

Gillian gave an admonishing shake of her head. "You need not be sorry, Brother Baldric." She couldn't help but feel guilty. The walk from the sparsely populated village was a long one, yet Brother Baldric made it as often as he could. "Indeed, 'tis most kind of you to help with food and fuel. I know that it takes away from your work with Father Aidan."

Father Aidan was nearly blind; since returning here, Brother Baldric had become Father Aidan's eyes. They sometimes walked for days to minister to those in the area, for the villages were few and far between.

She smiled faintly. "I am in your debt, as you well know."

"Debt?" Brother Baldric scoffed. "My first duty is to God. My second to your father, and he entrusted me with your safety, child. Speak no more of debt." He frowned suddenly. "You look fatigued, Lady Gillian. Are you ill?"

"Nay. 'Tis just that I did not sleep well."

"The storm?" he guessed.

"Aye."

"And other things as well, I vow."

"That, too," she admitted. "I worry about Clifton. He is so young. And he's been deprived of his family —"

"I understand your concern, but it was for your own good that your father sent the two of you away."

Her eyes shadowed, Gillian regarded the dark-robed man who had brought her here. "I know. But it pains me to think of Clifton alone."

"Not alone," he reminded her. "He is with Alwin, your father's chief retainer, and we both know that Alwin will protect Clifton with his life."

Though Gillian knew Brother Baldric meant only to comfort, there was no such comfort to be found for the endless, dragging heaviness within her . . . for what if it should come to that? What would happen to Clifton then?

Her eyes darkened. "If only we could have remained together!"

"It could not be. Your father was convinced his children stood a far better chance apart than together — and he was right, methinks. He dared not take the chance that

King John would find you — you or Clifton." Brother Baldric did not speak aloud what they both knew. At least this way, if one were caught, the other might live.

"I should have stayed with him. I should have stayed with Papa!"

"He would not have allowed it."

He was right. Her father could be so stubborn. Yet still the memory speared her heart, her very soul. From the moment she'd seen her father so many weeks ago, she had prayed for the best . . . all the while fearing the worst.

Alas, it had come to pass.

Events of the outside world were slow to reach this remote corner of the land, but earlier in the month Baldric had come with news. There was discontent among the barons; that they had ever come together at Running-Mead seemed a miracle.

But there was more . . . it was with obvious reluctance that he'd delivered the heart-rending news that her father had been caught . . . and was now dead.

Gillian could not help it. A hot ache filled her throat. She choked back a sob.

"Painful though it is — small comfort that it is — try to remember, it was God's will."

"God's will that my father take his own

life? God's will that he was buried in unconsecrated ground?" Her tone laid bare the bitterness etched deep in her breast.

"I can see why your faith would be tested. But I pray, do not do this, Lady Gillian."

"My father did not take his life because he was weak — because he was afraid. He took it rather than give up another to the king's wrath. Nay, he was not weak — it is I!"

"Nay, child, nay! I am proud of you, for not many could live as you do — here, alone with only an old man for companionship. You are strong, Lady Gillian. Strong enough to face the future."

Alone? That single word unspoken seemed to hover between them. For alas, she did not feel strong. Though she was a woman full grown, she felt weak as a mewling child. This austere existence was a far different life than she had lived at Westerbrook. . . . Fleetingly she wondered how King Henry's wife Eleanor had lived in exile for sixteen long years. Yet it was not what Brother Baldric thought. Nay, in truth it was not the loneliness that Gillian minded . . . but the storms.

"I leave with Father Aidan to accompany him to the east, Lady Gillian. But before I leave, walk with me a while. It will do you good."

Brother Baldric was right. She must not give in to despair. Nor would she cause him worry — indeed, it almost seemed as if the myriad lines in his forehead were etched even deeper as he gazed at her imploringly. In truth, she decided, surely she fretted enough for both of them.

"Ah, Brother Baldric. What would I do without you to guide me?" She reached out and gave his thin shoulders a quick, fond hug. He was a humble man; he'd grown to manhood poor and remained poor by choice.

Together they set out on the trail that cut along the edge of the beach. As they walked, she glanced over at him. "Is there news of the kingdom?"

Brother Baldric sighed. "All is unchanged, I fear. The barons rumble, yet King John remains unchallenged."

The soft line of Gillian's lips tightened. She was convinced there was naught but vile blackness in the king's soul — naught but darkness in the heart of John of England . . . or John Softsword as he was referred to in snide snickers by some of his subjects.

"John is a fiend." Her tears vanished and her eyes flashed as she voiced her opinion of the king aloud. "He promised his mother Eleanor when he captured Arthur of

30

Brittany that no harm would befall the prince. No doubt he thought he was so clever, for he showed those who had been captured with Arthur no violence. Yet they were given no food, and what is that if not cruelty? Arthur was never seen again once he was imprisoned in Rouen. How can there be any doubt that he was killed and his body thrown into the Seine? How can the people not know that John is a monster? He is a dangerous man. Ah, that we, his loyal subjects, should be subject to his whimsy. He cares not about his people — the people of England," she went on fervently, "but only of his own greed!"

"That is something the world may never know, Lady Gillian, and you must guard your tongue — even here, for it is said there are spies everywhere."

"How such a man commands loyalty, I know not."

"I fear gold can make many a man beholden to the sway of the king's wishes. And no doubt there are other ways as well."

'Twas the hand of fear that Baldric referred to — they both knew it. "And no doubt King John has employed such ways," said Gillian, "and of a certainty will yet again!"

Brother Baldric glanced at her sharply. "I

31

pray you, Lady Gillian, let us speak no more —"

Gillian heard no more, for just then a fierce wind ripped away his voice and stole it aloft; snatching at the voluminous folds of her mantle, the gust sent her hair rippling behind her like a streaming pennon, even as it pushed her back a step. The fingers of one hand clutched at the fastenings of her mantle to keep it from being torn from her shoulders. It was plain, of woven wool, as was her gown; there had been little time to gather her belongings that night at Westerbrook, and Papa had directed that she take warm clothing. With her other hand, she tugged a sable skein of hair from across her eyes and fought to regain her balance and her breath.

Still gasping at the icy sting of the wind, she felt Brother Baldric stop short as well. But it was not the wind that brought his step to a halt, and a stricken cry of horror to her own lips . . .

The storm had left its legacy.

They had just rounded the massive boulder that guarded the cove. Splinters of wood littered the beach beyond. Here and there, ragged swatches of sail clung to the rocks, fluttering in the breeze.

And the bodies of several men.

"Last night's gale," Brother Baldric's tone echoed her own shock. "It must have carried the ship too close to shore."

Before she knew it she was standing beside first one body, then another and another.

Shocked, she stared down into faces robbed of the vigor of life, white and pallid and bloated, their lifeless eyes turned to the sunbleached sky. Her stomach churned, as surely as the waves had churned throughout the gale. It was only too easy to envision the helpless frailty of their ship against the momentous forces of the sea — perched dizzily atop the crest of a wave, hurtling through the air, battered against the rocks that rose like jagged teeth just off the headland. Any craft, no matter how sturdily built, would have been as fragile as dried tinder.

"Do you know them, Brother Baldric?"

Baldric shook his head. "Nay. They are not from this area, I'm certain of it."

Refuge. The word played anew through Gillian's mind. Was it refuge these men sought as they sailed around the point? Yet there was no refuge for these men. Or perchance their families even now were patiently awaiting their return . . .

But they knew not that they were dead. Gillian felt sick at heart, sick to the very depths of her soul.

Something of her feelings must have been displayed. Brother Baldric shook his head.

"My lady," he said gently. "Do not look like that. You must remember, it is —"

"I know. God's will."

"Aye," he said heavily.

"Forgive me, Brother Baldric, but I cannot help but wonder at God's ways." She could almost hear the vengeful pounding of the waves surging against the rocks. A guilt like no other shot through her. She had cowered in her bed, fearing for her safety, while these men had perished so very near! Had they been alive, any of them, as the perilous waves carried them to this place upon the sand? Ah, but they were so very close . . .

If only she could have warned them of the danger of the rocks! If only she could have saved them. But alas, if they *had* been alive, the wind had masked their cries. And so, she hadn't heard them. Could she have saved them, if she had?

Her gaze rested upon the last man. Unlike the others, his eyes were closed. Heedless of the wet sand that soaked her mantle and gown, she slipped to her knees. Reaching out, she brushed the gritty sand from one lean cheek. The grayish pallor of death was upon his skin, yet it struck her that he was not so cold as she'd thought he would be. Was it merely the warmth of her own hand? Or but a wish so fervent it might have been true?

"A pity all of them died," Baldric lamented sadly. "I shall see to it that they are buried in the churchyard."

Gillian heard, but only distantly. Her attention was captured solely by the man next to whom she knelt.

Nay, she thought vaguely. It could not be. Shock stole her breath, the very beat of her heart. She could have sworn there was the veriest movement beneath her fingertips. But she did not snatch her hand back as every instinct compelled that she do.

"This man is not dead," she said faintly. "He is alive . . . Brother Baldric, he is alive!"

2

Brother Baldric stood numbly. His fingers knotted on the ties of his rough gray robe. "That cannot be. Lady Gillian, you have only to look at him to see he is beyond salvation."

"Do not say that!" Gillian's tone was fiercely adamant.

As if he heard, the man turned his head ever so slightly. A low moan emitted from lips that were dry and cracked, the sound long and raspy and filled with torment.

Brother Baldric still had yet to move.

"Brother Baldric, you must help me! Is there someone from the village who can help us move him to the cottage?"

"Aye," he said shakily. "The miller's sons Edgar and Hugh. They are strong lads, as strong as any in the village."

"Then fetch them, Brother Baldric, and hurry!"

Baldric did not move. A shiver played over

him. This man lay helpless in the sand — unable to move, unable to speak — and Baldric could not take his eyes from him . . .

"Brother Baldric!"

The urgency of her tone must have finally gotten through to him. With a nod he set off toward the village as quickly as his legs would carry him.

By the time he returned with Edgar and his brother, Gillian was nearly as pale as the man at her knees. Her tone low, she directed that the pair take him to her cottage. Within minutes, the man was lying on her straw pallet in the corner.

In troubled silence she and Baldric watched as Edgar and the other youth deposited the man on the bed. Baldric nodded his thanks before they departed. And when Gillian nearly scurried forward, he laid a restraining hand on her arm.

"My lady, wait."

There was something in his tone that made her regard sharpen. "What is it?"

He nodded toward the man lying prone. "My lady, I must remind you . . . we know not who this man is. This may not be wise."

"Brother Baldric, this man is injured!"

Baldric slipped his hands into the sleeves of his robe, his expression both grave and torn. He stared with shadowed eyes at the man stretched out upon the pallet. Heavily he spoke: "May God forgive me," and he briefly cast his eyes heavenward. "You should be wary of taking this man beneath your roof, for what if he knows that you are Lady Gillian of Westerbrook? In truth, I know this man not, yet I sense danger."

Gillian gave a shake of her head, sending a spray of dark tendrils across the delicate curve of her cheek. She brushed at it impatiently — and replied thusly as well.

" 'Tis not possible that he knows who I am."

"My lady, what if it is?"

"Nay, 'tis not." Clearly she shared none of Baldric's qualms. "This man was on a ship that was merely passing by, on its way to Wales or Ireland, mayhap. Besides, how could anyone know I am here on this far reaching corner of England? We were careful on our journey here. We spent the nights either out in the open or beneath the roof of the church. My identity is not my own. Those in the village do not know me as Gillian of Westerbrook. To them I am the widow Marian, come to spend my grief over my husband's death in seclusion."

Indeed, the story was one that Brother Baldric himself had concocted. Though Gillian abhorred such deceit, at length she had conceded that it was best.

"Nonetheless, I urge caution."

She remained adamant. "Brother Baldric, this is unlike you. You have dedicated your life to helping others. Why would you not wish to help this one? He may well die without it — indeed, he may die anyway!"

"Then perhaps it is God's will."

"God's will. God's will! 'Tis just as you said a moment ago. It was God's will that brought the storm — God's will that brought him here!"

"Aye. There may be some truth in your words. Still, I think we should not abandon caution. My lady, I would not speak ill of your father, for I admired him greatly. Yet when it came to King John, he was rash. We sought to save you by bringing you here. I fear for both you and Clifton . . . as I feared for your father. And indeed, I can hide it from you no longer. My lady, I have heard rumors that King John searches for you and Clifton — that he has dispatched an assassin."

She paled. "I do not know why he troubles himself."

"The king is a vengeful man. And no doubt he is angry still at your father's attempt on his life — your father and the other man."

"But *this* man cannot even move," she stated with calm. "He can do me no harm."

Gillian did not abandon her cause but swept an arm toward the corner. Her whole life she was ever one to lend a hand or a word to those in need. Did Baldric not understand her need, her resolute desire to help this man? For the sight of his shipmates, their bodies mangled and bloated, had been shocking. Baldric had gazed upon the solemn face of death many times, as she herself had not. And their desperate flight — and that of her brother Clifton — along with the tragic death of her father so recently, had wrought a change in her. Though she always greeted Baldric with a ready smile, there was an endless sadness that lurked within her now. Baldric frightened her anew with the statement that the king searched for her, but she tried to hide this.

Brother Baldric fretted aloud. "If only I did not have to accompany Father Aidan just now. But alas, those many years while the people of England lay under the Pope's interdict, there were those who abandoned the Church and have yet to return. 'Tis for their souls that Father Aidan wishes to minister."

"And rightly so. It is his duty," she agreed,

"and yours, Brother Baldric." Her eyes softened as they rested upon him. "As for me, I must tell you, you worry for naught."

"For naught? You will be alone with this man, this stranger. Oh, I should have had Edgar and Hugh take him to the village instead!"

"It is too far and he is too ill." She raised her chin, the picture of dignity and grace. " 'Tis the right thing to do. The only thing to do," she stated, the pitch of her voice low and musical. "I must help him, Brother Baldric. I must."

There was no use in arguing, and he finally agreed that she was right. With a sigh he took both her hands within his. "I must make haste, else Father Aidan will be convinced I have forsaken him. Is there anything you need before I go?"

"Only your assurance that you will keep yourself safe — and Father Aidan as well."

"And on that score I can only say that *I* will try. Take care, child. Take the utmost care."

"I will," she promised. "May God be with you, Brother Baldric." Leaning forward, her lips brushed his cheek.

His footsteps carried him to the door. He glanced back over his shoulder one last time. Lady Gillian was already at the stranger's side, lines of worry clearly writ on the smoothness of her brow. She appeared small and delicate next to the broad span of the man's shoulders.

Baldric shook his head, his expression grave. He mumbled, too softly for her to hear, "I pray I never rue the day I made this judgment."

Gillian bent anxiously over the stranger. Her pulse clamored wildly, for he was so still. So silent. Fear surged within her like the roiling of the sea. Dear God, was he dead then after all?

Swiftly she laid her ear on the breadth of his chest. Ah, he still lived! She could feel the beat of his heart; it lumbered slow and steady beneath her ear.

Slowly she drew back to look at him. A trickle of water dripped from his temple to the pillow beneath his head. What remained of his clothing was sopping as well. That would not do, she realized. Why, if he remained in these rags, he would surely sicken further.

Without thought, her hands moved to his body. She worked almost frantically at the laces of his tunic, parting it and shoving it aside to reveal his chest, tugging it from first one shoulder, then the other, and finally over his head.

His boots came next, followed by the tattered strips of his chausses. Fumbling a little, her fingers came to his drawers. At least they weren't completely ruined.

At last he was naked. Perchance a part of her was aghast at her daring, but this was no time for modesty, neither hers nor his.

And so she found out, as her gaze traversed the length of him. Her mind fleetingly registered a wide chest shadowed with curling black hair, limbs that were long and brawny . . . the unmistakable evidence that he was profoundly — starkly — a man . . .

Due to the nature of the task at hand, her inspection of that part of him was mayhap a trifle hasty. She guessed that all was well there and he'd suffered no injury nearby, though, in truth, Gillian could hardly be certain . . .

Now on to the other side.

She pushed and grunted and sought desperately to heave him to his stomach — and failed. Shoving aside the unruly tendril of hair that persisted in falling over one eye, she rocked back on her heels in frustration. Sweet mercy, but he was heavy! 'Twas not that she was so weak, she told herself. Though her stature was not large, neither was she frail. She'd grown used to hard work while living here. She fetched water from the well and carried wood for the fire, far more than she'd been able to when she'd first arrived. Nay, the man was simply too big! Indeed, his feet dangled over the end of the pallet.

Gillian's eyes narrowed. Her head tipped to the side in fervid consideration. Finally, she braced herself and pushed beneath his shoulder, peering at the top half of him as best as she was able. Now for the lower half. Biting her lip, she placed a hand on the bony ridge of his hip. Taking a deep breath, she felt her cheeks heat as she deliberately avoided focusing on his nether regions. Gingerly she cupped her fingers under one naked thigh and lifted his leg. In this way she was able to discern those injuries that were visible.

Indeed, it seemed they were countless. She sucked in a harsh breath. There was a massive lump on his temple; the skin was puffy and swollen, split by a jagged cut. Clearly he'd suffered a terrible blow to the head. His face was scratched and bruised. Various cuts and bruises marked his body all over. The worst was a ragged strip of flesh that had been ripped the length of his side. It began just under his left arm and ripped nearly to his waist, raw and oozing blood. As the ship had been flung and shattered against the rocks, it would seem that he had been cast as well. Had he been awake? Ah, but the brine of the sea upon his wounds must have been sheer agony!

To Gillian's eyes, it appeared as if the whole of his body had been beaten with a club. There was scarcely an inch of him that was not bruised and swollen. His right knee was mashed and bloodied. Her heart twisted. If he lived, would he ever walk again?

There was no hiding from the truth . . . she was not a healer; she knew naught of balms and potions. True, she'd often assisted the women of Westerbrook with various abrasions her father's men had suffered; she knew wounds must be kept clean and free of dirt. But in truth she'd never seen anything the likes of which this man suffered, and these were but the outward wounds.

Was she a fool to think she could save him? Perhaps. Yet even as the realization tolled through her, something crystallized inside her. She could not give in. *He* could not give in.

In a heartbeat she'd bounded to her feet. She raced to the well atop the hill for water. In her haste, she nearly tripped and barely caught herself from flying headlong onto

45

the mossy path. Her movements jerky, she lowered the leather bucket into the well. When she raised it and grabbed the leather handle, water sloshed over the edge — her hands were shaking.

"Calm yourself, Gillian." She scolded herself firmly. "Stay calm, else you cannot help him." The words screamed through her again and again as she returned to the cottage, then warmed the water and searched for a cloth.

Indeed, she told herself as she stationed herself beside him, she could do no more. She could do no less. Though he might well be beyond her power, it was just as she'd told Brother Baldric. If she did not help — did not try — he would surely die.

Lightly, her fingers skimmed his body, her eyes fixed on his face for any sign of reaction. In truth, she would have welcomed it. Alas, there was none. If she caused him pain, he gave no sign of it. Even when she scrubbed the gritty sand and dirt from the open wound on his side and his knee — ah, but it was stubborn! — he neither flinched nor winced. Nor did he move when she fetched a healing salve Brother Baldric had obtained for a cut she'd received on her leg during the journey, and rubbed it into his wounds.

Something twisted inside her as she finished bathing him, then wound a strip of cloth around his mangled knee. Dear God, how could Baldric believe this man might harm her? He posed no threat to her, nor to anyone!

Laying the strips aside, she turned back to him. An odd feeling tightened her throat. Only then did she realize what she had just done. . . . To think that she had been so bold as to strip the clothes from his body! A part of her was appalled. She had touched him . . .

He was starkly . . . unabashedly . . . naked. Though Gillian was a woman untutored in the ways of love and men, 'twas not a sight she found displeasing. Indeed, quite the contrary, for there was no denying he was a powerful man. Belatedly she acknowledged what she had not taken the time to note before. Pale though he was, his frame looked impossibly large; he filled the entirety of her narrow bed. His shoulders nearly eclipsed the width of the mattress, lean but padded with muscle — she'd felt the resilient tautness of that muscle beneath her very fingertips! Aye, she thought dimly. Under other circumstances, he was surely a man of considerable might.

Hastily she fumbled with the rough linen sheet at his ankles, pulling it up and following it with a blanket. His hair had begun to dry. The strands were thick and dark, the color of midnight. Biting her lip, she laid the back of her knuckles against the stranger's cheek before she knew what she was even about, the gesture one of comfort and compassion. A hundred questions tumbled through her.

"What brought you to this lonely stretch of England?" she voiced her thoughts aloud. "Do you come from some foreign shore? What is your trade? Are you a fisherman? Nay, perhaps not. You've not the tough, leathered skin of a man who weathers long hours of sea and sky. A tiller of fields then? Nay," she decided, tilting her head to the side and regarding him through narrowed eyes. "Mayhap you work long and hard at the forge." Indeed, he possessed the brawny arms of a man who could carry great weight with just as much ease.

That, too, she discarded, for there was a hint of arrogance in the aquiline flare of his nose, the set of his mouth. Nay, he was not a poor man, though he'd worn no jewels. She glanced at his boots; although slogged with water, they were finely made.

Her mind twisted and turned. Could it be that he was one of John's barons? God knew that John's greed had fired the minds of his

48

people with anger and resentment. Perhaps like her, he, too, fled for his life from the wrath of King John, only to be caught in a storm, much as she had been.

"Whoever you are," she murmured, "you must have a name. What is it, I wonder? Michael?" A slight smile curled her lips and she shook her head. "Nay. Oh, 'tis a fine name, to be sure, but not yours, methinks." She tipped her head first to one side, then the other as she studied him.

"I know. Walter. Or William. Ah, I know. 'Tis Edwyn. Aye, I do believe your name is Edwyn."

Thus she began to call him Edwyn.

He breathed . . . yet did not waken. He remained so motionless he might have been dead. As the hours wore on, many a time Gillian laid her ear to the breadth of his chest, assured that he lived only by the steady drone of his heart.

Was this a healing sleep that claimed him? She thought not. She feared not.

Time had been her most bitter foe throughout these long weeks of uncertainty. Yet now was it not her staunchest ally? *His* staunchest ally? Yes, she told herself firmly. The longer he breathed, the greater his chances of survival.

Throughout the day and night Gillian was

there beside him. The hours marched on. She sat beside him until her muscles grew stiff and cramped and her eyes burned with fatigue.

She talked. Of silly things. Of whatever chanced to wander through her mind. 'Twas odd, the ease with which the name sprang from her lips. Ah, she mused once, but what if his name was Edwyn in truth?

"I daresay you are a hunter, like my father. Oh, but my father was a great hunter," she recalled wistfully. "Many a day found him hunting with his gyrfalcon. When we could not find him we had only to look in the mews. My mother, before she died, used to say she feared Clifton would never spare the time to find a bride when he was old enough, for Clifton was almost always at Papa's side when he went hawking."

Her smile faltered. *Clifton.* Pain lanced through her heart, bled deeper. Would she ever find Clifton? Where was he? *Where?* Was he safe? Oh, if only she knew! But nay. She'd not succumb to despair. Papa was dead. But Clifton was still alive. She had to believe it. And somehow — someday — she would find a way to find her brother.

Rising, she moved to the window. Opening the shutters, she peered outside. Air whistled through the opening. Outside, the wind had begun to gust. Gillian could not help the thought that tore through her mind — she prayed there would not be another storm. Determined not to dwell on it, she threw another handful of limbs on the fire. Impatiently she brushed aside the curling strands of hair that swung forward, then started across the floor.

" 'Tis cold again today, Edwyn." With a rueful sigh she made the comment even though she knew he did not hear her. "I must confess, in Westerbrook where I am from, we have November days that are chill, but not like this — 'tis like the cold passes all through me."

There was a subtle movement beneath the sheet. Gillian felt her lips part. Why, he had moved! Or was it merely that she had sat too heavily upon the mattress and made his body shift?

There was no time to wonder, no time to think. A long arm swept the blanket to his waist. He began to thrash.

"Edwyn, no!" The name slipped urgently — unthinkingly — from her lips. "Be still else your side will begin to bleed. Do you hear me, Edwyn? Edwyn, you must be still!" She reached for his bare shoulders to push him down. It was then it happened.

His eyes flicked open. In the midst of

reaching for his bare shoulders to push him down, she found herself captured and seized. Strong male fingers shackled the fragile span of her wrist with a grip she'd never have guessed possible, given his state of just moments before. Despite his malaise, he was almost frighteningly strong.

"Edwyn," came a dry, hoarse mutter. "By God, desist from calling me Edwyn!"

Gillian gaped at him. She was stunned. Amazed. Overwhelmed . . . and all at once!

"Wh-what am I to call you, then?"

He tugged her close, so close she felt the warm mist of his breath mingle with hers, and she could clearly discern the flecks of gold in eyes that were the same lush green as the forest near Westerbrook.

Those eyes seemed to pierce into the very depths of her own. "Gareth," he said with utter fierceness. "I am Gareth."

And then he slipped back into unconsciousness.

3

Gillian gave a stricken cry. "Edwyn . . . Gareth." The name tripped awkwardly from her tongue, for already she'd grown accustomed to calling him Edwyn.

With both hands she shook him, be it roughly, be it gently, she knew not. She cared not.

"Wake up, Gareth! Wake up!"

A lean hand fell limply to his side. Her efforts to rouse him were in vain. Gillian wavered between buoyant exultation and a dragging disappointment, but it was just as before. As if all strength and effort had been bled from him.

But he had awoken. He had opened his eyes . . . and spoken.

She took up her vigil with renewed hope. With avowed conviction. Though the world beyond still summoned him, Gillian was suddenly determined. She would not allow death to stake its claim on still another man.

Not today.

Not tomorrow.

Not *this* one.

It was then she noted the warmth emanating from his skin. Heat seemed to rise from his body. Alarmed, she laid the backs of her fingers against his cheek. He was hot to the touch, and it had naught to do with the heat of the fire.

"Sweet heaven," she breathed, "you're ill with fever." No wonder he'd tried to push aside the blankets!

Once again she bolted for water, only this time she did not warm it. She dipped the cloth in it, then dragged it down his face and neck and shoulders, clear to his waist.

It was as if the fever had caught fire within him — as if it burned from the inside out and now raged out of control beneath her hand — before her very eyes. Beads of sweat broke out on his forehead and upper lip. His skin was no longer colorless but glowed with an unhealthy pallor. His chest rose and fell unevenly, as if every breath was a struggle . . . as indeed it was.

Gillian raged at the heavens — and at herself. There must be something else she could do, she thought frantically, but what? *What?*

Wringing the water from the cloth, she drew it down the side of his face, venting her despair. "Ah, Gareth, Gareth! If only you could help me!"

He turned his face into the cloth, as if he sought the coolness. It struck Gillian then. Was he thirsty? Of course he was. He had not drunk nor eaten throughout the long hours spent in her cottage. She chastised herself roundly for not realizing sooner.

Her mind vaulted forward. He could not chew or eat in his present state. But if he could but drink, perhaps later he might take the broth from the soup she had last eaten and thus gain strength.

Slipping an arm beneath his shoulder, she lifted his head and held the goblet to his lips. His head rested in the palm of her hand; lord, but it was heavy! "Drink, Gareth," she said softly. "Just a bit, that's the way."

Carefully she eased the goblet forward. He made a strangled, choking sound and began to cough. Hastily Gillian withdrew the cup, spilling half the contents as she did so. Water drenched the front of her gown, but she paid no heed. She would change it later.

Not to be dissuaded, she seized her spoon and dipped it into the cup, seeking to dribble it into his mouth. Like a willful child, he turned his head away. His lips pressed together, a stubborn refusal. Gillian tried patiently again and again, coaxing and cajoling, until at last she flung the spoon aside in fury and frustration.

Gritting her teeth, she regarded her patient. "You will not die," she pronounced. "I will not allow it, do you hear? And you will drink, even if I must pour it down your throat."

Where the idea came from, she would never know. Perhaps it was pulled from some insidious place inside her, culled by desperation.

The single beat of her heart forestalled the notion . . . then it was no more.

She crawled atop him, but not before dragging the sheet up over his naked limbs. Carefully she straddled him, nesting her knees beside his hips. A dozen things passed through her mind in that moment. She was heartily glad that Brother Baldric was not here to see her. The very thought made her want to smile, at a time when she'd never felt less like smiling! For what she was about to do seemed terribly intimate . . . yet terribly important.

Once more she reached for the cup. This time, however, she tipped it high to her own lips . . . then bent low.

Awkwardly her chin bumped his; she felt the bristly scrape of his beard against her tender skin, for he was no longer clean-shaven. It was a strange sensation of awareness, for such closeness with a man other than her father was utterly foreign to Gillian. Yet she did not allow it to hinder her.

Her heart knocking wildly, she closed her eyes and brushed her lips against his — his were warm and dry. At the contact, a jolt went through her. Yet in that timeless span between one breath and the next, Gareth's lips parted.

And so did hers.

Cool liquid trickled from her mouth into his. Hope bounded within her breast when she felt him swallow. Felt his lips part thirstily for more.

Thus he drank from her.

Thus he supped. Again and again, as if he was parched and could not get enough. A goblet full, and then another, and even a bit of broth from the soup. Only then was she satisfied. His breathing was not so heavy now, and he seemed cooler.

She eased away, her hand going to the small of her back. She was stiff and sore from bending over him so long, and a swirl of hair tumbled across her eyes. She pushed it away impatiently. Lord, but she must be a wretched sight to behold. Her gown was wet and wrinkled. Her hair, never truly tame, was a wavy, disheveled mass down her back and shoulders. With a sigh she moved to replace the goblet in its usual place on the rough-planked table before the hearth.

When she turned back, an eerie prickle raised the fine hairs on the back of her neck.

Her patient had shifted his head. His eyes were wide open and upon her — burning, as he had burned.

"Who are you?" he demanded. "Who are you?"

Her tongue seemed tethered to the roof of her mouth. "I am ..." To her horror, she had to grope for the name the villagers believed her to be. "I am Marian."

"You lie!" he accused. "Tell me who you are!"

Gillian could form neither word nor sound. At the iron flex of his jaw, a shiver of something very akin to fear played all through her. His countenance was black, his eyes glittering. She was somehow frightened as she'd not been frightened before. For one perilous, teetering instant, an awful feeling sent her world all atumble. Was Brother Baldric right? Did this man know the truth? Did he know that she was Gillian of Westerbrook?

She was spared an explanation, yet this was an explanation she would have gladly made, for in the very next instant his eyelids drooped shut.

Again he'd slipped away.

Gillian flew to his side. "Gareth!" Her fingers closed around his shoulder. Where before his skin was like fire, now it was like ice! Even as the thought took hold, he began to shiver. The whole of his body shook, as if the chill of the seawater had seeped into his bones. She nearly screamed in despair. Too hot. Too cold. Would he never be well? Would he never truly wake? Was he lost to this world forever?

She heaved the blankets from the foot of the bed and dragged them over him, yet still he trembled violently.

Gillian did the only thing she could think of that might help. Her fingers raced even as her mind raced. She clawed at her gown, stripping it from her shoulders; her wet clothing would do him no good. Clad only in her shift, she crawled into bed and wrapped her limbs around his, as if to guard him, to shield him, to give him warmth . . . to give him life.

Little by little, by subtle degrees, his shivering began to subside. His breathing went from hard and labored to slow and rhythmic.

Her fingers threaded through his hair. It was warm and soft and silky. "There," she whispered, "that's better, is it not?"

As if in agreement, his face turned into the hollow of her neck.

Evening came nigh and shadows crept into the cottage. Before long, she felt her body begin to loosen, her limbs begin to slacken. All at once she was incredibly weary. Oh, she'd dozed now and then, but how long since she'd slept, and slept deeply. . . . Even on the journey here, afraid the king's men would appear at any moment, she and Brother Baldric had been able to snatch a few hours of sleep each night. How long had it been? she wondered. Several days, surely.

Brother Baldric was right, she acknowledged hazily. She shouldn't have taken him in, for now there was nowhere to sleep. She really should rise and dress, then make her bed near the hearth. The prospect was not at all inviting, particularly when she felt so cozy and snug. Nonetheless, she told herself that she would, in just a few short moments.

But Gillian was suddenly too tired to think anymore. Too tired to move. Too tired to care. She felt herself drifting into the blissfully tranquil abyss of sleep, and could do naught to stop it.

★ ★ ★

His dreams were like none he'd ever dreamed before.

A creaking, tearing sound seemed to vibrate through his entire body. There was a massive, jarring shudder beneath his feet, followed by a heaving roll. Pain seared his lungs, his leg, his entire body.

All around were voices. Shouts. Screams of terror that shrilled to a piercing shriek, then fell eerily silent. Was any of it real? He hoped not. He prayed not. For he was drowning. Adrift in darkness, hemmed in by walls of numbing cold. Then suddenly his body was afire. When darkness threatened to close in all around him, he did not resist.

But then came another voice. This one was different. Melodious and dulcet and honeyed. The voice of a woman.

The hands of a woman, drifting over him, small and soft, blessedly cool. Lips, warm upon his, flowering open upon his.

She was the one he clung to. Those hands. That voice. The only light in a void of endless black.

Consciousness departed little by little, like newly fallen rain beneath the blanch of the sun. The scent and feel of warmth and woman swirled all around; soft, feminine curves melded tight against his side. He need not open his eyes to see the soft tendrils of hair coiled upon his chest and belly, as if he were wrapped in a silken cocoon. The mists of darkness beckoned anew, yet this time Gareth fought it. He might have gladly savored this incredible sweetness; it was a feeling not unknown to him, yet somewhere in the depths of his being lurked the certainty that it had been a long while since he'd lain thus with such alluring, womanly nakedness draped upon his form.

Alas, mingled with that sweetness was pain. And as he felt himself dragged from the lure of slumber, it was the pain which overtook him.

His companion stirred. Almost reluctantly, he pried his lids open.

Their eyes locked.

His thoughts were hazed. He grappled for her name, even as she seemed to grapple for breath. Thick, gleaming waves of darkest midnight tumbled over her shoulders, trailing upon the hand stretched at his side. She stared at him with eyes the same vibrant hue as a clear summer sky. Gareth had the oddest sensation, almost as if she were struck dumb by the sight of him. It spun through his mind that she was not naked, as he'd thought. Through the linen of her shift, round nipples peeped clearly visible. It was a sight that was a veritable invitation to linger — and indeed, he might have indulged the temptation had she not grabbed the sheet and snatched it to her breasts.

Good Christ, he thought. His head was spinning. It hurt to breathe. Was she not being ridiculously modest for one of her ilk?

He raised his head a fraction. "God's teeth," he muttered. "I do hope the night's pleasure was enough to warrant this morning's misery."

He spoke without being quite aware of it; he was almost startled to hear the rasping dryness of his voice. He could tell his lips were cracked and dry as the deserts of the East; his throat was parched.

Those incredible eyes widened. When she said naught, Gareth wondered vaguely if she'd been robbed of the ability to speak.

He tried anew. "Why do you stare at me so? Have you not been paid yet?"

Her chin came up. "Blessed be," she said faintly. "I am not a-a harlot!"

He hiked a brow, then promptly regretted it. God above, even that hurt! "Then why are you in my bed?"

"You, good sir, are in *my* bed!"

Gareth blinked. Sweet mercy, but he could hardly think. "Forgive me. Lovers then."

She gasped. "Nor am I your lover!"

She lunged upright. Clearly she was affronted. Clearly she intended to flee. Clearly he could not allow it, not yet.

He moved instinctively, capturing a handful of shining black hair. He gritted his teeth, waiting for the pain wrought by the movement to subside. "Wait," he said hoarsely.

She froze. "Release me!"

"And if I do not?"

The breath she drew was deep and ragged. Long, thick lashes swept low, shielding her expression from him, but not soon enough. The unmistakable sheen of tears stood high and bright in her eyes, darkening them to pure sapphire.

Gareth stared. His grip on the trailing ends of her hair was firm, but scarcely hurtful; he did not tug upon her scalp, nor had she jerked away. Why the devil did she cry then?

Her head lowered. "Please," she said, her voice so low he had to strain to hear it past the buzzing in his head. "Release me."

His fingers tensed. He crushed the lock of hair in his fingers, then slowly uncurled them. Wordlessly he let her go.

She was up and on her feet the instant he released her. Her gown lay on a small wooden stool near the head of the bed. Turning her back to him, she slipped it over her head and upraised arms. It shimmied downward, falling around her hips and legs in soft folds. For an instant, she remained very still, the set of her shoulders narrow and hunched. It spun through his mind that she appeared ready to bolt.

His mouth thinned. He tried to raise up on an elbow. Fire blazed through him like the flaming tip of a lance. He fell back with a groan.

In a heartbeat she was at his side. Small hands pressed him back. "Gareth, be still! Now tell me, where does it hurt?"

"Where does it *not* hurt?" He sought to raise his head, then let it drop back. The whole of him felt as if he'd been weighted and filled with iron. He ached in places he'd not known it was possible to ache. His knee felt as if a dozen knives had been thrust into it. What the devil had happened?

He spoke through lips that barely moved. "You know my name. How is it I do not know yours? Was I in my cups then?"

Wide eyes met his. "Nay! At least, not that I know. I-I am Gillian. And 'twas you who told me your name was Gareth."

"How did I come to be here? Why do I feel so wretched?"

Wispy black brows drew together over a dainty, upturned nose. "You were on a ship," she said slowly. "There was a terrible storm. The next morn the beach was strewn with bodies and wreckage." She had gone slightly pale. "You were the only one who survived. We moved you here, and I have been tending your injuries."

"We?"

"Brother Baldric and I. Brother Baldric lends his sight to Father Aidan, the priest in the village. Father Aidan is blind."

"I recall no storm. I recall no ship!"

A slight frown creased the smoothness of her brow. "Perhaps you were asleep when the storm arose."

His voice cut across hers. "Nay."

She studied him briefly. Gently she said, "Perhaps you should not be so hasty to judge. Remember that you have been ill . . ."

"Aye, that is the problem. I remember nothing!"

She frowned. "What do you mean?"

"I . . . remember . . . nothing!"

"That cannot be," she said.

"I tell you it is."

She faltered. "But . . . you said you were Gareth."

A cold sweat broke out on his brow. "I am. I am Gareth." He spoke with such convic-

66

tion that neither could doubt it.

He had gone very still. "By the blood of Christ, that is all I know" — there was an infinitesimal pause — "and all I remember."

4

He would live.

It was that which brought tears to Gillian's eyes, a burning ache in her breast. For a moment she'd been incensed that he thought her a harlot. Ah, to think she'd longed for him to wake with every pore of her being — and when at last he did, that she must bear such insult!

Yet Gillian could not help it. She ducked her head, battling to swallow the lump in her throat. At last she was certain he would not die. He would live. She knew not why it mattered so . . .

Only that it did.

I am Gareth. That is all I know . . . and all I remember.

"How is that possible?" she wondered aloud.

He gave a brittle laugh. "How the devil would I know?"

"There must be something else," she said slowly.

"I tell you there is not."

"Do not be so hasty. Think. Do you recall your mother's name? Your father's?"

"There is nothing," he pronounced flatly. "I know naught but my name. Where I am from, how I came to be here . . . 'tis gone."

Gillian sat back, stunned. The import of that statement echoed through her, like the ceaseless wash of the surf upon the shore. Dear God, she thought numbly. His body was broken . . .

And so was his mind.

"How long have I been here?"

"This is the fourth day."

"You said I was on a ship. We're near the sea, then?"

"Yes. The coast of Cornwall." Gillian divulged the admission before she thought better of it.

"Aye, of course we're near the sea. I can smell it. And hear it as well." His eyes closed and he grimaced. When they opened, eyes of sea green fire rested upon her. "You mentioned a storm. Tell me again what happened."

Gillian suppressed a shiver. Just thinking of the storm and the bodies she'd found made her blanch inside. "There are many storms here, but the gale that night was especially terrible. And the headland is treacherous. Perhaps your vessel was unaware of the jagged rocks there; perhaps it was, and the winds carried the ship straight into them. Judging from the debris, the ship was ripped apart."

It made sense, Gareth reasoned. That would account for the creaking, tearing sound in his dreams. The sensation of drowning, of numbing cold. Clenching his jaw and squeezing his eyes shut, he scoured his mind. There was nothing. Nothing abounded but questions for which he had no answers. What ship was he aboard? Where was it bound? Was he a seaman, then? Nay. He discounted the possibility instinctively.

I am Gareth. Just as instinctively he sensed there was more. Something he should remember. Something that eluded him.

Gillian sensed his frustration, like a ship without oars that turned in circles, traveling nowhere. Somehow, his injuries had wiped clean his mind; as surely as the dawn of a new day cleansed the night of darkness, so the storm had stolen his memories.

"Do you feel well enough to eat?"

He nodded, grimacing a little as he shifted. All at once he seemed to realize that beneath the covering of the sheet he was naked. His gaze swung immediately to hers.

Gillian swallowed. A flush that began in her cheeks surely spread to the curl of her toes in her slippers. Heat flooded all through her, and there was nothing she could do to keep it at bay. Dear God, she had undressed a man . . . *this* man. She had touched him . . . all of him . . . well, *almost* all of him. She was appalled . . . and embarrassed as never before.

"I . . . It was necessary to see how badly you were injured. And then . . . you were feverish, so I bathed you to cool the fever . . ." She felt compelled to explain, though he displayed no inclination for one.

"No doubt," he said with a lift of a brow. "Where are my clothes?"

Gillian had the disturbing sensation he was precisely aware what had gone through her mind. She bit her lip. "They were ruined. I burned them — all but your drawers. She pointed toward the hearth. "They are there, where I laid them to dry."

"Then perhaps you would be so good as to fetch them for me."

Her face flaming, Gillian did as he asked. She couldn't summon the courage to ask if he needed assistance. Turning her back while he struggled into his drawers, she crossed the floor and set about preparing food.

Moments later she drew up the stool beside him. She couldn't help but note his efforts at clothing himself had left him sweating.

In one hand she held a bowl of gruel, in the other a spoon. Her intention was obvious — to feed him. His expression grim, Gareth reached for the spoon impatiently. But he was clumsy from his weakness and lack of strength. His hand began to shake so badly the gruel sloshed onto his bare chest before it reached his mouth. He cursed rawly and dropped the spoon.

"Well," she said dryly, "I see you are a man of subtle words." Gillian dabbed away the puddle on his chest with a clean linen napkin. Her fingers brushed the crisp mat on his chest. Flushing slightly, she withdrew her hands and reached again for the spoon.

"Open," she ordered, holding it poised before him.

For an instant his mouth compressed stubbornly, as if to refuse. At last he opened and allowed her to feed him, but he was clearly displeased. The scowl returned, as blackly fierce as it had been before he truly wakened.

When she'd finished, his head dropped

back. He turned his cheek into the pillow. His lashes slipped shut. For a moment Gillian did not move. Her gaze traced ponderingly over the profile presented to her. What manner of man was he? she wondered. A sober man? A churlish rogue? She studied the flare of winged black brows. The set of his mouth was almost stern, his lower lip slightly fuller. A trifle arrogant, mayhap, she decided. A passionate man, of a certainty. Resilient, or he would never have survived the wreckage. Certainly a man of pride, judging from his reaction to her feeding him. Yet he had yielded, and by that very yielding, he had revealed a spirit and fortitude she could only admire.

He slept throughout most of the day. Several times Gillian bent over him anxiously, but his breath was deep and even, his brow cool, his color neither high nor pale.

Twilight's shadows began to creep within the cottage. It gave Gillian a start when she turned and found him fully awake. His eyes were open and fixed full upon her. Quickly Gillian prepared another bowl of gruel. No protest was forthcoming this time, though he made a face when he'd finished the last of it.

"Have you nothing more substantial than gruel?"

"You're hungry?"

The merest hint of a smile grazed his mouth. "Ravenous."

Gillian hurried to comply. His hunger was surely a good sign, she decided in approval. He ate every bit of the stew and bread left from her last meal.

Before the last of the light faded, she dressed his wounds. He drew in a harsh breath when she cleansed the long, deep cut on his side with warm water. She noted with relief that the redness had faded to pink, and the jagged edges had begun to close. She worked as quickly as she dared — as gently as she could — but she sensed it was still an ordeal for him. His lips were compressed and he was drawn tight as a bow. He jerked once when she began to smooth the unguent onto the wound. Only when she'd completed the task did he release his breath; the tension seeped from his muscles. She stowed the bandages away in a cupboard and emptied the water outside the door.

By the time she'd finished, it was night. The cottage was lit only by the yellow glow of the fire. Gareth slanted his head toward her.

"You look weary," he observed.

"I am," she admitted. "I fear I've not slept much these past days."

"Then sleep now."

Gillian bit her lip. All at once, the realization rose starkly. "There is but one bed," she said breathlessly.

Heavy brows rose inquiringly. "And?"

"And you are in it."

"Forgive me if I err, but did you not wake this morning in this very bed? Did you not wake beside me?"

Gillian flushed, flustered and uncertain. "Aye, but I did not know that *you* would be awake!"

"Where do you propose to sleep then, if not in this bed?"

"I . . . on the floor. Aye, on the floor."

"On the floor! You cannot sleep there." His voice took on a note of authority. "It's too damp. If you sicken, who will tend me?"

Gillian's mouth opened and closed. She had wondered what kind of man he was and now she knew — he was a man to think only of himself and never of others!

"It would seem you are a man accustomed to giving orders — accustomed to being obeyed." Perturbed, Gillian did not bother to disguise her annoyance.

"It would seem I am. But perhaps I am the one who should be wary of you."

"Of me! There is no reason you should be wary of me!"

"Perchance there is every reason. You stripped the clothes from my body. You crawled within this bed and lay upon me. As I recall, you've touched me as you pleased — bathed me — while I lay naked and unmoving and helpless beneath your hands."

Gillian gasped, then narrowed her gaze. "I thought you remembered nothing!"

Gareth nearly groaned. How could he forget that? He might be empty of mind, but he was not empty of awareness. Nay, it was not something that left a man easily, especially with a woman as beauteous as this one. Judging from the starkness of his surroundings, his caretaker was poor. The bed was crude, made of wattle with a grass-rope pillow. Yet there was some disparity between her clothing and the surroundings. Her gown was simple, yet most definitely not that of a pauper. It was well made, the material not extravagant but of considerable cost. Too, her features were dainty and finely molded. He must have been half out of his mind to have thought her a harlot. The by-blow of a lord, he wondered?

"I know the feel of a woman," he stated bluntly. "I knew a woman touched me. I didn't know the woman was you until I awoke."

He could tell from her expression that she wasn't certain if she should be insulted or relieved.

Her chin climbed a notch. "If I wanted to, I could sleep on the roof and you could not stop me."

"Precisely. And there is nothing I can do to harm you."

"Nay," she said slowly, "I suppose there is not."

At least in this, his weakness prevailed. He sighed and said, "You have naught to fear from me, Gillian. You may sleep beside me without distress."

Still she did not move, but regarded him warily. The stubble of beard that darkened his jaw lent him a dangerous look, but there were deep lines of strain etched beside his mouth. He was, she conceded, defenseless as a child right now.

Her hesitation ebbed. "You are right," she murmured. She placed a knee on the mattress, while he eased to the far side.

"Excellent," he said, and there was that in his tone which conveyed his pleasure in himself. "It would seem I am a man not only of subtle words but of subtle persuasion."

Gillian stopped short. She would have withdrawn if she hadn't glimpsed the quirk of his lips. Why, he was teasing, the wretch!

His smile waned. "Come," he said softly. "Methinks you need rest as much as I."

Gillian relented. The bed was so small that there was scarcely room for both of them, yet she managed to slip beneath the coverlet without touching him.

Shadows steeped the inside of the cottage, yet neither of them slept. She felt a rustling beside her, then his voice stole quietly through the silence.

"I must ask your forgiveness, Gillian."

Gillian turned her head slightly. His countenance was not visible, only the rugged outline of his form. "Forgiveness? For what?"

"This morning. I should not have assumed you were a harlot."

Gillian was glad of the darkness, for it hid the scarlet tide of color in her cheeks. Still, his statement was the last thing she expected to hear.

His voice came again, even more softly than before. "I did not mean to make you weep."

More unexpected still.

Her throat closed oddly. "It was not that," she said faintly.

"What then?"

She felt compelled to answer, yet for a heartbeat, she felt wholly unable to. " 'Tis

. . . difficult to explain."

"Try."

She could feel his regard, locked on her face in the thickening gloom. His persistence kindled tears afresh. Gillian was reminded keenly of the aching loss of her father. And Clifton — would she ever see her brother again?

"When we found you, Brother Baldric thought you were dead, like-like the other men on the beach. Then you did not wake, and you were ill with fever. And I" — she began to quaver — "I thought you would . . ."

In the darkness, a warm, hard palm slid against hers. Lean, brown fingers twined with hers. "I will not die, Gillian."

Swamped with emotion, this time speech was beyond her capabilities just now. It made no sense, the peace and comfort wrought by this man who was a stranger — yet no longer seemed a stranger.

Soon both slept. They touched nowhere . . . nowhere but their enjoined hands.

"So. He still lives."

As Gillian nodded, Brother Baldric glanced toward the wooden door of the cottage, propped slightly ajar. A fine gray mist drizzled from a leaden sky this morn, but the afternoon had brought a tepid sunshine and patches of blue sky. A fierce wind buffeted the waves against the headland. Overhead, black-headed gulls screeched and swooped.

"Who is he?"

"His name is Gareth."

"Gareth?"

Gillian took a deep breath. "That is all I know. That is all *he* knows." Her tone low, she told him how her patient had spent many of his days alternately sleeping, then waking. In the last week, his bruises had begun to turn a greenish yellow, and he'd gained a little strength.

By the time she'd finished, Baldric's expression was troubled. "I do not like this, Lady Gillian."

Gillian looked uncomfortable.

"What is it?" Baldric asked quickly.

"He knows me as Gillian."

Baldric groaned. "My lady, no! How could you be so careless?"

"I-I did not think quickly enough to hide it. He asked my name and I told him, though I did not tell him my father was Ellis of Westerbrook. Besides," she went on, her tone low and fervent, "I hate knowing that the villagers think of me as the widow Marian."

"Nonetheless, do not tell him you are

80

Lady Gillian of Westerbrook! Perhaps it is wise that you continue to stay far from the village. They are aware that you tend a man who was gravely injured in the shipwreck. I could not hide it, not with the lads Edgar and Hugh delivering him to your cottage. We can risk no questions, not from the villagers or this man Gareth."

A knot tightened in Gillian's chest. "You believe the king's men continue to search for me?"

"I believe so, yes. And Clifton as well." Gillian knew it must be the truth, for the monks were often the eyes and ears of the people.

"Gareth is not a common man," Gillian said slowly. "I can tell by the refinement of his speech." That and a dozen other things, she acknowledged to herself. The noble span of his brow. His compassion and consideration the night he'd been convinced he'd caused her to weep. And only this morning he'd tried to rise when he'd spied her carrying in wood for the fire. He had pushed the covers aside and swung his legs to the floor, only to immediately turn white as linen.

The bundle of wood had spilled to the floor. Gillian had rushed to his side and pressed him back.

"It is not right, that I lay abed while you work," he had argued.

Her mouth set sternly, Gillian had exclaimed in remonstrance.

Yet now, an uneasy sensation crept along her spine. She remembered his fierceness when he'd been ill with fever.

"I am Marian," she'd said.

"You lie!" he had accused. "Tell me who you are!"

"If he is not a common man," said Brother Baldric, "that is all the more reason not to trust him."

"Brother Baldric," she said gently, "I understand your loyalty to my father. But I do not understand your suspicion of this man."

"You believe him then? That he remembers naught of his past?"

"I do."

"It could be a ruse. A trick."

"Perhaps it would be best if you judged for yourself." She gestured toward the door.

With that Brother Baldric pushed back his cowl. Together they entered the cottage. Gillian approached the stranger's bedside. His eyes were closed, but at the rustle of sound, he stirred.

"Gareth," she stated with no ado, "this is Brother Baldric. He would like to speak with you."

The robed man stepped forward. Gillian retreated to stand in the shadows.

Gareth inclined his head in greeting. "Brother Baldric. Gillian speaks often of you."

Brother Baldric nodded. "Gillian tells me that other than your name, you have no idea of who you are."

"This is true," Gareth said.

"You know nothing of your trade?"

Gareth's mouth thinned. "I could be the king himself and I would not know it."

"An excellent choice of subject." Brother Baldric's eyes narrowed. "Do you know who is king?"

"No."

"John is king. Son of Henry and Eleanor, brother of Richard, youngest of the Devil's brood."

"The Devil's brood . . . King Henry."

"Yes."

"And Richard," he repeated, then suddenly it was as something opened inside him. *"Richard!"* he exclaimed. *"Coeur de Lion!* A great man with golden hair and vivid blue eyes."

"Ah, so you do remember. Have you been on Crusade?"

"I have," Gareth stated promptly.

"And what of King John?" Baldric surveyed him closely.

Gareth's response was a long time in coming. "I do not know," he said at last. "And yet I cannot deny the feeling that I *should* know." His voice carried a faint bitterness. "Then again, it would seem there is much I should know, but cannot remember."

"True," Baldric agreed.

"I can only hope that Gillian is right," Gareth stated quietly, "that as my body mends, my memory will as well." He glanced at Gillian. One corner of his mouth curled upward. "I owe the lady much," he said softly. "Indeed, I owe her my very life."

Baldric slid his hands into the wide gray sleeves of his robe. "She has a warm, giving nature. No man was more aware of it than her husband."

Gareth's gaze jerked back to Baldric. "Her husband?"

"Yes. She is a widow, you know. She still grieves deeply for her husband, who died when he was thrown from his horse. As she brought you here to heal, so did I bring her to this place to heal."

Gillian smothered a gasp. Why was Brother Baldric compelled to perpetuate that horrid lie — and more? she wondered wildly. There was no need, no need at all. She winced as she felt the touch of Gareth's eyes anew. Brief though it was, it was piercingly intent.

"You brought Gillian here?"

"I did. She felt the need to spend her grief in solitude." Baldric lifted a brow. "Have you a wife, sir?"

Gareth shook his head. "There is no one. I can feel it." His gaze slid back to Gillian. "A pity," he remarked, "that one so young as the lady here should find herself a widow already. Perhaps it is good that I am here, for now she need not be alone."

Brother Baldric's head came up. Each man found himself the object of a shrewdly measuring survey by the other.

"I wish you a swift recovery," Baldric said with a stilted smile. "Without doubt you must be eager to be well — and perhaps you will have remembered the rest of your past as well. I'm certain you'll then be anxious to return to your home, wherever that may be." With a bow he retreated toward the door.

Gillian followed him outside. Before she could say a word, Brother Baldric held up a hand. "I know what you will say, child. You think I am wrong. In truth, I know not what to believe about this man who calls himself Gareth."

"And I do not know why, but somehow I think he is a man of honor."

"And he may well be a man of honor. But there is something in the tilt of his head, his manner of speech, that leads me to believe this man Gareth is a bold man. A daring man. A knight in service of some powerful lord . . . mayhap even a knight in service of the king —"

Gillian protested. "He did not even know John was king!"

"So he said. But he remembered King Henry and King Richard. Therefore, you cannot tell him who you are, nor the true circumstances that brought you here. Your father was sharply critical of the king, and the less you tell Gareth, the better."

It was true. Her father had harsh words for the king, from the day he ascended the throne. His petty wars, his ceaseless demand for taxes from the people of England. . . .

"We cannot be careless, Lady Gillian. You cannot trust blindly. There is too much at stake."

A fierce gust of wind swirl whipped her skirts about her legs. Her gaze was drawn unwittingly to the sky. Alas, even now, the sky was seething. Black, threatening storm clouds hovered just above the choppy seas, a bittersweet reminder . . .

Ah, but if only Papa had been unjustly accused. Perhaps he might have lived. . . . Then she would not be here near the blustery shore where rain and wind and storms abounded.

The world seemed to blacken. Bleakness seeped through her. Her dreams had once been fanciful and full of the exuberance of youth, full of eager energy for what the future might bring. But now such thoughts of the future wrought only heartache and fear. Brother Baldric insisted that she was strong, yet Gillian felt as if the pain of a thousand fetters weighted her down.

Never would she forget the last time she'd seen her father, that bleak September night that thunder raged and sheets of rain thrashed the walls of Westerbrook — the night he'd swept into her chamber in the dead of night.

Never would she forget his last words.

"I've failed you, daughter," he had said with tears in his eyes. "I've failed you and Clifton. And I pray that you will forgive me, for I will never forgive myself for what I have done to you and your brother — for leaving you in such peril."

Gillian had known immediately that something was horribly, horribly wrong.

"Papa," she cried, "what is it?"

"The king visited William de Vries these last few days," he said heavily.

"Yes, I'd heard." William de Vries was a baron whose lands bordered Westerbrook's to the east. His wife Isabella had been god-mother to their eldest son.

"There was an attempt on King John's life today in the forest," he said.

As the words passed his lips, he did not look her in the eye. Gillian knew then . . . knew her father was the man responsible. A man of bluntness and bold action, Ellis of Westerbrook was ever a man to speak his mind — and he had been outspoken in his contempt of King John almost from the moment he came to power.

He had taken matters into his own hands.

A choking dread assailed her. "Papa," she whispered in horror. "Papa, no! Oh, dear God, it was you, wasn't it?"

Slowly he raised his head. There was a world of pain in his eyes, the eyes so like hers. "Aye, Gillian. It was I who loosed the arrow, but it missed its mark and struck the king's guard instead. Ah, what a fool I have been! I know it now, now when it is too late. All I could think was how England would be the better if our people were rid of him, for it has been a time of seething emotions and great unrest in our land. So many of us have grown weary and outraged by his unceasing demands for taxes and the call to arms, that John might regain his lands across the Channel."

His expression was tortured. "I was so angry when the Great Charter failed to rein in John's power as king. I fear it will but make him stronger, all the more determined to oppress the people of England. There are rumors that he seeks mercenaries from across the Channel; that he has promised them the castles and lands that belong to us, the people of England, in return for the defeat of those who gathered against him at Running-Mead."

He shook his head. "But once again, the barons can agree on nothing. I was convinced the easiest way would be to see John struck down now, and with the opportunity so close at hand . . . Ah, Gillian, I thought only of success, and never of failure. And in my zeal, I was reckless. You and Clifton are innocent, yet now I fear I have condemned you for the rest of your lives."

Gillian listened numbly as he seized her hands.

"We are in danger, all of us. I know the king, and he will not rest until he finds those responsible. Indeed, 'tis my worst fear that John may vent his wrath upon you and

Clifton as well, for he is a man of venom and spite. That is why we must flee, all of us, now while we cannot be seen."

"Now?" Her gaze slid apprehensively toward the shutters. She had disliked storms since she was a child, but as if to underscore the question, a flash of blinding lightning ripped across the sky; the crash of thunder shook the very walls of her chamber.

"Yes, child. I fear it cannot be helped." His hands tightened around hers. "But we cannot be together, Gillian, none of us. I have entrusted Clifton to the care of Alwin, for I know he will protect my son with his life. They have already departed." Alwin was his chief retainer.

"Where have they gone?"

" 'Tis better that you do not know. Brother Baldric awaits you in the stable," he said gently. "Gather several warm gowns and your mantle. There is neither the time nor the room for more."

Gillian was still reeling from all that had transpired. In the space of a moment, her life had changed forever, it seemed. "What about you, Papa?"

"Once you and Brother Baldric are on your way, I will make my own way."

"Alone?"

"It is best that way."

"Papa, no! Let me stay with you," she begged. "Let me help you!"

"Nay, Gillian." He was adamant. "It must be like this. At least this way, if one of us is caught, the others will live." He ran his fingers down her cheek. "Be wary, child. Put your faith in no one but Brother Baldric. If I am able, I will find you and Clifton."

But that was not to be. It was not to be, for as he'd predicted, he'd been discovered and caught by the king's men.

His life was forfeit.

At the remembrance, an odd prickle curled down her spine. Her father had not been alone in his endeavor to kill the king. He had shielded someone, but who . . . *Who?*

"The other assailant," she said slowly. "Has the king discovered his identity yet?"

Baldric sighed. "It would seem not," he said heavily, "and I do not know if that is a blessing or a curse. Your father gave his life to protect this other man. Was it worth it? May God forgive me, but there are times I wonder if Ellis did not give his life in vain." He shook his head. "Before he died, the king's guard swore that he saw two men when the attempt on the king's life took place. Yet what if he was mistaken? What if there was only one man?"

91

"My father." It was a quiet statement of fact, not a query.

Baldric winced. "Yes. What if the guard's eyes deceived him?"

Quietly she said, "They did not."

Brother Baldric peered at her oddly. "Why do you say that? How can you be certain?"

"The day before the attempt on the king's life, I entered the counting room to speak with Papa. I thought he was alone, but there was someone with him, behind the curtain. I heard Papa speak of the king — and hunting."

Fear leaped in Brother Baldric's faded blue eyes. "Lady Gillian, never tell me you know the identity of the other assailant — that you've known all along!"

"Nay. I saw but the shadow of a man. Yet I had the feeling I did not know him."

There was more, for in truth, something elusive nagged at her. More than once she'd experienced the unmistakable feeling there was something she should have remembered about that encounter, something vitally important. She struggled to remember, but alas, it would not come.

It seemed she was no better than the man inside the cottage.

"I was curious," Gillian went on. "Not

long after, I asked Papa who was there with him in the counting room. He was angry, Brother Baldric, and said that I was never to mention it to anyone."

"Do not," Baldric said in a strange tone. "Tell no one what you have just told me, Lady Gillian. *Tell no one.* Indeed, I pray you did not know him — I pray you do not remember — for it might place you in still more danger."

Gillian looked at him sharply. Was it the gloom of twilight and the coming storm, or had his skin turned a rather ashen gray? She was still striving to decipher both his meaning and his countenance when all at once he bent low, seized by a dry, hacking cough.

Gillian grabbed his arm. "Brother Baldric," she cried, "are you all right?"

It was some time before the paroxysm ceased and he raised himself upright, still more as he labored for breath and summoned the ability to speak.

"It has passed, child. Do not worry. Now, I must be on my way."

"Not yet. Please, Brother Baldric, come inside," she urged. "Wait until the storm passes before returning to the village." As she spoke, Gillian scanned his features. The sudden pallor of his skin was not due to alarm as she'd first thought, but to sickness.

"Nay. Father Aidan will be expecting me."

"Brother Baldric, you're ill!"

"I am not," he denied. Gillian had twisted her fingers into the sleeves of his robe, but he held himself firm. He straightened his shoulders and seemed to stand a little taller, and in the movement Gillian glimpsed a stubbornness that revealed itself but rarely.

" 'Tis a cough from a chill," he dismissed. "Naught to worry about, child. The days I traveled with Father Aidan were long and wet. I am well," he insisted. "Now go, Lady Gillian. Tend your patient. He is far nearer the grave than I."

But Gillian was suddenly stricken. A rending ache pierced her heart. Perhaps it was childish, but it was as if the world that had been so safe and secure her entire life had vanished.

Indeed, it had.

Her father was forever lost to her. Perhaps Clifton as well. Brother Baldric was all that was familiar, all that was left of that world. She could not bear the thought of losing him, too!

But she sensed there would be no dissuading him. She reached up and kissed his

94

cheek. "Look after yourself, Brother Baldric, else I will stand watch over you night and day and make certain that you do," she warned with mock severity.

He gave a rusty chuckle. "I do believe that you would." His smile faded. "I will bring clothing the next time I come." His gaze flitted briefly from the cottage, then back to her.

"Remember, Lady Gillian, do not trust lightly."

His meaning was not lost on her. Gillian stood motionless, watching as he weaved toward the tall grasses that led to the path.

Papa had urged much the same thing. *Be wary,* he had said.

An eerie foreboding washed over her. Gareth's image floated into her mind, dark hair, green gaze of piercing intensity. What part, if any, would he play in her life? she wondered. Would the future bring the return of his past? His future, she acknowledged suddenly, was no less uncertain than hers.

Neither of them had any choice. She could only wait, wait for whatever fate would befall her . . .

And Gareth as well.

5

"He doesn't believe me. Nor does he like me," Gareth stated flatly.

Gillian had done little more than cross the threshold of the cottage when she was hailed by Gareth's statement; it was readily apparent he spoke of Brother Baldric. She pushed the door shut, then turned to face him.

Gareth had pushed himself up to rest against the pillow. No semblance of a smile softened the grim line of his lips.

She considered his statement, a trifle unsure how to respond. "There are reasons for that," she said finally.

"And what might those reasons be?"

Ah, but she should have known he would persist. "I've known him since I was a child. He served my family long before I was born. He's been protective of me since my father's death —"

"And your husband's, no doubt." He made the interruption pointedly, and with decided coolness.

Gillian was uncomfortable. "Yes," she lied.

The corners of Gareth's mouth turned down. "He has no reason to distrust me."

"He is wary of you because you are a stranger."

"Isn't it the duty of a priest to —"

"He is not a priest. He is a lay brother in the service of the Lord. After the death of his wife and four children many years ago, he decided to dedicate his life to God."

"My point exactly. That he has never taken holy orders is irrelevant. He wears the trappings of a man of God, so is it not his duty to impart charity toward others? You claim otherwise, but I failed to see little hint of a forgiving, benevolent nature."

Gillian could summon no argument, save one. "There is much discontent in the country at present," she murmured.

His expression was a clear indication he was clearly unsatisfied with her explanation. Brother Baldric had urged caution; frantically she wondered how much she dare divulge.

"There are some who are not favorably disposed toward King John," she stated carefully, "some who fear John has spies afoot in every corner of the kingdom. The people of England have grown weary of the demand for taxes. Many believe King John wishes only to fatten his war chest, that he cares little about England and only wishes to retake the possessions he lost in Normandy."

"A time when loyalties sway like the wind. A time when it's every man for himself."

His perception was only too astute. Gillian nodded.

"My father used to say that even before the interdict, it was as if all of England lay hidden beneath a bleak cloud."

"And so King John is heartily disliked."

Despised, more like, she nearly blurted. She stole a glance at Gareth, only to discover that his features were almost guarded. Brother Baldric's warning clanged through her once more. *Do not trust lightly.* She hesitated, all at once afraid to say yea, afraid to say nay.

He indicated the stool beside the bed. "Sit," he said. "Tell me of the interdict."

There was a rustle of movement as Gillian obliged. "I was too young to remember, but there was much discord between the Vatican and King John when the archbishop of Canterbury died."

Gareth held up a hand. "The archbishop of Canterbury," he repeated. "It was Hubert Walter, wasn't it?"

"Yes. Pope Innocent refused to confirm the selection of the monks, Reginald, and also cast aside John's choice, the bishop of Norwich. The pope's choice was Stephen Langton. John swore he would never allow Langton to step foot on English soil. When John refused to give in, the pope placed England under interdict . . ."

". . . and so the church doors were locked and sealed," he finished grimly. "The bells did not toll. Altars were covered and sacred relics stowed away. But John at last swore allegiance to Rome and Stephen Langton was declared archbishop."

"Yes," Gillian affirmed. "It would seem you know far better than I the consequences of the interdict."

A lengthy silence prevailed. Gareth's gaze had shifted. He stared across the room into the deepening shadows. His profile was broodingly somber.

"How can this be?" he said after a moment. "How is it possible I know these things, yet my own past eludes me? Whether I come from the north, or the south, or London —" He broke off. His features seemed to freeze. "I've been to London," he said suddenly. "I've been there — and I disliked it heartily. The houses were crammed together, almost one upon another. The streets were dirty and smelled of the filthiest stable." His jaw clenched. "Christ, no wonder Brother Baldric doubts my every word!"

She could hear the frustration in his tone; at the same time, he sounded so tortured, so tormented, that Gillian's heart went out to him.

"It weighs heavily on you, doesn't it — not being able to remember."

"Sometimes it is all I can think of. My mind is never at rest. I try so hard my head aches. I dislike feeling so helpless. I feel . . ." He made an impatient gesture. "Oh, but I know not how to explain. As if someone holds a sword at my throat and I am incapable of defending myself." He glanced the length of his body. His mouth twisted in bitter self-derision. "Look at me! Were someone to roust this cottage, it would be *you* defending *me!*"

Gillian smiled faintly. Ah, but it was just like a man to liken any hint of weakness to battle. Was it so terrible to be beholden to a woman? Still, she could understand his feeling of vulnerability. She'd sensed his restlessness, his impatience with his malaise.

Her smile wilted. " 'Tis your wish to remember," she said quietly. "Yet sometimes I think it is better *not* to remember."

"Is that why you didn't tell me you were a widow?"

His directness startled her. Her gaze sped back to his, only to discover his scrutiny was as probing as his query. But before she could answer, he posed another.

"What was his name?"

"His name?" she echoed.

His gaze remained steady on her face. "Yes. His name."

Real panic raced through her, for Gillian was woefully unprepared to supply a ready response. She should have been, she realized — ah, why had Brother Baldric felt the need to perpetuate such falsehood?

"I . . . Osgood." God help her, it was the only name she could think of!

"How long has it been since he died?"

"Half a year," she said quickly . . . too quickly? She held her breath, for he appeared unwilling to abandon the subject.

"Is it true you still grieve?"

Gillian's mind sped straight to her father. Sudden tears blurred her vision. Her soul bled dark with the stain of her loss. She could not speak for the sudden ache that scalded her throat.

"I see," Gareth said softly. "So much that it is not your head that aches, but your heart."

She looked away, her tone very low. "Is that not the way of grief?"

"I suppose it is." It was odd, what her observation evoked. All at once a strange feeling washed over him. In some pocket of awareness deep inside, he was certain that he, too, had once harbored a grief that rivaled hers. But unlike Gillian's, the pain did not come, for the feeling was as fleeting as his memories.

Outside there was a distant rumble of thunder, signaling the approach of the storm. Gillian shivered. The storm was drawing close.

Gareth frowned. "You're chilled." He glanced outside, where the veil of night was already drawn over the earth. He held up a corner of the fur coverlet. "Come to bed where it's warm."

It should have been an innocuous enough request, considering they'd spent nearly every hour together the past week, both day and night. Yet all at once Gillian's heart was knocking wildly. She was starkly conscious of the fact that he was a man, and she was a woman . . . and they were alone. *Alone*. And she knew what men and women did, alone in the dark, alone in the night.

So did he. Though he'd displayed no such inclination — at least toward her — of that Gillian had no doubt. She suddenly admitted what she had been unwilling to admit until now — that Gareth was unquestionably the most strikingly handsome man she'd ever laid eyes upon. Black hair spilled jauntily over his forehead. His jaw was square and hard, his nose narrow and aquiline, his brows as dark as his hair and arched over thick-lashed eyes of green. Oh, aye, handsome he was . . . not just in face, but in form as well . . .

Firelight flickered over him. His body was angled slightly toward her, his strength clearly in evidence. A masculine tangle of hair darkened the plane of his chest. Gillian was well acquainted with the iron-hard tightness of his form and the breadth of his shoulders.

Her throat grew suddenly dry. Indeed, she thought shakily, what did she *not* notice about him? Her gaze drifted to his face; even in repose, his features had been strikingly arresting. Now her gaze locked onto the cleanly sculpted lines of his mouth. She glanced away in confusion, feeling her body flood with heat, remembering how she'd given him drink . . . recalling with almost painful acuteness the smooth feel of his lips beneath hers.

"I cannot." The refusal slipped out before she could even stop it. She stood so suddenly she knocked over the stool. As she spoke, she backed away several steps.

His mouth turned down. "Have we not had this discussion before?"

" 'Tis different now."

"Different how?"

"It is not right that I lay beside you."

"Because of Osgood?"

Osgood. For an instant her mind went blank. "Nay," she gasped before she thought better of it.

His gaze narrowed. He fixed her with a quietly measured look. "I begin to see." His silky undertone should have served as a warning. "It's because of the good brother's appearance this evening, isn't it?"

Gillian had no chance to respond. "You've slept beside me all these other nights. You've committed no sin. *We've* committed no sin," he emphasized. "Why so pious and virtuous now?"

Her chin angled high. A stab of anger pierced the hurt. "Do not tell me," she said stiffly, "you are a man who knows little of piety and virtue."

There was a silence, a silence that ever

deepened. "I do not know. Perhaps I am a thief. An outlaw."

Gillian looked at him sharply, but this time she detected no trace of bitterness. "I think not. You still have both your hands."

"Then perhaps I'm a lucky one. Now come, Gillian."

Outside lightning lit up the night sky. The ominous roll of thunder that followed made the walls shake. In a heartbeat Gillian was across the floor — and squarely onto the bed next to him.

He laughed, the wretch!

"Perhaps you are not an outlaw," she flared, "but I begin to suspect you may well be a rogue!"

He made no answer, but once again lifted the coverlet. Her lips tightened indignantly, but she tugged off her slippers and slid into bed. He respected the space she put between them, but she was aware of the weight of his gaze settling on her in the darkness.

"Are you afraid of storms?"

"Nay," she retorted. As if to put the lie to the denial, lightning sizzled and sparked, illuminating the cottage to near daylight. She gasped. Her gaze swung fearfully to the shutters. There was an answering rumble of thunder.

She tensed, half-expecting some jibe from

Gareth. Instead, his fingers stole through hers, as had become their custom. Thunder cracked anew, yet the fear she should have felt — *would* have felt if she were alone — did not appear. Oddly comforted, lulled by his presence, it wasn't long before she felt her muscles loosen and her eyelids grow heavy.

Within the hour, the skies railed and the storm vented its fury, a blasting tempest of wind and rain that pelted the world beneath.

Curiously, it was not the storm that woke Gillian, but Gareth. He was shifting restlessly, muttering something — she knew not what.

"I will not do it!" He shouted so suddenly she jumped. "It is wrong. By the saints, it is wrong!"

Gillian raised herself on an elbow and peered at him. The fire had burned down to ashes, but it cast out enough light for her to make out the iron clench of his jaw. His chest was bare; the blankets lay twisted about his ankles. He was dreaming, she realized, and it was no peaceful, easy dream that claimed him.

"Gareth," she said. "Gareth!"

He gave no sign that he heard. He swore, a

vile curse that made her ears burn. Then: "Sweet Jesus, what am I to do? I have no choice. I must find her. I must find her!"

Clearly he was a man who fought some inner struggle of his own. Her heart went out to him even as she wondered what woman he sought. Or was it a child?

All at once the hand at his side balled into a fist. He flung out his arm, and Gillian tumbled hard from the bed. A jarring pain wrenched through her, but she scrambled upright and crawled atop the bed. Gareth was still thrashing.

Without hesitation, she laid her fingertips on the raspy plane of his cheek. She knew he was not angry with her, but with some unknown presence visible only in his dream.

"Gareth." Urgently she beseeched him. "Gareth, wake up."

At her touch, his limbs ceased their questing. His head turned toward her. It gave her a start to see that his eyes were wide open, fixed on her unblinkingly. Before she could say a word, he reached out a hand and snared the cascade of hair that tumbled over her breast onto his chest. 'Ere she could draw breath, long arms caught her close — so close she could feel every sinewed curve of his chest, the taut line of his thighs molded against her own.

There was no chance for escape. No chance for struggle. No thought of panic. No thought of resistance, for Gillian was too stunned to even move . . .

His mouth closed over hers.

Never before had Gillian tasted the heat and warmth and possession of a man's mouth — the time she had pressed her lips against his to feed him was but a glimmer compared to this . . .

For this was a kiss of fiery intensity, of raw, untamed passion. From the shattering moment his mouth trapped hers, she knew instinctively that this was no kiss of gentle worship. It was a kiss that carried the sizzling flame of passion ungoverned, a searing kiss from lover to lover.

It was just as she'd always dreamed. How many times had she imagined this — being kissed in just such a way, by just such a man, a kiss that stole her very breath! Yet this was not the man of her dreams. This was Gareth, a man who knew naught but his name. A man with no past. Not the man she'd dreamed she would give her life and love and heart . . .

She cared not. She could only revel in the feel of his mouth upon hers, the arms that held her, both tender and strong.

There was nothing tentative in either his

kiss or his touch. His tongue traced the outline of her mouth. With torrid, breath-stealing strokes it dove boldly within, discovering the slick interior of her mouth, as brazen as . . . as the devil fingers that had taken up a tantalizing game at the neckline of her shift, which gaped low. Back and forth, back and forth, that bold hand teased and traced a flaming line across her chest. She gasped when at last he trespassed beneath, seizing with unerring accuracy the unfettered fullness of both breasts.

His mouth was sealed on the vulnerable skin at the side of her neck; her head tilted, as if in invitation — as if to oblige him further. Her heart bounded, yet everything inside went weak. Flames licked at the crests of her breasts; his thumbs were engaged in a taunting, evocative play that made her nipples harden and grow taut in something that could only be called eagerness. Sparks of a pleasure she'd never thought to expect — never even dreamed of! — burst from the peaks of her breasts. Unknowingly, Gillian's hands slid around to his back. Her fingers tightened. A thrill shot through her, for his naked flesh was as firm and sleek as she remembered.

She felt his hands in her hair, sliding through the tumbled darkness. A rush of air misted across her cheek. With his fingertips he combed through tangled, ebony skeins.

"Beautiful," he said hoarsely. "So beautiful. Soft and golden and warm. The color of bright summer sunshine . . ."

Gillian froze, as if the point of a dagger had penetrated her heart.

"Celeste," he breathed. "Celeste. God, how I've missed you."

The point drove home.

Gillian's heart squeezed. She tore her mouth away. Gareth raised his head and peered at her. An uncanny sensation prickled her skin, for he was still in the throes of his dream — it was not her he saw . . . but the woman Celeste.

"Sleep," she said shakily. "Gareth, sleep."

Something of her plea must have penetrated. His head dropped back to the pillow, but not before he'd reached for her once more, urging her head into the hollow of his shoulder. Gillian complied, but it was different now — now she held herself aloof, not in physical closeness, but in spirit.

The effort she made was valiant. Over and over she told herself it was shock that had stalled the rhythm of her heart. But in truth, she was wholly taken aback by the depth of her response to his kiss. In those heart-stopping moments when his lips fused hot and warm against hers, her pulse aclamor as never before, it hadn't mattered.

Now it did.

Her heart constricted. Disappointment flooded her. She couldn't blink back a fleeting mist of tears as she spied the dark lock of hair still gripped tight in Gareth's palm.

Beautiful, he'd said. But she — Gillian — was not the one who so enflamed him. For Gillian's hair was not the gold of summer sunshine, but the hue of the darkest winter night.

Ah, but she'd been a fool! She'd allowed Gareth to kiss her, to stroke her body in a shockingly bold way . . . with another woman's name on his lips. Another woman's image burned deep in his mind.

A woman named Celeste.

Nay, she was not the woman who filled his dreams.

And he was not the man of hers.

6

It was the splash of water that woke Gareth the next morning. Opening his eyes, he spied Gillian standing across the room. She was pouring a steady stream of water from the bucket into a washbasin. She'd restrained the incredible glory of her hair. Although it was confined in several braids which she'd fastened at her nape, still it gleamed with the shine of rich, polished wood. With stark, vivid remembrance, he recalled the way it had felt that very first day — soft, ebony silk sliding against the roughened tips of his fingers. He wished she might free it, that he might feel its dark splendor glide over his skin once more.

Even as he watched, the bucket was set aside, a linen cloth neatly placed beside the basin. Her intent to wash registered fleetingly in his mind, even as she loosened her gown and it settled on the flare of her hips.

Although she was now bare to the waist, all that was visible was the dimpled tuck of the slender lines of her back. Gareth meant to look away. He should have. But then she turned ever so little, affording him a glimpse of all that had remained hidden to him until now.

And then he could not look away if his life depended on it.

Slender arms lifted, tugging the braids forward. 'Twas a movement that outlined in perfect profile the alluring lines of her body — utterly enticing, unmistakably full and womanly. She was small, almost fragile looking, yet above the rising plane of her ribs, her breasts spilled forth in pale, supple splendor, crowned by pouting nipples the color of coral.

The cloth dipped, lifted and was drawn along her body. His gaze tracked its path. A trail of droplets shimmered in its wake, leaving her skin damp and dewy and gleaming with a luster that cried out for a man's touch. A glistening droplet of water clung to the very peak of one exquisite breast, puckered tight against the cold.

Hot, hungry desire rushed straight to his loins. Heat pooled inside him. His rod stirred to thick, almost painful erectness. His first thought was that Osgood had been a lucky man, to have a woman as lovely as Gillian in his bed. His second was the urge to snare her in his embrace, to divest her fully of her gown and bring her naked into his arms.

Were he an able man, he decided, he would do exactly that. Were he an able man, he would kneel before her, bend his head to the succulent fruit of her breasts, taste and tug those coral peaks until she could stand no more, until she cried aloud her pleasure. Were he an able man, he would run his fingers through the lush, dark triangle he knew would guard the hidden font of her womanhood. He'd run his fingers through the downy fleece and explore it to his most fervent desire — and hers. And then, when they were both ready, he'd bury his fiery shaft deep in the heat and heart of her.

Aye, an able man, he decided with dark, brittle humor, would have done just that. Little wonder, then, that he was given to ponder how long it had been since he'd made love to a woman.

Gillian was unaware of his perusal. It gave her a start when she turned and discovered his eyes wide open, fastened full upon her. Disconcerted, she hastily pulled the sleeve of her gown up over her shoulder. Her heart began to pound. Had he seen her? She prayed she'd been quick enough to shield herself.

Summoning a calm she was far from feeling, she stepped toward the bed and took a deep breath. "Good morning, Gareth."

No greeting was returned. A strong hand shot out and pulled her down onto the bed.

Her eyes flew wide. "Gareth! What is it?"

Lean fingers hooked into the neckline of her gown. Gillian gasped when he swept it down her arm, revealing the naked slope of her shoulder.

It was there his gaze now dwelled. "That is a fresh bruise," he observed grimly.

It was true. A dark purplish bruise marred the perfect creaminess of her skin. Gillian glanced down, then hastily dragged her eyes up. Her other hand fluttered up to cover the swell of her breast. She wasn't sure if she was more indignant or embarrassed.

"Can you not allow me some privacy?" she cried.

"I fear I have little choice in the matter," he reminded her tightly.

"Nonetheless, you need not spy on me!"

He dismissed her disparagement with an almost haughty disdain. "Where else would a man's eyes rest when a woman who looks as you do stands half-naked before him? I

115

am a man, Gillian, and I am not made of stone. But that is of no consequence," he went on. "Tell me how you came by that bruise."

She paid no heed to his demand, for her heart had fluttered, then resumed with thick, heavy strokes. Within that span, Gillian could neither think nor speak. Was he drawn to her, as she was drawn to him? She could deny the truth of what she felt no longer — the sensations sweeping through last night were all too real and remained all too vivid! Was he saying she was beautiful? A wave of darkness stole through her. Nay, she thought. It was Celeste he'd called beautiful.

" 'Tis nothing," she replied curtly.

"Nothing! By God, it is!"

Gillian's lips pressed together stubbornly. Green eyes clashed with blue in a wordless duel.

Gareth scowled, his lips thin, his features stony. "Was it Brother Baldric?"

"Brother Baldric!" Gillian was first astounded, then affronted. She defended Brother Baldric staunchly. "Why, he is the kindest, most gentle man on this earth! If you must know, then know this — it was you who did this!"

"Me!" Gareth was astounded. His anger

drained as suddenly as it had erupted, but he was no less determined. "How? When?"

Too late Gillian wished he had not seen her. Wished he had not spoken. Ah, but she was forever remembering that which she wished she did not!

"Last night," she said. "It happened last night." As she spoke, she realized he had yet to free her. Never in her life had she felt so awkward! She'd been intimate with him in ways she'd never been intimate with another man. Touched nearly every part of his body. And now he had touched *her*. Now he had seen her! She sought to tug the material of her gown back where it belonged, but his fingers twisted even more tightly into the material and held fast.

"I did this?"

She nodded.

A horrible feeling washed over him. The knowledge that he'd done this was like a red-hot knife plunged into his gut. "How?" was all he asked. *"How?"*

You were not yourself, she almost blurted. She did not, for she was all at once pierced by a prickly unease. Who was he . . . truly? And who was she to know him?

"You were dreaming," she relayed, her voice very low. "You seemed in some distress. 'It is wrong,' you shouted. And then

117

you seemed anxious to find someone."

Gareth listened intently. "Who?" A dream, she said. But was it a dream — or something more?

Gillian averted her gaze. "I do not know. 'I must find her,' " she quoted. "You were angry. And, in your anger, you struck out blindly." She faltered. "I . . . was knocked from the bed."

With the tips of his fingers he traced the outline of the bruise; his gossamer touch, so light she could barely feel him. "I am sorry, Gillian. I did not mean to hurt you."

"It was never my belief that you did."

"Then why will you not look at me?" His tone was very quiet. His fingers fell away. Free at last, Gillian dragged her sleeve upward, covering her exposed skin and rising at the same time.

She busied herself with bolting the shutter at the window, then moved to sit on the stool before the fire. She could feel his questioning regard, yet still she refused to meet it.

"Gillian?" An odd feeling gripped him and would not let go. Her shoulders were hunched tight, her hands clasped together before her. "I have the feeling there is more," he said slowly.

The fire seemed to hold the utmost fascination for her. *Perhaps because there is,* she thought wildly.

An even deeper fear began to sharpen inside him. "Dear God, Gillian, you begin to frighten me . . . what else did I do?"

Small fingers plucked at the fabric of her skirt; it was there she confined her attention.

"Gillian. Gillian, come here."

She shook her head, an ardent denial.

"Then I will come to you," he said grimly.

That brought her head up. Her gaze swung to his. "You cannot." It was less a taunt than a prediction, for she knew his weakness.

She was wrong.

The covers were thrust aside. He swung his legs to the floor and struggled to his feet. For one perilous instant, he wavered.

An almost feral satisfaction in his expression, he started toward her.

Gillian's lips parted. Shock brought her to her feet.

If she was taken aback, she couldn't help it. The closer he came, the more her neck craned, for he towered above her. When he'd been lying abed, she'd been aware of his strength and breadth. But somehow she hadn't been aware just how tall he truly was.

The effort was too much. One knee

sagged; swearing, he began to wobble. Gillian flung her arms around his waist, but his weight was more than she could bear. Together they toppled to the floor.

Gillian recovered herself in a heartbeat. But Gareth lay completely still, breathing heavily. His eyes were squeezed shut. White lines of strain were drawn about his mouth, and he'd gone a trifle pale.

"Gareth! Gareth, are you all right?"

It took a moment for Gareth to gather his breath and his strength. He opened his eyes. "Christ," he said hoarsely, "methinks I've given you a bruise to match the other."

Gillian made a swift, abortive movement. She would have twisted away, but he possessed the reflexes of a cat. Hard arms clamped about her back. He brought her close, so close she could feel the texture of the rugged mat of hair that covered his chest against the fabric of her gown. She lay on her side — and he on his. She stared into eyes the color of the forest.

"You've yet to tell me what else I did last night," he reminded her.

"All right," she said on a ragged rush of air. "You kissed me. You kissed me, Gareth!"

A confession. An accusation. Either way, the relief that poured through him was immense. He would have laughed, if not for the dismay so keenly writ on her lovely features.

"That is all? I kissed you?"

"Is that not enough?" Gillian fought a fleeting panic. God above, but she was not about to tell him what else he had done — that he had cupped the fullness of her breasts in his palms. That he'd even teased her nipples and made them ache in a way she did not understand at all!

Gareth paused to consider. For all that he knew she had been married, there was an air of purity and innocence about her that was puzzling for a woman who'd been wed. The way that she quickly, almost nervously, withdrew her hands when the need to touch him was complete, as if the feel of a man were something new, even disturbing. Or was he mistaken?

"Perhaps," he said slowly, "the problem is not that I kissed you, but that you kissed me back."

"What!" she gasped.

"Did you return my kiss?" Quietly he posed the question.

Gillian floundered. Her cheeks burned painfully. The truth was that she'd hardly endured his kiss. The truth was that in those dizzying moments with his lips upon hers, she'd been wholly captivated. Entranced. But she was not about to divulge such feelings to him!

"You should not ask such a thing!" Her hands came up between them. She strained away, longing for escape. Alas, there was none, for his arms tightened.

" 'Tis a fair question."

" 'Tis most *un*fair!" Her cheeks were burning. She glared at him, perturbed at his insistence.

"But you remember and I do not."

"Ah, yes, how could I forget," she said on a note of bitter reproof. "You remember nothing but your name."

"And you've yet to answer my question."

Gillian's breath dammed in her throat. Ripe within her breast was an odd tumult. How it happened, she knew not. Why it happened, he knew not. That it did . . . they both knew.

His lips hovered perilously near hers. Gillian's fingers curled and uncurled against the mat of hair on his chest. A lock of black hair had fallen onto his forehead, lending him a roguish look. She was devastatingly aware of his gaze traveling slowly over her features, settling for a long moment on the curve of her mouth.

"Do not look at me so," she said on a ragged breath.

All traces of teasing departed his features. "Why? You have no husband, Gillian."

Nor did I ever, she longed to screech. Why did she have the awful feeling that untruth would come back to haunt her?

He lowered his head so that their lips almost touched. "I am sorry I hurt you" — his gaze flickered briefly to her shoulder — "but I am not sorry I kissed you."

Her heart wrenched. His declaration only made it harder. It made no sense, that the thought of him with another woman should bother her. Yet it did. It hurt unbearably.

"You do not understand," she said wildly, for suddenly that was how she felt. As if her emotions were as blustery as the seas which had brought him here. Though it pained her to think of him with another woman — to speak of it — Gillian knew what she must do. Perchance it might jar his memory.

"In your dream, it was not *me* you kissed. It was another woman, a woman with golden hair." Gillian couldn't bring herself to say the name he had breathed aloud, nor to tell him he'd called her by name. "A woman with hair like summer sunshine, you said. You praised her beauty. You whispered how you'd missed her. And for the life of me, I cannot help but wonder if she is real . . . a part of your past, Gareth. You told Brother

Baldric you had no wife, but perhaps you are wrong."

He did not deny it. For the space of a heartbeat, something surfaced in his eyes, something that might have been remembrance.

Yet neither did he affirm it, either. Gillian was acutely aware of the way he'd gone very still.

"Do you remember her? A woman with golden hair?" She held her breath and waited — waited forever, it seemed.

"Methinks 'twas but a dream, Gillian. It does not mean such a woman existed."

But he had glanced away as he said it, and a shiver went down her spine. Her heart began to thud. He had come here a stranger — indeed, he was still a stranger, for what did she truly know of him? What secrets, she asked herself, lay hidden behind the screen of his eyes?

She started when a lean finger trailed along the line of her jaw. She would have pulled away, but strong fingers captured her chin, forcing her regard to his. His was level and unbending.

"Why do you flinch? You've naught to fear from me, Gillian."

Gillian's chest labored with the rise and fall of her lungs. "At times it's almost frightening," she confided, her tone very low. "Forgive me, Gareth, but I cannot help but wonder who you are. If you are a man of honor and truth."

" 'Tis my hope that I am. In my heart, I feel that I am."

She wanted to believe him. Longed for it desperately. Yet what if she was wrong? She searched her soul . . . along with his.

His gaze was so steady, his eyes so green.

Little by little, her fears slipped away. For in that moment, Gillian believed in him. Believed in him with all of her heart.

7

To Gareth's dismay, his efforts that day were not without cost. When he tried to get out of bed again, he discovered he could barely lift his head from the pillow. He ached almost as badly as he had that very first day. Gillian chastised him roundly for even trying. It was then Gareth acknowledged that willpower alone would not dictate his recovery; his body simply needed more time.

It also brought home the somber realization of how perilously near death he had come.

Those first few attempts to rise brought a sweat to his brow and a giddiness to his head; without Gillian's help, he might surely have fallen again and again. But his limbs gained strength as he cautiously hobbled around, first across the cottage floor, and then outside, a little farther each day. Brother Baldric had returned on several occasions, the first time bringing clothing for him to wear. He had little to say, at least to him, and Gareth sensed his disapproval.

Sometimes his knee ached abominably at the strain of his weight, yet after such confinement as he had endured, the pain was almost welcome. His side was still tender, the jagged edges of the wound red and still rough. Most likely he would bear the scar the remainder of his days.

He found it frustrating when several days of constant, miserable downpour and unceasing wind kept them indoors. A steady stream of water puddled in the corner near the fireplace. Gareth chafed inwardly at the confinement but swallowed his frustration.

His reward came the next day, which dawned with nary a cloud in the sky. Wind and rain no longer poured from the heavens. Gillian needed no further urging when he suggested they venture outside.

They walked in silence for a time, an aimless path along the sands. Before long they came upon a small, half-moon beach. Tall grasses edged the sand. The tattered corner of a sail caught beneath a log whipped in the breeze.

His gaze narrowed. He paused, aware of an odd sense of awareness sweeping over him.

"This is it, isn't it? This is where you found me."

From the corner of his eye he saw her gaze on his profile. "Yes," she murmured. "It appears as if the tide has taken much of the wreckage."

He glanced toward the headland. Beyond was the open sea. His lips compressed, for it was a sobering sight. A sheer granite cliff rose high in awful grandeur. It was all too easy to see how a vessel might be carried helplessly straight into the massive rocks that lurked beneath. Even now, a wave crested and rolled. With a thunderous roar, it crashed against the rocks. Mist sprayed high and foam surged and swirled, a churning, deadly current at the base of the rocks.

He was aware of Gillian watching him closely. "Is there anything?" she asked quietly.

Cursing silently, he shook his head. Whatever it was that had brought him aboard this ill-fated vessel was lost. Questions resounded in the cavern of his mind, the questions he'd examined a hundred times; as before, all that resulted was an echoing well of emptiness.

His body was mending.

His mind was not.

Oh, on occasion, a jumbled assortment of images paraded through his consciousness. But they were all fleeting, and little else accompanied them. They vanished almost before he was aware of it — a castle that raised twin towers aloft in majestic splendor. The shoulders of a forest richly green and verdant. . . .

But there were many such castles throughout the country. And England was covered with forest land.

And Gillian had been so convinced he'd dreamed of a woman from his past. A woman with golden hair. A woman with hair like summer sunshine. She'd said he whispered how he missed her. Again and again, he struggled to remember a face. A form.

But the only face he could see was Gillian's, her features dainty and fine, framed by soft, rich waves of darkest midnight. He could only conclude it was just as he'd said . . .

Just a dream.

I am Gareth. Gareth . . . Again he chased the elusive sensation that there was something more, that he was on the verge of something momentous. Something critical that he should have remembered, that would unlock the clouded blur of his past.

"The others," he said. "How many were there?"

"There were five."

Who were they? Gareth wondered. Captain? Crew? Friends? Reason warred with guilt. He regretted their tragic end, but he would not burden himself with guilt. For God above, he was suddenly heartily glad that he was not among them — that he'd been spared.

He was lucky to be alive. Lucky to have survived. But so very, very glad he had lived.

"Where are their bodies?"

"Brother Baldric saw to it that they were buried in the village churchyard."

He nodded. "They were given a proper burial then. That is good."

"Aye. 'Tis important to-to have a Christian burial."

There was a faint bitterness etched in her tone, a sudden darkening of her eyes that brought a shadow to her expression. Once again Gareth was struck by the sensation that while he was unable to remember, there was something she wasn't telling him, something she did not divulge.

Sometimes I think it is better not *to remember.*

What had she meant? Was it Osgood? Her possessions were few — he'd already noted she had but two gowns. But he could not put aside the incongruity of her clothing and the wretched starkness of the cottage. Brother Baldric had stated she'd been brought here to heal, but he couldn't help but wonder if there was another reason.

It bothered him that she had asked if he was a man of honor and truth. He could have sworn she was almost frightened of him . . . He'd given her no cause to fear him, had he? No cause for distrust?

No cause? a part of him scoffed. She was a woman alone. He was a man, a stranger who had washed ashore with naught but the clothes on his back — nay, not even that! A man who knew not from whence he had come, where he journeyed, or even why. No cause, indeed!

But he wanted her to trust in him. He wanted her to confide in him, to tell him what was wrong, if anything.

And so he waited, hoping she might offer more explanation. But she did not, and he would not demand it.

They did not linger at the site, but left the somber scene behind. Further inland, the wintry winds did not bluster so fiercely. Indeed, the sky above was a brilliant blue dotted with fluffy white clouds. Gareth made his way toward a fallen stump. He lowered himself to the ground, which was spongy with moss and bracken, and glanced around.

He inhaled deeply, filling his lungs with fresh air. Sunlight had banished the misty chill of the morn. Rabbits popped madly from the grass, darting to and fro. The twittering, warbling song of a skylark filled the air, reminding him of warmer days. It was a lovely place, and he could almost envision the panorama of summer. The field surrounding him would be filled with wildflowers, pink and purple and brilliant yellow.

Gillian did not join him, but walked idly about. Gareth was not surprised. Her manner had been most restrained. Directly meeting his eyes seemed an ordeal she could scarcely manage. It was the kiss, he knew, the kiss he did not remember — and perhaps the loss of this memory was the one he despaired the most! Their midnight encounter had been discussed no more — but it had not been discarded, he was almost certain of it. Aye, he strongly suspected she strived very hard not to think of it . . .

Christ, it was all he could think of.

And indeed, his head turned slowly as he searched for the object of his thoughts.

He frowned. "Gillian?"

No answer was forthcoming, but there was a rustle in the grasses nearby.

He tried again. "Gillian?"

A brow crooked as he weighed her silence. Was the lady determined to ignore him?

In truth, Gillian was not. But the cottage was small, and finding herself in such close quarters with Gareth after what had happened between them was difficult. Her nerves were screaming. It seemed she had only to turn and he was there behind her . . . before her . . . beside her!

He was so broad, so tall he had to stoop to step through the door. It still seemed strange, to see him standing on his own. So vital. So tall and broad. So intensely masculine, no matter that he limped slightly. She couldn't forget the way he'd held her. Caressed her. The hot brand of his mouth upon hers . . . It mattered not that *he* did not remember — of a certainty she did! Nay, she could not forget. Indeed, it was almost preferable when he'd been lying helplessly abed!

"Gillian!"

Her head swivelled toward the tree stump where she'd left him. Where the devil was he?

"Gillian!"

The call came again. This time it betrayed an unexpected urgency. She picked up her skirts and started toward the spot where he'd last been. Instinctively her steps quickened.

He lay on his side, his head pillowed on one arm. Her heart lodged in her throat. She dropped to her knees beside him.

"Gareth! Oh, I knew it! I knew it was far too soon for you to —"

Warm lips trapped hers 'ere she could finish. Strong arms locked tight about her back and she was swept against a hard male form. There was no escaping the blazingly thorough possession of her mouth.

When he raised his head, she glared up at him, willing aside the peculiar heaviness that had gathered in the pit of her belly. He'd frightened her half to death — and now had the audacity to appear quite pleased with himself, the wretch!

"What the devil do you think you're about!" she cried. "Do you think you can make free with me just because you kissed me once —"

"Twice," came a reminder accompanied by a wolfish grin.

She thumped her fists against his shoulders. Her lips pouted as she prepared to deliver a stinging denouncement of his brashness.

It never happened. His mouth closed over

hers yet again. His fingers slid through her hair, binding her to him and holding her captive to his will. He allowed no room for retreat — and Gillian could summon no denial. But there was naught of force or plunder in the way he kissed her, only a subtle, seductive persuasion that was both hot and sweet and sent tendrils of fire to every part of her.

She was trembling inside when at last he released her. A blunted fingertip traced the outline of her lips.

"And now thrice," he whispered.

It was no small task to summon her breath and garner the courage to meet his gaze. "Do you mock me, sir?" she asked quite seriously.

"Neither mockery nor insult was intended, lady."

Despite the swiftness of the vow, the corner of his mouth curled in lazy amusement. Gillian ducked her head. She wished she could present some pretense of anger. Swamped by confusion, she found herself unable to look at him. Perhaps such teasing play as this was familiar to him, but it was new to her — and heartily disconcerting.

That wicked fingertip now tucked an errant strand of hair behind her ear. "Why so shy, sweet maid?"

Maid, he called her. But only in jest. Only in jest . . .

"Are you embarrassed because you've kissed a man who is not your husband? Because you lay thus now with a man who is not your husband? There is no need, Gillian. I know how lonely you have been. I have only to look at you to know the pain you have endured since you lost Osgood. But it's just as Brother Baldric said. You were brought here to heal."

Her heart constricted. An almost hysterical panic seized her. If he knew the truth, that she'd never lain thus with a husband, with any man, what would he say? If he knew she'd lied — that she was not a widow at all — what would he think of her then?

She drew a deep, ragged breath. "I do not need healing."

"A woman who grieves does indeed need healing."

Perhaps she did. But not for the reason he thought.

"Osgood is dead, Gillian. I am here and I am alive. You brought me to life" — he was quietly intense — "you healed me, Gillian. Can I not do the same for you?"

She shook her head. "It is not that," she confided. "Truly, it is not. I-I am fine."

To her consternation, she couldn't disguise the tiny break in her voice. Gareth read into it far more than she wanted him to know.

"What then? What troubles you?"

His tenderness, his concern, tied her insides in knots. Shame poured through her. Shame at her lies. At Baldric's. At the way she'd deceived him, the way she'd pretended that the memory of Osgood pained her grievously.

The truth was like a burning, oppressive weight upon her breast. She despised herself for the deception. She longed to confess everything — that she was hiding from the king — that she was Gillian of Westerbrook. How her father had tried to kill the king and she'd been forced to flee — but something held her back. She longed to tell him the truth, longed for it with every fiber in her being. The prickle of warning in the back of her mind was all that stopped her, something she could not put a name to.

She looked away, afraid he would see past her feeble defense — afraid he would see beyond to the truth hidden deep inside.

Tears pricked her eyes. "Do not ask me," she said unsteadily.

"Why not?"

"Because I cannot answer."

She could. 'Twas simply that she chose

not to. But he would not push her, Gareth decided. Not here. Not now. Not yet, for there was something almost fragile about her just now, something that made him want to shelter her. Protect her and shield her from any and all hurt.

Nay, he thought again. This was no time for demand, gentle or angry or otherwise. There was time enough for such things later. For now, he was content to relish the moment, savor the gladness of simply being alive . . .

The feel of this beauty right here in his arms.

He lowered his head. His lips brushed the petal-soft lobe of one delicately shaped ear, the curving sweep of her jaw to the delicate point of her chin. Her fingers curled into the front of his tunic. His chest swelled when she turned her cheek into the side of his neck. He could feel the damp, wispy heat of the tremulous breath she released, the fringe of long, dark lashes against his throat.

His knuckles beneath her chin demanded that she meet his gaze. "Do you remember," he said softly, "when you asked me what sort of man I am?"

She nodded. Gareth was well aware of the wariness that flitted across her features, but she made no effort to break the hold of his eyes . . . or his embrace. Her lips parted, still moist from his earlier possession. Eyes of sapphire regarded him, framed by long, thick lashes. A rending ache shot through him. Christ, but she was lovely!

His arms tightened. He made a faint sound deep in his chest. "Methinks I am a selfish one," he whispered as his mouth captured hers.

There came the veriest hesitation . . . then slender arms crept around his neck. She surrendered her lips with a muffled sound deep in her throat. What was intended to be a kiss of sweet reassurance caught fire in a way he never expected. He reveled in the way her breathing quickened. Consumed by a hot, molten passion, he wondered vaguely if she could feel the thick, straining ridge of his manhood.

The urge to push her to her back and plant the searing heat of his rod deep within her welcoming softness was nearly overwhelming; the very thought made his head roar and his blood burn. His hands were sorely tempted to stray where perhaps they had best not. . . . Reluctantly he curbed his need, for somewhere in the back of his mind Gareth was afraid that if he did so, he would risk trespassing on the boundaries of her vulnerability . . . and he had dared much already.

To take her here and now — here on the cold, hard ground . . . True, it might ease the hunger in his loins, but it was not the way to prove it. Not to her — or to himself.

Little did he know that he could have . . .

Was it merely the desperation of her situation that drew her to him — the need to be near another? Nay. Gillian knew instinctively it wasn't only because his presence eased the loneliness.

It was him.

His kindness. His gentleness. Aye, from the very beginning there had been a sizzling awareness between them. Yet this day had brought still another fear. He was almost well. She could scarcely deny it. What would happen next? Would he leave to find the truth of his identity? He had no reason to remain here, and the thought was like a knife twisting in her breast.

Guilt burned through her. It was not he who had been selfish, but she. What if she hadn't withheld the name he had whispered the night he'd first kissed her? *Celeste.* Oh, she hadn't meant to deliberately deceive him. But if she had, would it have freed the darkness in his mind? Would he have remembered his past? His longing for another woman?

It was wrong, she knew. But she hadn't

wanted it then, any more than she wanted it now. It might have taken him from her even sooner.

She didn't want him to leave. She'd lost her home. Her family. God above, she didn't want to lose Gareth, too. . . . Her emotions tumultuous, she yielded her lips with wild abandon, for his arms were a haven, a haven from the agony of past and present — and aye, even the future. For Gillian suddenly cared not about tomorrow, or the future. Only now — now with the intoxicating heat of his mouth upon hers, the swirl of his breath in her mouth. A jolt went through her when his tongue touched hers, but she welcomed it eagerly. Her lips parted. Her fingers caught at the hardness of his shoulders. She pressed herself against his length. Her heart leaped at the unmistakable feel of jutting male desire, but she did not withdraw.

Instead, it was Gareth who dragged his mouth away. He ran a finger down the pert curve of her nose. "Do you know," he said with a shaky laugh, "how much you tempt me?"

It was not a question that beseeched reply; even if she'd been of a mind to, Gillian could not have said a word in that instant. She buried her face against his shoulder and clung to him, suddenly atremble like a leaf in the wind.

He sighed and rested his chin atop black, shining waves. "Someday you will tell me what is amiss," he murmured against the soft skin of her temple.

Someday, he said. *Someday*. A pang shot through her. Her throat ached. Perhaps when she was ready, he would not be here to listen.

He held her until her shaking subsided, then helped her to her feet. Gillian flushed when he tugged a leaf from her braid. She could not lie to herself — deep inside she was shocked by how easily she could have been swayed by the demands of his lips and arms. Did he think her wanton? Bold?

Flexing his knee, he grimaced slightly when they arose. A frown immediately appeared between Gillian's brows.

"We had better return to the cottage," she said worriedly.

Gareth was not of a mind to return so soon, and so he stated. He gestured toward the path that wound to the east.

"Let us walk that way."

Together they set out. The pathway skirted through a copse of trees. Though the air was crisp and cold, sunlight shimmered down from the sky, gilding the treetops with a halo of gold.

Before long Gillian complained of a stone in her slipper. Sitting on a flat-topped rock, she paused to remove it. Gareth wandered idly about. He'd picked up a branch that had fallen from a nearby tree. He weighted it in his hand; it was thick and round. His hand curved naturally around it. He whipped it in several quick circles through the air. He stepped and turned, as if to thrust and parry.

A rustle behind him made him pull up short. Gillian stood regarding him with her hands on her hips. A slender brow rose askance, as if in remonstrance. He fully expected a mocking jibe. Feeling rather foolish, he started to return a sheepish smile, but then he noticed her gaze had flitted beyond his shoulder.

Gareth turned. It seemed they were not alone. Brother Baldric stood before them on the path.

The old man trod slowly forward. He greeted Gillian, then bowed rather stiffly to Gareth.

"You appear quite well," he said upon straightening. "I should guess it will not be long before your recovery is complete and you leave us."

Beside him, Gillian felt as if an icy wind blew across the center of her heart. She held her breath and waited.

Gareth inclined his head. "I thank you for your observation, Brother Baldric. I'm feeling quite recovered indeed, but for the loss of my past. As for my plans, I fear I've made none yet."

"Well, my son, you brandish this" — Baldric nodded toward the branch Gareth still held in his hand — "with a deftness that leads me to believe a sword would be a weapon you would wield quite well. Indeed, I should guess you could be quite deadly did you possess a sword rather than a stick."

Gareth's smile was pleasant. "And were it true, would you condemn me?"

"That would depend on the circumstances. But come, what are your thoughts? You may have no knowledge of your past, but you must have an opinion, sir. Are you a man who abhors killing?"

Gareth's reply was as unfaltering as his regard. "This is my opinion, Brother Baldric. Not every man must choose between the sword and the staff, but for those who do, he must do what is in his heart — what is right. A man who uses his sword and his might to crush others when there is nothing at stake is not a man at all. But there may well come a time when a man must do whatever he must to defend his home and his family, his

144

country and his beliefs, whether it means the sword or otherwise.

"Indeed, consider the Crusades. The Church looks to the sword to defend our faith, but a man who condemns another for killing outside of the Lord's name may indeed judge far too quickly — and perhaps far too harshly. 'Tis my belief that respect should be earned by deed. Yet there are those who would argue that respect can be earned by fear as well as force. I cannot agree."

"Nor can I, Gareth."

Gillian couldn't help but notice this was the first time Brother Baldric had addressed Gareth by name. Now he bestowed a long, measuring look upon the younger man, then tipped his head to the side. He opened his mouth as if to speak.

"You surprise me with such wisdom. But tell me this, my son . . ." he paused, as if to carefully weigh his next words. A hand drifted up to rest on his chest. There was a puzzled look upon his face. He did not finish.

He could not.

Without a word he pitched forward, straight toward the ground.

"I knew he had been ill. He said nothing,

but I could hear it in the thinness of his voice. Dame Agnes confided that he eats but little of late. And on many a night he coughed until dawn." Father Aidan hovered near, his sightless eyes sliding to and fro, wringing his hands. Like Brother Baldric, he was a small man but more sturdily built in the chest and shoulders. "I was afraid this illness would see the best of him. Alas, he insisted he was well!" Reflected in his tone was the same anxious worry that Gillian felt the moment Brother Baldric collapsed.

The three of them — Gillian, Father Aidan and Brother Baldric — were in the tiny cell off the church sanctuary where Brother Baldric slept. It was Gareth who caught him as his limbs gave way — Gareth who had heaved him into his arms and carried him to the village.

Gillian knelt beside the pallet where Baldric lay, her expression frantic. Sparse lashes lay upon Baldric's gaunt cheekbones. She slipped her fingers between his. There was an unhealthy gray pallor to his lips. His skin looked like parchment.

"He has no fever," she said. Leaning forward, she lay a hand upon his brow. "Brother Baldric," she pleaded. "Can you hear me?"

Brother Baldric did not awaken. There was a rattle in his chest that sent fear spiraling all through her.

Father Aidan shook his head. "Ah, Mistress Marian, he has been a Godsend to me. I cannot imagine that I should lose him. Alas, I hate to say it, but perhaps I should prepare him for last rites . . ."

Gareth's brow puckered. *Marian,* the priest said. Had his ears deceived him, or had the clergyman mistaken her for someone else? It would have been easy, considering his blindness. That must have been it, he decided.

He also took quiet note of the leap of fear in Gillian's eyes. He laid a hand on Father Aidan's sleeve. "Perhaps, Father, your prayers would also serve Brother Baldric."

"Perhaps you are right." Father Aidan tipped his head to the side. "Your name, my son. Can you tell me again?"

" 'Tis Gareth, Father. I am Gareth."

Father Aidan clasped his hands together. "Will you join me in prayer, Gareth? Prayer is God's tool, and one that is oft neglected. Mistress Marian, please forgive me for taking our leave of you."

Gillian was too distressed to even notice that Father Aidan had called her Marian — or the way Gareth's eyes suddenly narrowed

147

on her. Even if she had, all of her being was focused on Brother Baldric.

A halo of pain shrouded her heart. He was so thin, his eyes seemed shrunken into his head. He lay motionless, his breath rattling in his chest. That he might not live was a possibility she could not voice aloud. She could not bear to think otherwise. She raged at herself inwardly. Brother Baldric had been unwell the last time he'd visited the cottage. Oh, but she should have checked on him, made certain he was taking care of himself as he should.

There was nothing you could have done, chided an inner voice. *Besides, Gareth needed you, too.*

How long she sat beside him and held his hand, she could never have said. She was vaguely aware of Gareth and Father Aidan entering and leaving several times. Once Gareth pressed food and drink into her hands.

It was hours later when there came a touch on her shoulder. Gillian raised her head. Through the tiny window set high in the wall, she spied the glimmer of a full moon.

It was Dame Agnes, the plump-cheeked matron who often helped prepare meals for the two men.

"Mistress Marian," the woman said firmly, "you must rest else you will sicken, too. Go home and sleep. I will sit with Brother Baldric. I promise, I will not leave him."

It was then Brother Baldric squeezed her fingers. "Go, child," he said in a hoarse whisper, so low she had to strain to hear. "When you return, I will still be here."

Her heart twisted. Ah, but he was so weak! It was in Gillian's mind to adamantly refuse, to insist on staying where she was, but such argument might drain what little strength Brother Baldric possessed. Trying to smile, she bent and kissed his forehead.

She didn't see the way Gareth's eyes cleaved straight to her . . . or the sudden tightening of his features as he took her arm and led her from the cell. Nor did she notice his brooding silence on the trek back to the cottage, for her thoughts were solely of Brother Baldric. Once they were inside the cottage, her fingers lifted to rub the throbbing between her brows. Sleep, she thought. Sleep would ease the pounding ache in her head. Overcome by weariness, she started to make her way toward the bed in the corner.

Gareth barred the way, his arms across his chest, his feet braced wide part.

A tired sigh escaped. "Gareth, I am weary.

Step aside, if you please."

"I think not."

Her head came up. Were it not for the abominable ache in her head, she might never have snapped at him. "For pity's sake, what the devil are you about?"

His smile was thin. "Mayhap you should tell me" — green eyes locked fast with hers — "Mistress Marian."

8

Mistress Marian.

Her heart lurched. Her legs felt like melted tallow. She'd been caught, as surely as a hare in a trap.

"I know not what you mean." She sidled back. Her breath trickled to a wisp of air.

He stepped boldly forward.

"I find myself vastly puzzled. Brother Baldric called you Gillian. But Agnes and Father Aidan called you Marian. So I must ask . . . should I call you Gillian — or Marian?" His dark head tipped to the side as if he were puzzled, his smile ever-so-pleasant, but the hard light in his eyes told a story far different. "Or perchance there is yet another name you prefer?"

Gillian's stomach twisted, for he hit dangerously close to the truth.

"What, lady, nothing to say? I find my patience wearing thin."

"I am Gillian." Struggling for composure, she feigned a calm she certainly did not feel.

"Then why did Father Aidan address you as Marian?"

"You are mistaken."

"I think not."

Gareth's eyes never left her. Her feeble denial but fueled the anger mounting within him. Did she truly think he was such a fool? Aye, perhaps he was, for he had believed her — he had believed everything! He derided himself fiercely. Yet who would have doubted a man of God — especially one conjoined with a woman of such beauty? A dark, brooding anger slipped over him, an anger quickly masked.

His smile turned icy. "I heard him," he said softly. "Twice I heard Father Aidan call you Mistress Marian. *Twice.* And Agnes did as well. *Agnes did as well!*"

Gillian swallowed. "You are right," she admitted. "Father Aidan and Agnes called me Marian. When we came here, Brother Baldric and I told the villagers that my name was Marian. But — in truth my name is Gillian." Uncertainty welled within her. That, at least, was not a lie. Ah, if only she knew if she could tell him she was Lady Gillian of Westerbrook. Brother Baldric had warned her to stay far from the village. Oh, but she should have listened! He'd been so afraid someone would learn that she was Lady Gillian of Westerbrook. . . .

"There were reasons, you see, that we did not wish it known that I am Gillian —"

"What reasons?"

Gillian shook her head. An awful dread had begun to churn her insides. "Those reasons have not changed," she said.

"Nonetheless, I would know the reason for such secrecy." A brow hiked imperiously. A wide — aye, and very deliberate — step breached the distance between them.

Hers widened it anew. "And I say again, I cannot tell you."

Gareth stared at her, and in that span of a heartbeat, a half-clouded suspicion began to blossom in his mind.

"And I find that I heartily dislike secrets. However, I will oblige you. Since you are so unwilling to talk about yourself, I suggest we talk about Osgood . . . how long did you say it has been since your beloved husband died?"

The bite in his tone as he spoke her name made her wince inside. "Why?" She shifted nervously. "I fail to see what —"

"Nonetheless, refresh my memory, if you please. You may recall, it ever eludes me."

"A year," she said quickly. Her reply was

made in part-hope, part-dread, part-prayer that he would not glimpse her dismay as she frantically sorted through her mind. Aye, that was it — a year.

His smile had turned utterly wicked. "No," he said, and it was a distinctly unsettling sound.

Gillian inhaled sharply. "I did. I told you — !"

"Half a year," he finished tautly. "You stated half a year had passed since he died."

Gillian made a muted sound of rage, both at her own folly and his deliberate plot. "You miserable wretch!" she sputtered. "You tricked me!"

This time it was she who closed the distance between them. Hands and fists raised in a temper such as she'd never known before, she launched herself forward. Gareth's arms shot out. He caught her and brought her up hard against the solid strength of his form.

"Ah, lady," he proclaimed with false heartiness. "All these questions give rise to still another. Are you a widow or no?"

She would not give him the satisfaction of an answer! "You are a man with no memory — a man with no heart!" she flung at him. "I will tell you nothing."

His mouth clamped shut. His jaw hardened. That smile that had been aught but a parody of a smile from the very beginning had vanished.

"A man with no heart, she says." The cast of his jaw was rigid, his mouth thin. "By God, lady, I pitied you. I comforted you in what you claimed was your grief. I believed the shame you felt to lie beside another man in the wake of your husband's death — but now I begin to wonder if you've lain beside *any* man! So let us see once and for all if you've ever had a husband, shall we?"

Hard arms snaked about her waist. Gillian felt herself bodily turned and spun through the air, her slippers leaving the ground. He sat upon the stool — and her upon him! — and dragged her down upon his lap. For one mind-spinning instant, her skirts swirled about them both. In shock she realized a bold male hand trespassed beneath. That same brown hand clamped the slender flesh of her thigh and insinuated itself between. Devil-fingers skimmed tender flesh untouched by any man, on course for a relentless journey straight toward the forbidden place that guarded her womanhood.

For one shattering instant Gillian could not even contemplate what he dared . . . what he sought. When she did, panic took wing inside her. "Nay!" she cried, twisting wildly. Her struggle proved futile. Her arms were trapped against her sides by a sinewed, muscled forearm. Her back was flush against his chest. She was a prisoner in his hold as surely as an animal in a snare.

"Yes," he said through his teeth, for in truth Gareth had lost all patience with her lies and denials. "Yes, lady! You may not speak the truth, but by the Cross, I will have it!"

And aye, a single accursed finger was already parting soft, golden fleece and dainty, pink folds. She was bitterly aware he sought the tellingly fragile barrier of her maidenhead.

"Stop!" she cried.

His starkly daring foray ceased. His gaze delved sharply into hers.

"Why?" he demanded.

"Because you need not confirm what you already know!"

His lips compressed. He pushed her from his lap and set on her feet. It was over almost before she knew it . . . in her mind it lasted forever. With shaking hands, Gillian smoothed her skirt down. For a moment she stood mutely. Eyes downcast, she could not move for the scalding humiliation that washed over her.

"So the widow is not a widow at all," he

observed. "But come. Why so shy, sweet maid?"

That brought her head up in a flash. Her spine stiffened and she turned. His gaze flickered over her dispassionately. He'd spoken those very words once before, and then there had been only gentleness, both in his manner and his touch.

'Twas not the case now, and Gillian was suddenly furious. He had the truth he sought. He'd had it his way, damn his hide, yet now he dared to taunt her! Her anger boiled over. Before she could stop it, her hand shot out. With all the force she could muster, she dealt a stunning slap to the hardness of his cheek.

Gareth stood his ground unblinkingly, feeling the sting of her hand against his face. Though he was still fiercely angry at her deceit, he would allow her the blow. He could understand her ire, but he would certainly not allow it again . . . ah, but that was precisely what she intended! With a low growl he snatched her against him, catching the offending wrist in the binding vise of one hand and raking it behind her back.

"You are a beast!" Gillian cried.

"And you are a liar," he said grimly. Glittering jade eyes rained down on her. "Tell me true and tell me now . . . Gillian or Marian?"

She pressed her lips together.

With his hand he prodded her chin up. "Answer me!"

Her gaze faltered beneath the fiery demand of his. She looked away. "I told you. 'Tis Gillian," she said, her voice very low. "Lady Gillian of Westerbrook."

"It's true that Brother Baldric brought you here?"

Wordlessly she nodded.

"Why did you hide who you are? Why *do* you hide who you are?"

His voice hammered at her, swift and unrepentant. It was pride alone that kept her upright — either that or the steely band of muscled arm about her back. She preferred to think it was the former.

"Because the king searches for me, and for my brother Clifton."

"The king!" His eyes narrowed. "Why?"

"Because he would see us dead. Because our father is . . . *was* . . . Ellis of Westerbrook."

Gareth gave an impatient shake of his head. "The name means naught to me."

There was no point in disguising her father's actions, she decided bleakly. By now, it was surely common knowledge across the whole of England. "Were it not for your illness," she said painfully, "no doubt you would remember the failed attempt on King John's life early in the autumn. It was Ellis of Westerbrook who loosed the arrow that missed its mark and instead felled the king's guard . . . my father."

"Sweet Christ. Your father . . . !"

"Yes."

He released her, only to grab her hand and tug her to the bed. "Tell me what goes on," he demanded tautly. "And by God, there had best be no secrets now."

Gillian's eyes darkened, but she was resigned to her fate. "King John came to visit William de Vries, a baron in the nearest shire," she began. "It was late when Papa came to my chamber." She shuddered anew, hearing once more the ominous rumble of thunder. Dear God! she thought starkly. Would that night ever leave her?

He listened in stony silence as she continued. "He was preparing to flee, before he was found out. He commanded that Clifton and I leave as well. I was to accompany Brother Baldric, and Alwin, his chief retainer, would take charge of Clifton."

"He sought to conceal you from John's wrath?"

She nodded miserably. "He feared the

king would take his revenge on us."

"What happened to your father?"

"He was captured several weeks later." Raw heartache bled onto her soul, but she held it in check. "He killed himself rather than reveal the identity of the other man involved. There has been no word that the other assassin has been found."

She didn't disclose that the other man had been closeted with her father in the counting room the previous day. Brother Baldric's warning clanged in her mind. *Tell no one,* he'd said. Besides, what did she know? Nothing. She had no idea of the man's identity. Indeed, Gareth might well accuse her of lying anew. She defended the decision staunchly, smothering a brief pang of guilt. Nay, it was neither a lie, nor an omission of truth.

"What of your brother?"

A hot ache constricted her throat. "I have no idea where Clifton was taken" — her breath caught, for it was so hard to say it, to even think it — "or if he still lives."

Throughout, Gareth listened, his jaw so hard it might have been hewn in stone. Rising, he stared at her, his expression implacable.

"You should have trusted me, Gillian. Why didn't you?" He gave her no chance to

160

answer, but went on. "You should have."

Stung by his harshness, she struck out. "And what good would that have done? What could *you* have done, you who could not even move from the bed!"

His lips thinned. "There was no need for such deceit, especially in light of what passed between us."

His coolness pricked an anger that had eased but not abated. Her jaw opened and closed. "In light of what passed between us?"

"Aye. And I do not mean what happened just now. Indeed, I think you know precisely what I mean." His gaze resided meaningfully on her lips.

His utter calm only made her more furious. She leaped to her feet. "Oh, the devil take you!" she flared. "Need I remind you who it was you first kissed? 'Twas just a dream, you said. But of a certainty it was not I you kissed so passionately!" She plucked at the sable ribbon of hair that lay upon her breast. "It was the woman with hair like summer sunshine," she quoted feelingly. "It was Celeste, as I recall. Aye, it was Celeste!"

Her jibe had an effect she could not have foreseen . . . did *not* foresee.

Their battle receded. Gareth went absolutely still. Before her very eyes, the color seeped from beneath his skin. "Celeste? I called her Celeste?"

"Aye." Her knuckles pressed against her lips as a horrified inevitability swept through her. "Oh, God. You said there was no one. But she is your wife, isn't she? Celeste is your *wife*."

"My wife is dead," he stated without hesitation. "She is dead."

Her heart twisted. Silently she raged. Ah, but she was a fool! Instinct had warned he was wed; she simply had refused to believe it! She'd been too caught up in the magic wonder of his kiss . . . "How do you know? How can you be certain?"

"I do. I am. She is dead. I cannot say how or when, but I know she is dead." Gareth's head was buzzing. She asked how he knew, but he could not explain. He had only to hear the name . . . *Celeste* . . . and awareness shot through him with the sizzle of lightning, as if some mighty, unseen force pierced him like the shaft of an arrow.

Gillian knew it, too. Her breath caught. "You know who you are, don't you?"

"Aye," he whispered. "I am Gareth" — there was a heartbeat of silence — "lord of Sommerfield."

162

9

It was uncanny, the way it happened. Why it happened — or how — he could never have said. It was as if a single beam of light had slipped through a crack, then opened wide to allow a thousand shimmering rays to pour through him, clear to his soul. The gladness that filled him was indescribable. Yet just as quickly, with the suddenness of a candle being snuffed out, the crack sealed shut. The light inside him was extinguished and he knew no more.

It was enough. He knew that Celeste had been his wife. Dear Lord, his wife! Yet he could not have said how long they'd been wed. If she had in truth possessed hair like summer sunshine, he could not say. He couldn't even claim that he'd loved her . . . indeed, that he had not!

Yet he knew his home was Sommerfield Castle, a grand fortress perched high upon a hilltop in the northern shires. Half a dozen shimmering lakes were visible from the south tower, nestled between green hills that swept to the eastern shores.

"Gareth?"

A low, feminine voice drew him from his reverie. His gaze was drawn to the wide-eyed, dark-haired beauty before him. He was Gareth, lord of Sommerfield, he thought, filling his lungs with air, as if for the very first time.

The maid before him was Gillian of Westerbrook, daughter of Ellis.

If only she'd told him earlier, he might have remembered far sooner. But she was right. He'd thought it was just a dream.

Just as suddenly darkness filled his mind anew — but this time it was darkness of a different sort. The clouds in his mind shifted and swirled. The hairs on the back of his neck prickled.

"Sweet Christ," he whispered.

Something in his expression must have given him away. "What?" Gillian cried. "What is it?"

"You cannot stay here."

Gillian stared at him, feeling her insides curl into a cold, hard knot. Her control was tenuous at best. She felt as if she'd been thrust into the midst of a tempest.

"What do you mean?"

"You must leave. Now. Tonight."

A sudden crash of thunder split the air. The walls shivered . . . as she was suddenly shivering. It was so much like that horrible night her father had come to her room that Gillian could no longer bear it.

She clamped her hands over her ears to shut out the sound of his voice. " 'Tis a trick. You mean to frighten me!"

"No, Gillian, no!" He tore her hands away from her ears and held them at her sides. Though his hold was not hurtful, he was adamant. "You must listen to me! You cannot stay here. It is not safe."

She was trembling from head to toe. "Were you sent by my father's men?" The question emerged, tremulous and quavering.

"Aye." Gareth cared not that he lied. In truth he had no idea how or why he had come to be here. Some little known instinct inside him compelled his urgency. "You cannot remain here," he said again. "We must leave as soon as we're able, Gillian. With every moment you linger, you risk discovery by the king."

"You say I should leave, but I have nowhere to go. Brother Baldric brought me here to keep me safe!"

"And I will keep you safe now. I will take you to Sommerfield. I can protect you there." His hands came up to rest on her shoulders. "You've naught to fear from me, Gillian, I swear. I will not harm you."

He was grim, so very, very grim. Gillian battled a spiraling panic. Never in her life had she felt so helpless, not even the night she'd been forced to leave Westerbrook. God help her, she knew not which way to turn! Always before there had been someone to guide her. Her father. Brother Baldric. Now Gareth was asking her to place her faith in him — a man she'd known but a span of days — a man who, in truth, scarcely knew himself! Though she despised her weakness, all she could do was pray she made the right choice.

She drew a deep, ragged breath. "What about Brother Baldric?"

"He is too ill to travel." Gareth made the declaration flatly. That Brother Baldric might well succumb to the hereafter was a notion he kept to himself. "Now hurry and gather your things."

Gillian shook her head. "I cannot leave without seeing Brother Baldric."

For an instant she thought he might refuse. Finally he capitulated with a nod.

It was close to midnight when they returned to the church. A stub of candle cast a wavering light on the damp stone wall. Agnes was dozing in a chair at the bedside. As the door scraped the floor, she woke with a start.

Gareth gestured Agnes aside. Gillian eased down on the pallet. She clasped Brother Baldric's gnarled hand between both of hers. His skin was chill as the wind.

"Brother Baldric," she whispered. He was so pale. Fear struck a chord, for he lay so still and unmoving. For one agonizing moment she thought he was dead.

Heavy eyelids lifted. There was the faintest grasp of gnarled fingers around hers.

"Brother Baldric, something has happened . . . Gareth believes I am in grave danger if I remain here . . ." In hushed tones she told him what had happened.

Baldric's gaze lifted to Gareth, who stood near the door. "So," he said in a voice that sounded like the rasping of leaves across a cobbled street. "You are the lord of Sommerfield."

"I am." Gareth stepped forward. There was that in his tone which sounded as if he expected the old man to contest the statement.

"You will take care of Lady Gillian? You

will guard her from the king's wrath — keep her safely away from the king's hand?"

"I will."

"Swear it, for I would have your oath."

"I swear it." Gareth's oath was unfaltering, deeply resonant. "I will guard her from the king's wrath and keep her safe from his hand."

"So be it, then."

Baldric's gaze returned to Gillian. Gillian could hear his breath waning. Her eyes clung to his as she rubbed his leathery hand against her cheek. He felt the dampness of her tears.

"Do not weep, child."

She gave a dry sob. "If only you were not ill, then you could travel with us. Oh, I-I hate this wretched illness that plagues you!"

"It will pass," he said.

"And what if it does not?"

He smiled faintly. "Then it is —"

"I know. God's will," she finished bitterly. It was so easy for him to accept, yet not for her. Her tears choked her. There was a crushing heaviness in her chest.

Behind her, footsteps shifted on the floor. Gillian felt Gareth's presence and sensed his impatience to depart.

"Gillian," he said.

She ignored him. "Brother Baldric,

promise me you will not give in. That you will not go easily. That you will try and best this wretched illness . . ."

"You have my promise, child." Baldric's lips formed a feeble smile as his gaze briefly encompassed Gareth. "A word of warning, my lord. I sense in you a steady purpose, but it may not be wise to cross the lady, for I fear she can be as stubborn as her father."

Gillian stiffened as she felt Gareth's gaze drift coolly over her profile. A glance from the corner of her eye revealed a tight smile. "I shall do well to bear that in mind, then," he said.

Brother Baldric surprised her by offering his hand to the younger man.

"Remember, my lord, I have your oath."

Gareth briefly squeezed his fingers. "I will not forget," he said quietly.

Brother Baldric's hand fell limply back to his chest. He grew weaker by the breath. His eyelids drifted shut, as if he no longer had the strength to keep them open.

"Brother Baldric!" Gillian cried.

"Hurry, child. I should hate to think our ordeal was for naught."

Gillian bent and pressed a kiss upon his cheek, her eyes streaming. Tears clogged her throat, tears she somehow managed to keep at bay.

An imperious hand cupped her elbow. Gillian knocked it aside, feeling as if she would break apart inside. "Leave me be," she cried.

Gareth's hand fell to his side. His lips thinned. "As you wish, lady."

Her chin angled high, she brushed past him and out into the night.

Outside the wind gave rise to a keening howl, then fell eerily silent. Tears clogged her throat, but she refused to let him see the ripeness of her despair. Her cheeks were wet, whether from tears or rain, she knew not.

They walked until Gillian longed to sink down in sheer exhaustion, ready to declare defeat. When Gareth announced they would sleep for a few hours, she sank down and was asleep almost immediately.

By noon the next day, Gareth's face was drawn and gray. He was limping badly, yet still he forged ahead. Whether they went east or west, north or south, she knew not. She was too tired to care.

They slept longer that night, but shadows still shrouded the treetops when they set off again. Near dawn, Gareth stopped her with a tug on a fold of her cloak.

"Methinks I've just found a way to hasten

our travels," he said.

Gillian glanced ahead. They approached the outskirts of a tiny hamlet. A wisp of smoke curled from the squat chimney of a small, thatch-roofed wooden building. The door was propped ajar, allowing the escape of rowdy male voices and gales of laughter.

Gillian couldn't hide her exasperation. "We have no coin for such —"

"Not there," he said. *"There."* He gestured to where several horses had been tethered near the back wall of the inn. At the sound of their voices — and perhaps gleaning their scent — a chestnut stallion turned its head. Its ears pricked forward.

Gillian gaped at the sudden gleam in Gareth's eyes, the smile of pure satisfaction that rimmed his lips.

"He looks to be a fast, impressive steed, does he not?"

It would have served him right if the animal had bolted. It would have served him right if the animal had neighed and raised the alarm. As it was, Gillian could only watch and wait as Gareth crept forward. The stallion snorted as Gareth eased upright from his crouch. Her breath caught as man and beast beheld each other face-to-face. One lean hand caught the tether. With the other he ran his palm over the stallion's deep, powerful chest. The animal's skin quivered as Gareth eased closer. He blew through his nostrils, his tail raised high.

Seconds later, the pair cantered to a halt before her. From his lofty perch high atop the stallion, he gazed down at her with a decidedly rakish grin.

A black brow cocked high. He extended a hand. "Your carriage awaits, my lady."

Her hesitation was fractional. She swung up behind him. "I do believe you are a thief after all," she said outright.

"Ah, now she protests!" He lifted his eyes heavenward. "I assure you, the horse will be returned, and with ample recompense."

"By then the owner will have long since departed."

"In that case the steed will belong to the innkeeper, and he will have earned a goodly profit for the night."

'Twas a point she could not argue against, nor was she inclined to, for he was right — their journey would be completed much more quickly, and with far more ease on horseback than on foot.

Hours later she wasn't so sure. At a fork in the road, she glanced up just as he brought the stallion to a halt. He looked first to the right, then the left, then back again, a furrow of concentration etched deep between his brows.

She was so tired she could have screamed; her bottom ached abominably and she was certain she'd never been filthier. "What, has the lord of Sommerfield lost his way?" she inquired.

Such shortness did not set well. Gareth was sorely tempted to snap that in truth he'd lost his mind. . . . He pointedly ignored her, rubbing his jaw in mute consideration. He had the feeling he'd traveled this very same road before. If he wasn't mistaken, the fork to the right twisted and turned among the hills, while the one to the left was a more direct route to Sommerfield.

Gillian grew impatient. "Perhaps you are not who you claim to be at all. Perhaps you are not the lord of Sommerfield. Indeed," she went on, "we ride upon a horse you stole —"

Gareth drew a sharp breath. "Lady," he began warningly.

"— so perhaps 'tis just as you once said and you are an outlaw, too!"

"An outlaw, eh? If we were to encounter the king's men this very moment, it would be you and not I who would be thrown into the nearest gaol."

It was a petty reminder. One look at the

shattered defeat in her eyes and Gareth knew it. He cursed himself harshly, for he'd quelled her outburst in a way he'd truly never intended.

Throughout the remainder of the day, she was quiet and subdued. She ate little of the hare he trapped and roasted that night. Afterward she stared into the fire, her eyes downcast, her posture as lonely as the wind. Finally she murmured a goodnight, laid down, and curled into the folds of her mantle. Not once did she meet his gaze.

How long he stared at the slender lines of her back, he knew not. His hands curled and uncurled as he battled the impulse to reach for her, to draw her near. All that stopped him was the way she wielded the acid lash of her tongue — and wielded it well indeed! Nor could he deny the part of him that still smarted at the way she had deceived him and played him for a fool.

At length he stretched out beside her, near but not touching her. It was, he decided grimly, a trying end to what had initially promised to be a fine day.

Sunlight was flirting with the day when Gillian awoke. For a moment she lay very still, watching hazy golden spears fill the glade where they'd stopped for the night.

The pungent smell of dirt rose all about her. Frost fleeced the ground all around. With a sigh that seemed dragged from some empty little place inside her, she gathered her mantle more tightly about her, but it was of little help; the dampness had seeped through her mantle. The root of a tree dug into her hip. Her muscles protested mightily when she scooted farther away from the tree trunk. Oh, how she longed for the softness of a real bed. Even the crude pallet she'd slept upon those many weeks at the cottage would have been welcome. The realization dawned slowly . . .

She was alone.

She surged upright, galvanized by a surge of panic. Her heart bounded. A movement in the far edge of her vision snared her attention. Almost blindly she ran toward it, pushing her way blindly through a thick tangle of chest-high bushes. Thorns pricked her hands as she thrust them aside, but she paid no heed.

Wide black oaks guarded the waters of a tiny lake, quietly serene. In the early morning sunlight, a golden sheen trembled on the surface. The stallion, she noted dimly, was nearby. He raised his head at her intrusion, then went back to idly munching a tuft of grasses beneath the trees. But it was not the steed that made her come to a stumbling halt.

It was Gareth. He stood not far from the shore, his back to her. The water just barely covered his buttocks, buttocks that she knew were hard and round and tight. She stared at the smooth, sculpted line of his back. His hair was black and glossy.

As she plunged through the thicket, he glanced back over his shoulder with a frown. "Why do you run, Gillian?"

"I thought you'd left me," she blurted.

He turned to face her fully. To her surprise, a slow smile spread across his lips. "A pity," he remarked. "I thought perhaps you were eager to join me."

Gillian's cheeks burned scarlet. "Men and women do not bathe together!"

"They not only bathe together" — his eyes gleamed knowingly — "but they bathe each *other.*"

Gillian was aghast. She longed to dispute such a claim, but in truth, she had no way of knowing it was *not* true!

It was almost as if he read her mind. "Ah, but it is remiss of me to forget so quickly," he said softly. "Lady Gillian, being a maid, has no experience with such things. And the widow Marian" — he spread his hands wide — "well, she is no doubt far too wise and well aware of where such play would lead."

It was his first reference to her duplicity since they'd left the cottage. She reminded herself that she had no reason to feel guilty; he had no right to make her so. He toyed with her, and she resented him fiercely for it.

A daring smile rimmed those handsome lips — a roguish smile, oh, but an infuriatingly smug smile! Gillian raised her chin aloft. "Do you know," she stated sweetly, "I do believe I liked it better when you were not awake and could not speak."

He laughed, the sound low and hearty and oddly pleasing to the ear. "Well, if you will not come in, then it seems I must come out."

Gillian gasped and spun around. She heard the slosh of water. He whistled a merry tune, then there was nothing.

She jumped when a hand clamped down on her shoulder.

"Gillian," he said softly.

"What is it?" Her heart clamored as he turned her to face him. Was he still naked? She resisted the urge to squeeze her eyes shut and reminded herself she'd seen him naked before . . . naked, aye, but never naked upon his feet!

He was not, praise God. The top of her head was level with the dark tangle of masculine hairs that curled into the hollow of his throat, and it was there her gaze settled. Her heart tumbled to a standstill. His hands were warm and hard upon her shoulders. The remembrance of how he'd cupped her breasts — touched her bare skin — sent scorching heat all through her.

His statement was not what she expected. "I should not have said what I did yesterday — that you would be hauled off to gaol, and not I."

Her eyes darkened. "Why not? It's true," she said, her voice very low. "Indeed, perhaps it would be best if you leave now, while you still have the chance, lest we are captured and the king decides he will have your head as well."

"I won't desert you, Gillian."

Her mouth grew tremulous. She pressed her lips together in an effort not to betray such weakness. Deliberately she looked away. "How long before we reach Sommerfield?"

"Four to five days, I suspect."

His answer dragged her gaze back in an instant. "Four to five more?"

She sounded so forlorn he was tempted to reach out and stroke her cheek. "Aye," he said. And aye, it was after nightfall on the fifth day hence that they approached Sommerfield. Gillian had not complained even once; he was oddly proud of her mettle.

Gillian dozed behind him as they neared the castle. He could feel the limpness of her form. Her arms had loosened around his waist. Her head lolled against his back.

He reined the stallion to a halt at the crest of a gently sloping hill. All at once it was as if the world stood still.

Moonlight spilled down from the sky, casting the world below in a silvery glow. The dipping, rolling hills were poured in deep shadow. Four lofty towers rose in gleaming splendor against the glory of the night.

This was it, the place he'd dreamed of . . . Sommerfield Castle.

Mayhap it was selfish, but he was almost glad that Gillian was not awake, that he might be allowed this first glimpse of Sommerfield with only the night to bear witness. An almost painful ache caught in his throat. For so many days at the cottage, he'd felt like a ship without a rudder, lost and adrift to the mercy of the waves.

But now his restless soul had found its fortress.

He was home, he thought, and suddenly he felt like shouting. By sweet heaven . . . *he was home!*

10

Within minutes the gates were heaved high and massive doors creaked wide. As Gareth cantered across the drawbridge, torches began to light the courtyard, one by one. A hound bayed in the distance.

"He is back! Our lord has returned!" All around there was an excited clamor of voices. A dozen knights rushed over to greet him. Behind him, Gareth felt Gillian stir.

Gareth leaped lightly to the ground. He turned, but helping hands had already reached for Gillian. As she was set on her feet, her gaze swept in a half-circle. Gareth's chest swelled with pride at the way her eyes widened in awe. Even now a cupbearer hurried toward them with two silver goblets.

Gareth readily accepted one. He offered the other to Gillian. She declined with a shake of her head.

His gaze never left hers as he set it back on

the tray. "Are you hungry?" he queried.

She smiled slightly. "I am more weary than hungry."

He beckoned to a maid who had appeared. He stared hard at her. "Lydia," he began slowly.

The maid blushed. "Lynette, my lord."

"Aye, of course. Lynette. Lynette, this is Lady Gillian of Westerbrook. Please see that she is escorted to a chamber and her needs attended to," he directed.

Lynette curtsied. Gareth's eyes followed Gillian as she crossed the courtyard and climbed the wide stairs that led to the great hall. Her gown was rumpled, the hem stained — no doubt he was as disheveled as she — yet there was both grace and poise in her bearing. He chided himself soundly. There was no doubt that she had been born and gently bred, yet he had been blind to it! The corners of his mouth turned down with something that might have been disapproval. It was impossible not to note that his was not the only gaze that followed her progress — and sure enough, the others were not only curious, but rife with admiration.

In the great hall, they all gathered round while food and drink was brought.

" 'Tis glad we are that you are back,

181

milord." The comment came from Sir Marcus, the handsome, chestnut-haired knight who was charged with Sommerfield's defense in Gareth's absence.

His attention diverted, Gareth's gaze encompassed the assemblage. There were many, he suspected, who were long since abed in the barracks. But he recognized Irwin, his steward. Sir Ellis and Sir Godfrey, who had also served his father and now watched over the armory with a practiced eye, along with several others. Yet his mind was blank as it skipped over several others.

He gave a rusty laugh. "Ah, Marcus, 'tis glad I am to *be* back."

Marcus gazed across at him earnestly. "We kept all in readiness for your return," Marcus said, "but I confess, never did we think the king's business would keep you away from Sommerfield for so long!"

Gareth's smile withered. The king's business? A tingle of apprehension snaked up his spine. He didn't like the sound of that. As they had traveled, he'd witnessed for himself the fright Gillian had spoken of. Women stared with wary eyes, hurrying their children inside whenever a stranger approached. King John was a tyrant, he suspected, and England's people were but a toy he used for his own amusement — and to his own advantage.

"I fear much has changed since I left," he said slowly. "An accident at sea wiped away my remembrance of the past. 'Tis only of late that I've begun to recall some things . . . I count myself lucky that I was able to make my way back to Sommerfield. Indeed, if not for Lady Gillian, I might not have lived to see this day.

"It was Lady Gillian who found me, washed ashore, half-drowned and nearly dead. She took me in and nursed me back to health."

Sir Marcus looked solemn. "My lord, you called her Lady Gillian of Westerbrook. Is she the daughter of Ellis?"

"Aye," Gareth said levelly. "Ellis of Westerbrook, the man who attempted to slay King John. It seems that before Ellis fled, he arranged for her and her brother Clifton to be taken from Westerbrook. They went into hiding from the king, for Ellis feared John might seek revenge through his children. And I tell you again, were it not for Lady Gillian, I might never have survived to see this day. She saved my life, and I brought her to Sommerfield to save hers." He glanced around at his men. "It would be foolish to try to keep her identity secret forever, and so I decided not even to try. But the rest, I tell you in confidence, and I trust it will remain so."

All who were gathered round nodded their agreement. "Is her brother safe?" asked one man.

"No one knows. He and Gillian departed separately. Ellis thought it would be safer that way. Even Gillian does not know where he is."

Sir Godfrey spoke up. "Before you left, my lord, you told us the king had sworn you to secrecy regarding the business you must attend for him. We have respected your vow to him, my lord, and rest assured, we will continue to do so. And indeed, it seems we have much to thank Lady Gillian for."

There was another signal of assent.

Gareth smiled slightly, then looked at Godfrey. "You must forgive my forgetfulness, but can you tell me how long I've been absent?"

"Some three months, I believe."

"Three months!" Gareth was astounded.

"Perhaps it will ease your mind to learn we've had word that young Robbie is doing quite well 'neath the king's protection."

There was a strange tightening in his chest. "Young Robbie?"

"Aye, milord. Though he be as fair as his mum, he's a strong, stout lad, every bit his father's son." Godfrey grinned. "We have every faith he'll grow to be as fine a knight as you, milord."

Gareth could not move. For one perilous instant, he feared his legs would not hold him. For with Godfrey's words a vision flashed in his mind. He saw himself before the hearth in this very hall, tossing a young lad high into the air. A lad with blond, sun-kissed hair and laughing green eyes . . .

His eyes.

He had a son. Good Christ, *he had a son.*

But his son was not beneath the king's protection. He was the king's hostage. Despite Godfrey's choice of words, they all knew it. A fierce, black anger shot through him, and with that certainty came another . . .

One that made his very soul grow cold.

For Gareth knew, with precise awareness, why he'd left Sommerfield . . . who he had sought . . . and why.

His mouth twisted. With blithe confidence, he had assured her she had no cause to doubt him.

He couldn't have been more wrong.

Scathingly he derided himself. Busy with the king's business indeed . . .

He had no choice but to tell her. Yet what the devil was he to say?

She would hate him. Fear him. And just

185

when she had begun to trust him.

It was not, he decided tiredly, a task he envisioned with relish. Nor was it one that he would pursue this night. The morn was soon enough. Aye, in the morn . . .

He arose from the table, forcing a smile. "I fear I must bid you good night, gentlemen. It has been a long and tiring day."

He turned and started toward a darkened doorway in the far corner of the hall.

Behind him there was a quietly discreet cough. He turned to behold Sir Marcus, who inclined his head to the left. "Your chamber is that way, my lord."

Gillian woke to the crackle of a fire casting out warmth to every corner of the chamber. She didn't rise straightaway, but stretched her limbs and buried her face in the pillow, luxuriating in the scent of fresh linen sheets, soft, furry blankets, and the down-filled mattress that enveloped her. It might have been a trifling thing to some, but never again would she take for granted food and shelter and such comfort as this.

A long sigh escaped. It was not a sigh borne of weariness, for she'd slept soundly the night through. A faint shadow crept over her, for her thoughts veered inevitably to Brother Baldric and Clifton. Was Brother

Baldric still alive? She prayed to the depths of her soul that he had survived.

Then there was Clifton! Was he hungry? Cold? Was Alwin still with him? 'Twas not so vital that she see him, touch him — though she longed for it dearly! Nay, if only she knew that he was alive and well, a little of her anxious fear might have lessened. Yet neither could she deny that she felt safer than she had for a long, long time. With their arrival at Sommerfield, a tremendous burden had been lifted from her shoulders.

There was a knock on the door. It opened a crack, and the maid Lynette peered in. When she saw that Gillian was awake, she stepped inside.

There was a tray in her hands. "I've brought food for you, my lady. I hope you're hungry."

After the girl had shown her to her chamber last eve, she'd helped Gillian undress. Gillian had liked her on sight. Wisps of drab brown hair escaped from beneath her cap, but bright, shining eyes lent her a warm vivacity.

Gillian obligingly sat up, and Lynette slipped the tray onto Gillian's lap.

Gillian blinked. There were two huge hunks of bread dripping with honey, several wedges of cheese and a dish of stewed figs.

"My heavens, I am but one and there is enough here for at least two!"

"Well, you did miss your meal last eve, my lady. And milord said your nourishment had been lacking of late, so I made sure you had good hearty servings."

There was no doubt that worry had cost Gillian a goodly bit of flesh since she'd departed Westerbrook. Her meager store of gowns hung limply from her shoulders and hips, and gaped wide at the neckline, where before they'd fit her form perfectly.

Gillian was adamant. "I cannot possibly eat all of this." She held up the plate. "Would you like some, Lynette?"

For an instant the girl appeared taken aback. "Oh, I could not —"

"Oh, please do! Unless, of course, you're afraid the master will beat you if he finds out. I should hate to land you in trouble because of me." Gillian found herself holding her breath. She had a hard time envisioning Gareth bullying the servants, but one never knew.

To her surprise, Lynette laughed. "Oh, 'tis not that," she announced cheerfully. "The master is hardly likely to beat us, nor will he allow anyone else to beat us. Our lord is surely the most kind, generous lord in all the land. I daresay, there is not a man, woman, or child here at Sommerfield who is not amply fed and warmly clothed. But I thank you, Lady Gillian, for your generosity. 'Tis simply that I broke my fast not long ago. If it would please you, though, when you are done, I'll see if one of the kitchen boys wishes to finish what you do not eat."

"An excellent idea, Lynette." The girl's response affirmed Gillian's initial assessment. "It would be a shame for it to go to waste, and I vow I cannot possibly eat all of this." As she spoke, Gillian broke off a chunk of bread and dipped it in a swirl of honey.

It fairly melted in her mouth, warm and yeasty and sweet. In all her life, Gillian didn't know when she'd tasted anything so delicious.

Lynette hid a smile as she whisked the tray from Gillian's lap a short while later. Gillian had devoured all of the bread, and nearly all of the cheese.

"Would you like a bath, my lady?"

"A bath would be lovely."

"I'll see to it then. Oh, and I cleaned your gown, my lady."

Gillian felt herself redden. "Thank you, Lynette. That was most kind of you." She darted a quick glance at the girl, but her expression revealed little. If Lynette thought it odd that she had come to Sommerfield with no trunks or servant of her own, she kept her opinion to herself.

Left alone, Gillian glanced around curiously. The chamber she'd been given was not overly large, but it was well furnished. Rich tapestries adorned the walls. There were rugs on the floor to guard against the cold. The small seat beneath the wide arched window was strewn with plump, inviting cushions.

Slipping from the bed in her shift, she peeked through the shutters. Sommerfield was a grand castle, far grander than Westerbrook. The timbers that stretched across the huge expanse of the great hall had widened her eyes. Now in the light of day, she saw that knights, squires, and pages swarmed the courtyard.

Before long, there was a second knock. Gillian leaped back into bed and drew the covers up to her chin before she called out for the newcomer to enter. Several girls traipsed in with buckets of hot water. Another hauled out a wooden tub and screen, wrestling it toward the fire. By then, Lynette had returned to help her bathe.

Gillian very nearly dismissed her. It was awkward, having someone to assist her after so many months alone, but Lynette's openness and ready smile banished her reluctance. It felt wonderful to have the dirt scrubbed from her hair and scalp, and the leisurely soak in fragrant, steaming waters did much to ease the soreness that had settled in her muscles from the journey.

Lynette had just finished braiding her hair when there was a tap on the door. The girl went to answer it; a young squire stood there. The conversation they exchanged was brief and low-voiced.

Lynette turned back to her. "The master would like to see you belowstairs. Would you like me to show you?"

Gillian nodded. Her mouth was suddenly dry as parchment.

Lynette ushered her into a room just off the great hall. Two men flanked Gareth as they stood behind a wide table, but all her attention was captured by the man between. This morning in the bath she'd wondered how she would feel when she saw him again, but she had deliberately put it from her mind.

But now she knew. Her palms were damp and her pulse quickened madly. The very sight of him stole her breath. The tattered clothing in which she'd grown so accustomed to seeing him was gone. He was richly dressed, clad in a forest green tunic that deepened the color of his eyes and clung to the breadth of his chest. It seemed so odd, seeing him in a different light, that of lord of the castle. . . .

He had straightened upon seeing her. "Lady Gillian," he said. "May I present two of my knights, Sir Marcus and Sir Godfrey."

Both men bowed and greeted her warmly. Sir Godfrey, she learned, was the elder of the pair. Sir Marcus was of an age with Gareth, she guessed, but not quite so handsome.

"Marcus, Godfrey, do you mind?" He directed a faint smile toward the pair. "I must speak with the lady."

The two knights quickly withdrew and they were left alone.

When Gareth turned to face her again, the smile was gone. He gestured her toward the chair and closed the ledger with a snap. "I trust you slept well."

Gillian lowered herself to the chair and folded her hands in her lap, but her legs were poised as if she were prepared to flee.

"I slept very well, thank you."

But Gareth had not. He grimaced, for it had proved a night where thought after thought ran rampant through his mind. God's blood, who was he trying to fool? It wasn't just the dilemma that faced him. It was her. *Her.* In truth, he'd missed the feel of her beside him, for it had grown vastly familiar in these past weeks.

But Gillian was convinced that of a certainty he did not appear glad to see her. His mouth had tightened, as if in disapproval. The seconds ticked by as he continued to regard her. For a fleeting instant she had the oddest sensation that he knew not what to say.

But then she heard his voice. "There is no easy way to tell you this," he said abruptly, "so I must simply come out with it. You confided that your father sent you and your brother away from Westerbrook because he feared for your safety — and Brother Baldric heard tales that John had sent an assassin to scour the country for you."

Gillian clasped her fingers together to still their sudden trembling. "Aye," she said.

He gazed at her unblinkingly. "You were right, Gillian. There was indeed a man dispatched to seek and find you."

A strange feeling crawled up her spine. "You're certain?"

"I am."

Gillian went cold to the tips of her fingers. "How?" she whispered. "How do you know?"

"Because I am that man," he said at last. "I am the man the king sent" — there was a taut, ringing silence — "to be your executioner."

11

For one awful moment, Gillian feared she was surely losing her mind. Numbness befell her. She regarded him in shocked, frozen silence. Unbidden, she recalled the days after she'd found him . . . idly talking when he lay still and unconscious, praying that he might hear. She'd guessed that he was a hunter like her father . . .

Never in this world had she dreamed that *she* was his quarry.

She could feel every drop of blood drain from her cheeks. "Holy Mother Mary," she whispered. "You were sent to murder me."

"Aye." There was no denial, no apology, just a flat pronouncement of fact. He was so calm, so matter-of-fact that it ran through her mind that he would do the deed here and now.

She lowered her head. The hand she lifted to her temple wasn't entirely steady. Gareth flinched, for he'd glimpsed the flare of panic that leaped in her eyes, the slump of her slender shoulders. Her countenance was stripped of all color. He thought she was defeated — after all she had endured, this had finally broken her.

He was mistaken.

In an instant he was up and rounding the table. He extended a hand toward her, his only thought to comfort her. All at once she was on her feet, propelled by anger. Taken wholly by surprise, her shoulder struck a jarring blow against his chest; he grunted and stumbled. Her attack took him wholly aback.

"You tricked me!" Her eyes blazed with the fire of her fury. "You told me I was in danger. What you neglected to tell me was that I was in danger from you!" She launched herself at him anew, venting aloud her outrage.

He captured one flailing hand before she could claw at his face, then managed to snag the other. His arms imprisoned hers, hard and unyielding. With the weight of his chest he trapped her against the wall, holding her fast. Gillian struggled and screeched and swore.

"You brought me here to kill me, didn't you? You dared to call me a liar — to make me feel the guiltiest sinner on this earth for allowing you to believe I was a widow. But you are the one who lied. You said you would protect me, while all the while you meant to kill me!"

"Nay, Gillian. That is not true."

She tried to wrench from his hold. He wouldn't let her. "That's why you were on the ship, isn't it?"

"Aye. I was on my way to you. But the storm tore apart the ship, and when I woke I recalled nothing of my mission, nothing but my name. The rest you know. When I sensed you were in danger, I brought you here to Sommerfield."

Her lip curled scornfully. "Oh, that is rich. You've only just recalled the king would have you kill me."

His face was lined and drawn, but she was too incensed to notice. "I have been gone for three months, Gillian. Three months! But not until we arrived last eve did I remember the reason for my departure."

"No matter when or where or how you remembered, it seems you are still one of the king's lackeys!" She delivered the words with stinging disdain.

Gareth's lips compressed to a thin line. "I am not the king's lackey."

"Oh, but I think you are, my lord. I confess, I'm curious . . . what was the price of my life? What sum did the king pay you to murder me? A fair price, I do hope."

His teeth clamped tight. Lord, but she could be infuriating! "He paid me nothing," he said curtly. "I agreed only to save my son."

"Your son!" Her eyes opened wide, then narrowed in blatant suspicion. "You have no son. You said your wife was dead!"

"She is." He was grim-lipped and abrupt. "I don't know how or why, but I know it as surely as I am here at Sommerfield. My son is a lad of nearly five. His name is Robbie." His eyes darkened. "May God forgive me, but I recalled nothing of him until my return here."

Gillian released the storm in her heart and soul. "You expect me to believe you?" she cried. "To pity you? Do you seek to arouse my sympathy? Well, I will not put aside the truth! You are a fiend. A toad. The most disgusting rodent on this earth cannot compare to you!"

Deep down, he knew she was terrified. Stunned and furious. It was no more than he expected. No more than he deserved. For that reason alone, he bore her tirade for as long as his patience held out.

"That is enough!" he said harshly. "Your

point is taken. Now calm yourself."

"Calm myself, he says! By God, if I were a man, I'd run you through!"

"Then I shall give thanks ever after that you *are* not and *cannot*."

With that he whirled her around and placed her in the chair. When she would have jumped up, he clamped his hands around her wrists, staying her movement.

"Sit!" he thundered.

She was momentarily quelled, but by no means beaten. She glared up at him mutinously as he straightened.

"You wish the truth and so you shall have it. We are far from court here, but I had heard of Ellis of Westerbrook's attempt to kill King John. I was aware of the rumble of discontent throughout the land during John's reign, but I had no patience with the way the barons argued incessantly among themselves. I find myself amazed that they united and were able to force King John to sign the Great Charter! I had gone on Crusade with Richard. I had done my duty to the Crown and it was my intent to hold myself distant from the squabbles of the kingdom as much as I could. For the most part I succeeded — until the night the king and a small party of his advisors passed by Sommerfield on their way to the north and sought shelter for several nights. I could hardly tell him to be on his merry way, for one does not refuse the king."

His voice took on a note of grimness. Tell her, he would. Spare her, he could not, not one detail. If he was merciless, it was because she demanded it. "I learned from the king's party that Ellis of Westerbrook had been captured and was being held at Rockwell, near the Scottish border. Apparently John was intent on discovering the man with whom your father conspired to kill him, but torture did not compel your father to confess the other man's identity."

Torture! Gillian nearly cried out. A rending pain ripped through her, as if a lance had pierced her heart. "He thought he could save England from the king's tyranny. That is why he tried to kill John. And in the end, he took his own life rather than bow to John's will."

"Aye. The king is clever. I will give him that. Perhaps John already suspected that your father would not yield to such tactics, for it seems he had already ordered his men to Westerbrook. No doubt it was in his mind to seize you and your brother Clifton to blackmail your father into revealing the name of the other man responsible for the murder attempt.

"John did not foresee that Ellis would take his own life before surrendering another. A messenger came here that night, Gilbert of Lincoln, to pass along the news that Ellis had killed himself. He relayed how the king's men discovered Westerbrook was deserted when they arrived there. I was present, along with Gilbert, and two of the king's advisors, Geoffrey Covington and Sir Roger Seymour. I remember watching Gilbert from that very corner." He gave a slight nod. "As he delivered the message, the poor man quaked so badly his knees knocked together. And aye, the king fell into a vile rage — 'tis true what is said about his vicious rages — for he'd been duped . . . duped by a dead man. Now he might never know the identity of the man your father protected."

Gillian froze inside. Her father *had* shielded someone; she recalled distinctly the shadow of a man behind the curtain that long-ago day in the counting room.

"He cursed Ellis. Reviled him over and over. He ordered that Westerbrook be burned to the ground. No matter that he was dead, he charged that Ellis would pay for having cheated him out of carrying out his death — of discovering the other assailant. I've never seen such blackness in a man's heart. Death was not a great enough punishment, John raged. Ellis's treason must be punished. He vowed that no sons or daughters would be born to *his* son and daughter. Only then would he be avenged."

Gillian shuddered. The king was surely a monster, to plan such a despicable act upon two innocent people! Yet even as the certainty crossed her brain, she wondered . . . who was the more despicable? The king . . . or the man who would carry out such a despicable deed?

Her chin lifted. "And that is when you offered your services?" The question was uttered in a tone of near frigid politeness.

At that moment, Gareth could have cheerfully throttled her. He gritted his teeth. "I did not *offer* my services," he refuted with icy precision. "I was chosen because I was present — because the king chanced to spend that wretched night here at Sommerfield — because the king would not sully his own hands with such an abhorrent task, nor the hands of his ministers!"

"Yet you agreed, my lord Sommerfield."

"Only because he took my son hostage to the completion of the deed. Regardless of what you may think, my Lady Gillian" — he mocked her as surely as she had mocked him — "my knights are no match for the forces of the king. And should you chance to find it in your heart to care, King John *still* holds my son hostage!"

Gillian's conscience stabbed at her, but she ignored it. "And what of my brother?" she demanded. "Is Clifton alive? Or did you hunt him down and murder him before you came for me?"

There was an endless, hollow silence. "I think not," Gareth said at last.

The truth? Another lie? Or simply that he didn't remember? Gillian searched his face, his very heart — but could find no answer. "Don't you know?" she asked scathingly.

A muscle ticked in his jaw. Color seeped beneath his skin. "Nay," he said.

"You don't know! Your memory serves you most conveniently, my lord." Gillian hurtled upright from the chair, unable to disguise her ire. "I cannot help but wonder if you recall how you were able to find me!"

"It was not an easy task. Your father's people scattered far and wide, for they feared the king's wrath might be directed at those who served beneath him as well. I could hardly reveal my intent, and so I spent days searching for anyone willing to speak with me.

"Finally I paid a fat purse to a former stable-boy at Westerbrook. He saw your father, your brother, and you depart that night, and all in different directions. In time I came to learn of an aging friar who had served your father — and a woman who had been seen with him." Levelly he met her gaze. "The memory is not sharp, but I believe I was near a port on the North Sea. I boarded a ship to hasten the journey to Cornwall where Brother Baldric had taken you."

"The men on board the ship. Were they the king's men, too?"

Something flickered across his features, something she might have deemed regret had she been inclined to feel generous toward him.

"They were the ship's crew," he said quietly. "I traveled alone. I acted alone. Only the king and two of his advisors were aware of my mission. Not even my knights know the full truth."

His acknowledgment had rendered her pale as winter's first snow, yet her chin climbed aloft.

"I do believe you are right, my lord. One does not refuse the king. So what is to stop you from finishing your task here and now — now that you have me at your mercy?"

Gareth's lips tightened. "You know me better than that, Gillian."

"I do not know you at all! You are not the

man who woke in my cottage." Her tone was blistering. "This is what I know. You are Gareth, lord of Sommerfield, defender of King John, a puppet to do his bidding. It seems your son has great reason to be proud of his father."

Gareth was incensed. "Puppet bedamned!" he swore. "I was his pawn!"

A rallying anger pounded within her. "And still are!" she declared bitterly. "Why should I believe anything you say? You deceived me. You said you would not harm me. You said you would not desert me. Oh, and to think I defended you to Brother Baldric. I touted you as a man of honor and truth!" In her desperation, she had believed him. But no more. No more! "You said I had naught to fear from you, when in truth I have *everything* to fear from you. And by God, I will not stay here!"

Her announcement met with a snort of disdain. A brow quirked high.

"Where would you go?" he challenged baldly. "Brother Baldric is most likely cold in his grave. Westerbrook is burned to the ground."

Gillian caught her breath, for his words lacerated her very soul. "What!" she said in a tone of acid sweetness. "Will you hunt me down anew? In that case, I would be a fool

205

to tell you, wouldn't I?"

This time she suspected it was she who wounded him. His gaze flickered and he made no reply. Squaring her shoulders, Gillian picked up her skirts and stepped deliberately around him.

Or tried to. Long arms reached out and snatched her up against him.

"Release me!"

"So you can run again? I think not."

Gillian's head came up. His half-smile grated. Her fists came up between them as she sought to twist away. His arms merely tightened their steely hold until her breasts were crushed against the solid plane of his chest.

Her eyes blazed her fury. "Oh, I knew it. I perceived it that very first day while you slept. You are a lout — an arrogant lout!"

"Arrogant, perhaps. But a lout?" He shook his head. His smile turned devilish. "Never in this world."

Why, the braggart! She could almost believe he was enjoying this. Her lips parted as she prepared to heap upon his head the full measure of her wrath.

"My lord! I must speak with you!" The shout was accompanied by an insistent banging.

Gareth's smile vanished. "Not now," he

called over his shoulder. His gaze never wavered from her face. Desire unbidden cut through him, an arrow of shooting fire that veered straight to his loins, leaving him uncomfortably full and straining.

Sweet Jesus, he thought, but she was just as beautiful angry as when she was not. Color bloomed high on her cheeks. Her eyes flashed like twin sapphires. Her lips — ah, her lips — were tinted with the first pink blush of summer roses. His heart pounded. He longed to drag her into his hungry embrace, cradle her hips against his so that she could feel the pulsing of his rod. He wanted to smother those pouting lips with his, kiss away her fiery resentment and melt her anger into heat of a far different sort.

His head lowered.

Again the pounding. "My lord, methinks this cannot wait!"

With a muttered curse, Gareth released her. He strode to the door and threw it open. "Not now, Marcus!"

Marcus flushed, but held his ground.

"I thought you would want to know, my lord, that a message was just delivered to the guards at the gate. The king sends word that he will arrive within the hour."

Gareth hesitated but an instant. "Wait for me in the hall," he directed tersely. He swung around to face Gillian, only to find she stood just behind him.

Never in all his days would he forget the terror he glimpsed in her eyes.

"Oh, God," she whispered.

It was odd, he reflected later, how the bleak vulnerability etched in her soul were revealed in but two simple words ... 'twas as if she'd been run to ground. The breath she drew was ragged and belabored. Before his eyes, she swayed giddily. She would have fallen had he not reached out and caught her. It was almost as if he could feel everything collapsing inside her.

His mind was racing. Christ, this was his fault! He'd thought to save her by bringing her here. Instead he'd led her straight into the mouth of the lion himself.

All at once she surged upright, as if she'd been stabbed in the back. Her gaze darted to the door. "I must leave before the king arrives!"

Gareth sensed her rising hysteria. Winding his fingers around the narrow span of her wrists, he pulled her close. "No," he said. "There is no need."

"There is every need!"

"I can help you, Gillian."

"Help me? Oh, I think not. I came with you to Sommerfield because I thought you meant to help me. Instead you mean to hand me over to the king and save your son." As soon as the words spilled forth, Gillian despised herself. It was selfish and small, petty and wrong to envy the life of a small boy, yet she couldn't deny the terror that burned in her heart at that moment.

Gareth's mouth tightened. "You cannot spend the rest of your days in hiding."

"Better to spend them in hiding than to lie cold and lifeless in a grave like my father!" The words echoed her desperation.

"There is another way."

"There is *no* other way!" It was a choked, stricken cry.

"There is." He tugged her into the passageway. "Marcus!" he bellowed.

The young knight came toward them. He halted before Gareth, crisply alert. "Yes, my lord?"

"Fetch a priest, Marcus. And hurry!"

"Aye, my lord." Marcus broke away at a dead run.

It was the last thing in the world Gillian expected him to say. A sickly dread spilled all through her. All she could think was that he intended to kill her after all; out of some misguided sense of honor, he wanted the priest to administer last rites. Through sheer effort of will she forced her lips to move.

"Why do you call for a priest?"

"Why else?" he said grimly. "You're going to marry me."

12

For the veriest heartbeat, Gillian could neither move nor speak. She was caught squarely between laughing hysterically and sinking to the pits of hell. She wrenched free of him with a cry of rage, infuriated by his pronouncement.

"I will not," she said fiercely. "I will not marry the man who sought to murder me!"

Gareth's jaw locked. His hands clamped down on her shoulders. "If you do not," he said harshly, "your life will surely be forfeit. Is that what you want?"

Tension charged the air.

His voice prodded her, stabbed at her.

Gillian swallowed. Her throat burned as she struggled to speak. She hated her helplessness, her inability to fight back . . . to fight the king. But he had stated it well and true. He was lord of this sprawling, grand castle, but even he could not fight the king.

"Nay," she said raggedly.

"As your husband, I can protect you in a way I cannot otherwise." He spoke with brittle truth. "Now make your choice, for there is no time to ponder. Will you marry me or not?"

Gillian's breath came unevenly. A violent tug-of-war was being waged deep in her chest. He was right. Where would she go? Mama and Papa were dead. She knew not where Clifton was. Westerbrook was gone. She had no one — no family, no home. Her throat burned rawly as she blinked back tears, blinked back a wrench of despair. She would not cry, she told herself. She would not weep.

She withstood the cold demand in his eyes as long as she could, then dragged her gaze away, unable to bear it any longer. "Aye," she said tonelessly. "I will marry you."

It happened in a daze. Almost before she could clear her mind of the enormity of what was about to happen, she stood in the great hall. The priest — she discovered his name was Father Paul — appeared just a trifle harried as he smoothed his hand over his portly belly and gave a nod, signaling that he was ready to begin the ceremony. If he had any opinion as to Gareth's hasty compulsion to be wed almost immediately after his arrival, he kept it to himself. Sir Marcus and Sir Godfrey stood near as well. A bevy of onlookers, all agog, watched from a doorway.

She stood woodenly as Gareth took his place beside her. Staunchly upright, she sensed in him the same gripping tautness that had driven him but a short time ago. Father Paul cleared his throat and began to speak.

His words were but a blur. Panic swamped her. Dear God, she thought frantically, what was she doing? Was she mad? If she could have escaped, she would have. An inner tremor shook her. She quelled it with stringent effort, then stole a glance at Gareth, an act instantly regretted. Their eyes caught and held. His regard was cool, almost distant.

Hers was the first to slide away.

When it was time for the vows, Gareth displayed no hesitation; he spoke his with utter conviction.

Hers could barely be heard.

Then it was done. It was no accident that Gillian turned away from Gareth. She didn't notice the way his lips creased with displeasure.

Marcus stepped into her line of vision.

"On behalf of all my lord's knights, we wish you well, my lady." The words were accompanied by a slight bow. Sir Godfrey was not so shy. He seized her hand and carried it to his lips.

Her head was still spinning. From the corner of her eye, she saw a young knight approach Gareth. "My lord, the king and his party are nearly at the gates."

Gillian's head jerked up.

"Well, then, my bride and I should welcome them." His gaze encompassed Gillian. "Come," was all he said.

At the bottom of the wide stone steps that descended to the courtyard, they stopped. The lord of the manor awaiting his king! she reflected bitterly.

But you are now the lady of this manor, chided a niggling little voice in her mind.

She was still reacting to the enormity of that knowledge when she heard a jingle of spurs, the clank of steel and armor that heralded King John's arrival. She longed to look away, as if she would be tainted if she did not. Yet it was almost as if she were riveted by a power beyond her control. A small party of riders cantered beneath the towering arch. Her eyes widened at the array of noisy carts that lagged behind. She wasn't aware of Gareth anxiously scanning the king's entourage, skimming the horses and the carts.

It wasn't difficult to spot the king, though Gillian had never seen him when he'd visited their neighbor, William de Vries. John's mount was a majestic steed of pure white, but it spun through her mind that he looked neither noble nor kingly. Nay, the man perched atop was far less grand, despite the splendidness of his garb. The ermine-trimmed mantle did little to hide the bloat of his belly over a tasseled silk belt, his frame given to obesity. Matching fur circled the top of his boots. It appeared his wife Isabella and her ladies did not accompany him.

Several men, clearly of some consequence, dismounted first, then moved to aid the king.

"Gillian."

She glanced up at Gareth.

"Take my hand," he said tersely.

Gillian instinctively retreated a step.

"Take my hand and smile. And by God, if you want to save your soul, do not argue or disagree with me, no matter what I say or do."

Their eyes collided. His were fiercely commanding, while hers reflected her uncertainty. When she hesitated, the muscles in his face seemed to tighten. Within his gaze glimmered a warning she didn't fully comprehend, yet knew intuitively she dared not question.

Without a word he extended a hand.

Trembling, she laid icy fingers within his. His hand closed around hers. She nearly snatched it away, but didn't dare. All at once she felt trapped as never before. His palm burned like fire against hers. A stab of anguish shot through her, for it was so very different from those nights at the cottage . . .

He led her forward. Together they halted before the king. Broad and squat, his black beard framed a square face and concealed some of the heaviness of his jowls.

"Your Highness," he stated, "your arrival is most fortuitous. I've only recently returned to Sommerfield."

The king's dark eyes glinted. "Fortuitous indeed, for I have sent several messages to you of late and received no reply. I thought I would see what has transpired since our last meeting." He gestured to the man who flanked his right, who was slim, with hair of russet brown. "You will recall Lord Geoffrey Covington" — he indicated the other, gray-haired and heavy-chested — "and Lord Roger Seymour."

"I do indeed." Gareth gave a slight bow. "My lords."

The king had diverted his attention to Gillian. His black eyes were gleaming and lust-filled — and abhorrently revolting to Gillian.

"I do not recall this beauteous lady," he said with a bold leer. "Did you hide her away that night, Sommerfield?"

"Nay, my lord." Gareth's laugh was falsely hearty. He held their joined hands high. "I should like to present my wife, Lady Gillian of Westerbrook."

Gillian envied his calm, yet she could feel every muscle in his body coiled tight. Her stomach churned and her limbs quailed, for this might well be the last day she would see on this earth.

Somehow she willed the tremor from her voice. "Sire." It galled her to greet him courteously, but she bowed her head and dipped into a curtsy. It was all she could bring herself to say.

There was a suffocating silence. She heard King John's sharp inhalation of breath, saw the menace that contorted his features as she straightened. Geoffrey Covington and Roger Seymour were clearly startled, then ill at ease. In that moment, she had no doubt of the black vileness that stained the king's soul, that he was capable of any and all atrocity.

Only Gareth was seemingly unperturbed. John's gaze fastened upon her, as scathingly condemning as his tone. "Lady Gillian." He spoke the name as if it were a vile curse. "You are the daughter of Ellis of Westerbrook?"

Gillian pressed her lips together bravely. Though she quavered from head to toe, she would not cower nor cringe openly before this hateful man. Yet neither would she fall before him, pleading for mercy and begging for her life.

"I am, sire." She spoke with quiet dignity.

The king's gaze swung to Gareth. "We must speak in private," he said brusquely.

"Doubtless we will, my lord . . . after I see my son."

Gillian was stunned by his daring.

"Your son is well," the king said curtly.

"I would see for myself," Gareth answered easily.

"He is not here." John dismissed him impatiently.

"Pardon me if you please, Your Majesty, but it would seem that since you are so busy with your affairs, you must have overlooked his presence." He turned and pointed to the very last cart in the procession. A golden blond head was just barely visible. "I see him there, my lord, with his nurse. I must express my gratitude once again, for allowing the woman to accompany the boy."

Gillian was both amazed and appalled. Oh, but he was glib. He would give and take almost in the very same breath.

John bared his teeth. "By God's teeth, you dare much! But since I am feeling particularly generous this day, I will allow it." He raised a hand, and Roger Seymour stepped away to convey the message to one of the other knights present.

Within seconds, a big, raw-boned woman with a matronly air about her crossed the courtyard, holding the young boy's hand. When the pair reached them, the woman curtsied and seized Gareth's hand, pressing a kiss upon it.

"My lord Sommerfield," she cried, fairly beaming. " 'Tis good to be home again."

"Indeed it is, Edith." He acknowledged her salute with a faint smile. "You'll be amply rewarded for taking such good care of my son." He addressed the woman, but his gaze never wavered from the lad, who peered up at his great height.

His hand fell away from Gillian's. He sank to his knees before the lad. His gaze roved over golden, silky hair and plump, rosy cheeks. He laid his hands on the boy's small shoulders.

"Robbie," he said hoarsely. "My son. My boy."

The boy stretched out a small hand, just barely touching the raspy hardness of Gareth's cheek. "Papa?" he said tentatively.

It was a moment before Gareth answered. Gillian saw the way his throat worked, saw the way he struggled to speak. "Aye, lad," he said rustily. "Aye!"

In the next instant, he'd clasped that small, sturdy body fast against his chest. With no hesitation, the boy laid his head against his father's shoulder.

"A touching reunion" — the king's voice resounded mockingly — "but it has gone on quite long enough, Sommerfield. Geoffrey" — he beckoned to first one knight, then the other — "Roger." His gaze settled on Gillian. "You may as well come, too, girl," he informed her haughtily, "since it is your fate I'll be deciding."

Gareth had swept Robbie high in his arms. Gillian had the feeling he was on the verge of refusing, but then Edith stepped forward.

"I'll take him, my lord."

"Thank you, Edith. Perhaps the cook can find some tidbit for him."

Within minutes, the five of them were closeted alone in a chamber above the hall

220

— King John, Gareth, Geoffrey Covington, Roger Seymour, and Gillian. Covington and Seymour removed themselves to stand at the far end of the chamber near the wall. Gillian hid her hands in her skirts to hide their trembling as the short, stout monarch took the chair that Covington had brought forward to the center of the room.

He wasted no time. Thin lips twisted into a snarl. "Are you a traitor?" he demanded.

"I am not, Your Majesty."

"Then why didn't you put her to the sword as I ordered?"

Gillian's heart pinched. The ground seemed to sway beneath her feet. So it was true. Not that she'd doubted Gareth's claim that he was to kill her, but to hear the king state her fate so cruelly made her long to plummet to the innards of the earth.

The king continued his fuming. "Why is she not dead?" A disdainful finger flicked her way. "Can you tell me, my lord Sommerfield, why you should not be condemned as a traitor for your failure to slay her?"

Gareth's smile was taut. "I've no desire to see your royal troops surround Sommerfield, my lord, but I pray you, hear me out."

Oh, but he was clever. He knew just what to say to keep his head from the block.

221

"Get on with it, then!" snapped the king.

"I was able to indeed hunt down the lady to the place where she had fled. I boarded a ship to hasten the journey, but just as I would have reached her, the ship broke up in a storm. Strange as it may seem, when I awoke, I remembered nothing of my past save my name — Gareth. When I awoke, Lady Gillian was there. She tended me while I recovered."

"So you married her out of gratitude. Because she rescued you — because she saved you?" John rolled his eyes. "God's teeth, Sommerfield, what blithering nonsense! I'd heard tales that you'd grown hard and bitter and cruel upon the death of your wife, that you cared about naught but your son. When you lost your past, did you lose your spine as well?" Beneath John's denunciation laced an acid bite.

Gillian's eyes flew wide at the king's scornful affront. She wondered fleetingly how he would respond to the king's jeer.

She was not given to wonder for long. He erupted into an easy laugh. "Hardly that, sire. I was taken with the wench. I wanted her."

The declaration was not what she expected. Gillian very nearly swung her gaze upon him in startled surprise. Was it true?

The thought had barely skittered across her mind when a hard arm slid around her back. With the other he blatantly ran a trespassing finger along the neckline of her gown, even skimming down — nay, between! — the valley of her breasts.

The impudent rogue! Gillian bristled. She girded herself, for the urge to jab an elbow into his belly was immensely tempting. If not for the king's presence, by God, she would have! Her lips compressed in mutinous ire. Spying it, Gareth gave a mocking laugh and pulled her tighter against his side.

John slammed a fist against the ornately carved arm of the chair.

"So why didn't you just bed her and be done with it? Why the devil did you have to marry her? She carries her father's blood!"

"And my seed," he said with soft deliberation.

Gillian reeled. A hundred things ripped through her in the mind-spinning aftershock. Horror. Disbelief. In some faraway corner, she marveled that she was able to remain upright; mayhap it was because Gareth's fingers bit almost painfully into her arm. Her mind was racing. What the devil was he about? Why had he made such a claim? Yet now, she realized numbly, she understood his warning that she was not to argue with him, not to dispute him.

He stepped away. A half-smile lurked upon his lips. His gaze raked down her form, lingering on the swell of her breasts beneath her gown — a brazen insult. Despite her best intentions, Gillian flushed.

"She was a maid when I first saw her," he said almost lazily. His smile widened. His eyes were hard. "But not for long, eh, lass? Ah, yes, she came willingly into my arms every night while I healed."

Gillian felt her face flame scarlet. How dare he do this, she railed in furious indignation. She began to smolder inside. He taunted her. He taunted her most cruelly and there was naught she could do! He was aware that she would not denounce him — not before the king. Fear of her life prompted her silence, for she could not predict what the king might do if he knew the truth, that she did *not* carry his babe. Dear God, his babe!

Nor was he finished. "I daresay you've an eye for a fair maid, sire," he went on blithely, "and so do I. Look at her, my lord. She's a tempting morsel — and a tasty one, at that." Slowly he began to circle her. All the while, that maddening smile curled his lips. "Is it any wonder I took her to my bed? Or perhaps I should say *hers* . . .

"I touched her as I pleased," he continued baldly. "I wanted her — and I had her. And if you doubt me, sire, you've only to look at her to see the truth, to know that she lay with me. When I was well again, I discovered I was not yet ready to end such . . . pleasurable nights. I brought her with me to Sommerfield, and it was then I recalled my mission. But by then, I'd discovered she was with child. I could hardly kill her," he said with a shrug.

Gillian could scarcely believe what she was hearing. Hot shame poured through her. When, she wondered achingly, would this nightmare end? Oh, but he was a master of cunning . . . a master of deceit, for the lies poured from his lips with ease. Behind that irksome smile was a man she did not know. Worse yet, she detected a seething current of something dark and dangerous . . . The teasing rogue from the cottage — the tender man who held her hand throughout the night — might never have been.

He'd halted behind her now, so near she could feel the rise and fall of his chest.

His voice rang out above her head. "You see the dilemma that faced me. To kill her would be to kill my own child, something I was not prepared to do . . . will not do." He moved so quickly she nearly cried out. A hand clamped suddenly on her belly, pulling her against him. His fingers splayed wide — as if he owned her, she decided bitterly. As if she were naught but a possession.

Deliberately she held herself rigid, trying to strain away. For an instant, the hand on her belly tightened. Then he abruptly released her.

Gareth had braced his legs slightly apart. "I will have no bastard child, sire," he said with a distinct undercurrent of steel. "I had no choice but to wed her."

"What of her brother? Do you know his fate?"

"Nay, sire, I do not." Oh, but he delivered the words with just the right amount of regret, the snake!

John made no answer. His black gaze had shifted to Gillian. "Your father tried to murder me," he said flatly.

And your lackey would have murdered me! she longed to screech.

"Did you know of your father's attempt before it happened?"

Gillian shook her head.

"He did not act alone. Do you know the man who conspired with him?"

"I do not, my lord." Her heart drummed painfully as she thought of the man behind the curtain. But then resolve hardened her heart. Her father had died protecting this man. Even if she'd known who he was, she wouldn't have confessed to him!

"Do you know your brother's where-abouts?"

The king's tone was almost pleasant, but Gillian was not fooled. It was but a way to coax her cooperation. Her fingers inter-locked before her as she raised her chin. "I do not, sire. He left Westerbrook the same night as I, but he did not accompany me. My father thought it would be safer that way."

John looked to Gareth. "Does she speak the truth?" he demanded.

"She does, sire. The plotting and scheming were left to her father, and the other man involved."

A hush borne of tension descended. Gillian had heard tales of the king's pen-chant for jewels — that at his coronation, even his white gloves were adorned with sapphires. No doubt it was true; there was a ring upon nearly every finger, laden with precious stones — emeralds, diamonds, and sapphires. A huge, brilliant ruby dangled on his chest; suspended from a heavy gold chain, it glittered with every turn of his fin-gers. He toyed with it endlessly, until she longed to tear it from his thickset neck that he might stop.

It was Gareth who broke the silence. "You need not worry that she will cause you such trouble as her father," he stated smoothly. "I will keep her in check, Your Highness. Nor will she flee, even if it means keeping her under lock and key."

Such arrogant presumption earned him the seething regard of his wife.

John's eyes narrowed as he studied her. Thoughtfully he stroked his beard, so meticulously trimmed and waxed. "I am reluctant to release my vow that Ellis's kin be wiped out. But indeed, 'twould seem that a mere woman and a boy can hardly pose any threat to me — and in truth, her brother may well be dead already."

Gareth was forgotten. The king's speculation that Clifton was dead tore into her breast like an arrow, clear to her heart. *No,* she cried in silent anguish. *Please, God, no!* It was beyond bearing that Clifton was dead.

John transferred his gaze to his ministers. "Geoffrey . . . Roger . . . what is your counsel?"

Covington frowned. "It may well be," he began slowly, "that perhaps we should take the girl's survival as a sign —"

"By all the saints, Geoffrey, you sound as

if you've gone over to the Church! Spare me such drivel."

Geoffrey's fair cheeks reddened. "What I mean to say, sire, is that it may not be wise to harm the girl. What if someone should discover you gave the order to slay the daughter of Ellis of Westerbrook? The barons might —"

"The barons . . . Lord, but I wish someone would rid me of every one of them. I gave in to their demands and signed the Great Charter at Running-Mead, yet still they grumble. They are like a nest of vipers. They will not be content until I give up my crown, and I will not give in to them again, I tell you. I will not!"

Gillian's skin prickled. She turned her head to see that she was the object of Roger Seymour's scrutiny. Her pulse skittered. How long had he been watching her? He did not smile or desist when their eyes met. Her heart skipped a beat, for she sensed his dislike keenly.

He surprised her by echoing Geoffrey's sentiment. "We can deal with the barons, sire, but Geoffrey may be right. Even if you were to throw her into prison, some of the barons might seize on just such a move. It's probably wise not to give them cause to incite their passion anew. And further bloodshed will do little to rally the people to your side."

"So you believe I should let her go," the king mused aloud.

Gillian held her breath. Seymour stared at her in a way that made her heart drum painfully.

"Aye," he said at last. "My counsel is to let the matter rest and leave her to Sommerfield for now."

For now. Those two simple words made her blood run chill. But it appeared John's anger had begun to abate. He gestured Gareth forward.

"Very well, then. I leave her in your hands." He leaned an elbow on the arm of the chair and fixed those small black eyes on Gareth. "But what of the money you owe me? You borrowed a goodly sum when last I visited here."

Gareth's lips compressed. Gillian was close enough to see the sudden sizzle in his eyes. "Much eludes me still, but I recall that night most distinctly. I am certain I owe you no coin, my lord."

The king's mouth assumed a petulant droop. "Perhaps you are right." He glanced at Geoffrey. "We'll not be staying the night. Send for the boy."

Again Gareth intruded. "For what purpose, sire? He is but a boy and has no further need of your . . . care. Lady Gillian is no longer in hiding. She is here, and I have vowed I will keep her under control. The boy belongs with his father."

Gillian's gaze bounced from Gareth to the king. John stared hard at Gareth.

"The boy has done very well with me."

"I do not dispute that, sire, and for that I thank you."

"If I leave your son with you, I have no assurance that you will not join with the rebel barons."

"You have my word," Gareth said quickly. "My every assurance. But if you doubt me, leave some of your men here to assure that I comply."

"I could do that," the king said slowly.

"I have never been disloyal to you, sire," Gareth reminded him. "I must ask that you not disregard my request. I merely do what is best for my son."

John pursed his lips. "I suppose you are right," he said shortly. "The lad is indeed of a tender age." Thus relenting, he got to his feet, tugging his surcoat over his girth before returning his attention to Gareth. "I do trust that you will be ready to serve me as the need arises?"

Something flickered across Gareth's features, something she could not decipher. He gave a low bow. "As the need arises," he confirmed.

King John swept by without another glance at Gillian. Geoffrey Covington and Roger Seymour followed in his wake. The door closed with a hollow thud. Gillian swallowed, fighting to slow the thunder of her heart.

Gareth stepped up beside her. "You did well," he murmured.

"And I would commend you for your performance, if you were not such a lying blackguard!" Air left her lungs in a scalding rush. "You must be mad to tell the king such a tale." A part of her was still aghast. "It is not possible that I carry your — your child!"

"Very true," he drawled. "And there is only one way you can *be* with child."

"Precisely," she snapped. "How then do you intend to fool the king?"

A slow-growing smile crept across his lips. "I don't," he said very softly.

All at once Gillian could scarcely breathe. "What do you mean?"

A thick black brow climbed aloft. "Come, now," he chided. "Surely you know the ways of the world." He gave an exaggerated sigh. "But if you insist, I will be happy to explain further . . . nay, mayhap it would be better to show you . . ." He reached out to grasp her arm.

She jerked it away with a toss of her head. "Don't touch me!" she cried. "I will never allow the man who would have murdered me to lay a hand on me! I'd sooner bed an adder than bed with you!"

She didn't bargain on his reaction. He snatched her to him with a suddenness that ripped the breath from her lungs; the fierceness of his hold betrayed his wrath. With thumb and forefinger he captured her chin, demanding that she look at him. His features were implacable; the harsh line of his mouth exactly matched his voice.

"Perhaps you should ponder on this, then, lady. It will be in your best interest to get yourself with child — and quickly, for that will be the only thing that saves your life."

Gillian blanched, going utterly cold inside. He released her abruptly, as if he could no longer stand the sight of her. Without another word, he strolled from the chamber and slammed the door.

She stared at the oaken portal. A sickly dread clutched at her. Sweet Mother Mary, she thought shakily. Was it a prediction he made . . . or a threat?

Vivid in her mind's eye was the way he'd looked as he stormed away. His tightly constricted features betrayed a ruthlessness that was frightening.

It was the face of a stranger, she thought vaguely, the face of a man she no longer knew . . . for in truth, she knew this man not at all. Bitterness welled up inside her, for the hell of it was that he was right.

If not for his protection, she'd be fast in the clutches of the king.

13

Gillian spent the remainder of the afternoon in her chamber, alternately stewing, then chafing over his high-handedness. He was quite an accomplished liar, this new husband of hers, and if she didn't have to face him until the other side of forever, it was too soon!

She was lying on the bed, trying to sort through the tumult of the day, to bring some order to all that had transpired when a knock sounded on the door. Gillian sighed. She very nearly called that she didn't wish to be disturbed, but then the door opened slightly.

"My lady?"

It was Lynette. The girl stepped inside. "My lord bid me to come and ask you to join the celebration in the hall."

A frown drew Gillian's brows together. She very nearly queried the girl as to why there was a celebration going on. Then she remembered . . . this was their lord's wedding day . . . *her* wedding day.

And Gareth was her husband. *Her husband.*

Lynette had crossed the floor to close the shutters. It was later than Gillian realized. The steel-colored sky had turned almost black. Snowflakes had begun to float toward the earth.

Refusal leaped to her lips. But she wouldn't put it beyond him to come and fetch her. Besides, it wasn't right to shift such a burden to Lynette. Gillian was not afraid of him, and she would not cower and hide as if she were!

"Would you like me to comb your hair before you go down, my lady?"

Gillian hesitated, then gave a nod. She sat quietly upon a bench beneath the window, with Lynette behind her. No doubt Lynette expected a brilliantly radiant bride, but there was no joy in her heart this day, no wild elation. How could there be?

Lynette set aside the comb, separating Gillian's hair with her fingers deftly. "Your hair is lovely, my lady," she said wistfully. "So dark and shining."

There was a painful catch in Gillian's breast. Her mind sped straight to Celeste. What was it Gareth had said? *As if you could forget,* scoffed a needling little voice inside.

So beautiful, he had praised. *Soft and golden and warm. The color of bright summer sunshine.*

Celeste. Gareth's wife. But no, *she* — Gillian — was now his wife.

It seemed so impossible. When she woke this morning, she'd never thought the day would end with Gareth as her husband. And the little boy, Robbie. Gareth's son. Ah, but it was so difficult to comprehend . . . he was now her son, too!

To become wife and mother, and all at once . . .

Something inside her cried out. Perhaps it was selfish. Perhaps it was wrong. Aye, he was a beautiful little boy, but . . . it wasn't supposed to be like this, she thought wrenchingly. It wasn't the way she had dreamed it would be. She'd hoped for joy and love and laughter on the day she became a bride, but there had been none of that.

Quietly she posed the question to Lynette. "Does Robbie resemble his mother?"

Lynette's nimble fingers stopped their movement. Gillian glanced over her shoulder, not surprised to find the girl's expression a trifle uncertain.

"You needn't look like that, Lynette. I know of Gareth's wife, Celeste."

Some of Lynette's unease seemed to lessen. "Aye, Robbie resembles Lady Celeste," she admitted. "He has the same fine golden hair. . . . I've always said it looks as if it had been sprinkled with fairy dust." Her fingers began to move swiftly through Gillian's hair. She stopped long enough to smile. "He is asleep now, the little mite. My lord scarcely let him out of his arms this afternoon. My lord was so unhappy after his lady died, but already 'tis different here in the castle. Now that he is back — and Robbie is back — it no longer seems so empty." Almost shyly she added, "And now he has you, too, my lady."

Gillian said nothing. Gareth's feelings for his son were unquestionably apparent. The heartfelt emotion in his eyes as he sank down on his knees . . . the way Robbie had clung to him . . . it was enough to make her throat achingly tight once more.

But his feelings for her were quite different from what Lynette imagined — quite different indeed.

"There, my lady, 'tis done. I do hope it's to your liking."

Gillian had to refrain from a cursory examination in the mirror the girl held up.

Lynette was so anxious to please that Gillian couldn't bear to disappoint her. Looking into the mirror, she saw that Lynette had caught it up and twisted it into a long rope, then wound it atop her head.

"It looks lovely, Lynette." She smiled in genuine pleasure. "Thank you."

She made her way to the hall alone. She felt rather awkward standing alone in the doorway — and this her wedding day! She wondered belatedly if it was a calculated move, sending Lynette after her. Had Gareth done so deliberately in order to put her to some sort of test?

All around was the sound of boisterous merrymaking. The lilting tune of a lute carried through the air. Her eyes scanned the revelers, searching for Gareth. At last she spied him. He stood near the dais, surrounded by his knights, a striking figure clad in boots and a tunic of forest green. The material stretched across his shoulders, bringing to the fore the latent power that lurked beneath. Despite her best efforts to quell it, her pulse began to clamor. Seeing him with the others made her acutely aware of how tall and broad he really was. He was laughing and seemingly well amused by something Sir Godfrey had said.

He must have sensed her arrival, for he

raised his head and gazed over to where she stood.

His smile withered. He clamped his hand on one man's shoulder, then turned and began to close the distance between them, his strides long and easy. As he reached her, she saw that his lips were compressed, as if he were displeased. He barely gave her a glance.

" 'Tis about time," was all he said.

For the space of an instant it was as if he trod upon her heart, but then a saving anger flowed through her. Oh, but he was hard to the bone and she was a fool! For several moments upstairs, she'd allowed herself to soften. Yet now it was instantly regretted; in its stead simmered a fiery resentment. If he was determined to show his indifference, then so would she.

Without a word he curled his fingers around her elbow and led her to the high-backed chair in the center of the dais. A hush had gone over the assemblage when they mounted the steps. He did not seat her immediately, but reached for her hand and held it high.

"The lady of Sommerfield," he said simply. A cheer rang out and shouts still echoed throughout the hall when Gillian took her seat.

Gareth had thought it best to send Lynette up for her, for the lady had been rather contrary when they parted. He had no wish to enjoin another battle. As he'd approached her, he noted that her eyes were not red-rimmed and swollen — 'twas a vast relief to know she hadn't spent the afternoon giving in to tears. In truth, Gareth was still smarting from their last stinging encounter. She'd made her feelings about this marriage — and him — abundantly clear. He would not play the love-sotted fool who doted on a wife who had nary a care for him.

The day had taken a turn he'd never expected. In the back of his mind, he'd had the feeling John would swoop in when the king discovered he was back. What he hadn't expected was that it would be so soon.

He didn't know how the solution had come to him, only that it had. In that shattering instant when Marcus announced the king's arrival, his gaze cleaved straight to Gillian's stricken features. He seized upon the first thing that spun into his head.

There had been no time to consider, to weigh and ponder. There was much he had to learn about himself, but somehow Gareth was aware he was a man of decisiveness, a man who would act upon his instinct and stand behind his commitment.

Nay, there could be no regrets. Indeed, as they stood before the priest, an odd elation had swelled his chest. The king's arrival had forced his hand, yet Gareth was almost glad. He wanted her. He'd wanted her from the beginning, when he woke in her bed. He wanted her and what better way to have her in his bed than as his wife? Yet earning her trust would not be easy.

God knew he did not wish to be beholden to the sway of the king's will, but so be it. He had accepted the fact that he had done what was right. He'd had no choice but to fall in or run afoul of King John. Though he was now consigned to do John's bidding, it was a trap of his own doing. He disliked having to submit to the presence of two of John's men — Stephen and Alexander now sat near the fire — but that, too, had been his choice. Yet he would also be wary of the king's tactics. That John had tried to trick him into handing over his coin made him furious!

But he'd kept Gillian safely within reach. He uttered a fervent prayer that now would see an end to John's vengeance toward her father.

And he'd managed to regain control of his son. He couldn't describe what he'd felt in that moment when he'd first laid eyes on Robbie. He'd felt . . . as if his innards had turned to mush. As if someone had reached inside and grabbed at his heart. He could neither speak nor move nor breathe. The feel of that small body against his chest, the shining green of the eyes that were but a reflection of his own. Guilt rampaged through him like wildfire. He would never forget the wrench of shame that slammed through him, shame that he'd spent the last weeks wholly oblivious that he had a son.

There had been shame, too, on the journey here, the same deep, scalding shame he felt with Robbie, for his mind had dwelled often on Celeste. To his unending frustration, he could recall nothing of her, not even when he'd seen Robbie.

Was it because she was dead? The king had said he'd grown hard and bitter after Celeste's death. He must have loved her then. He must have mourned her, so why couldn't he remember? He berated himself harshly, for he couldn't even recall how she'd died! Some might have called him too prideful, and perhaps he was. Yet he couldn't even ask how she'd died, for he was ashamed to admit such a memory had fled.

Ashamed that he could feel no sadness. No pain.

In time, such remembrances might return. Aye, perhaps now that he was home.

Yet no matter that he couldn't remember his past, he could not afford to dwell on it, he acknowledged silently. He must first see to his future.

And that meant seeing that Gillian and Robbie were kept safe. On that note, he returned his attention to his wife.

As soon as they were seated, servants swarmed from the kitchens. Supper proved a sumptuous affair. There was roast capon with cumin, huge platters of fish, loaves of bread, and an array of cheeses. Gareth ate and drank heartily, his appetite keen. The day had certainly not started off well, but it had ended reasonably well, and he had no aversion to enjoying it.

A maid offered another serving of pigeon pie, but he declined. Sated, he leaned back in his chair. It was no accident that his gaze drifted to his wife. Silently he studied her. Pale and still, she sat stiffly in her chair, sparing him neither thought nor glance nor word. She had eaten little, merely picked at her food, moving it around on her trencher.

He tipped his head to the side. "Is the food not to your taste, wife?"

Wife. The word was laced with mockery; his barb struck home. She longed to retort that it was not the food which was not to her taste, but the husband to whom she'd been shackled!

Her gaze cut to him sharply. Her rebellious aspirations must have shown. He propped an elbow on the lion head carved into the chair's arm, and bent his head to hers, so that only she could hear. "Sulk if you wish, Gillian, but do it in private — do not convey your ill humor to my people. They believe there is cause to rejoice and you will indulge them."

Their eyes locked in combat.

"And you?"

"And me," he reiterated flatly.

"I see," she said sweetly. "You wish me to be merry and gay?"

"Aye," he said shortly. "You've sat beside me like a stone. Perhaps a dance might be in order —"

"I do believe you are right."

Satisfaction rimmed his smile. Perhaps she was thawing. Perhaps her coolness was not coolness at all, but a shy reserve. After all, she knew no one but him. And perhaps this night would not bring about the cold reception he'd fully expected to receive. But before he could rise, she'd flounced from her seat.

In truth, Gillian despised him for his arrogance . . . his calm, for her stomach was twisted in knots at the prospect of what lay ahead this night. She much preferred to keep such thoughts at bay. Her gaze lit on Marcus, who had just stepped away from a group of knights. He had been kind, and she liked his gentle manner.

She stepped before him, her irritation at Gareth lending her courage. "Forgive my boldness, Sir Marcus, but it would please me if you would dance with me."

She didn't miss the surprise that sped across his handsome features, but he quickly set aside his ale.

"You honor me, my lady. I should be glad to accompany you." With a winsome smile he offered his hand, palm up. Gillian laid her fingers within his.

He spun her to where some of the others were dancing. Before long, a faint frown appeared on his brow. "What is it, Sir Marcus? Come, tell me," she encouraged lightly. "I will not bite, you know." His lord might, she decided tartly, but she would not.

"My lady," he said earnestly, "I do not mean to intrude upon your affairs — either yours or my lord's — but knowing that you are the daughter of Ellis of Westerbrook, I want to assure you that all here welcome you."

Dismay shot through her. She could

barely find the courage to meet his regard. "So it's common knowledge — that my father tried to kill the king."

"Aye, my lady."

There was a sharp stab in her breast. Even if she were to somehow find a way to leave Sommerfield, would she be ostracized? The prospect lent her no ease.

" 'Tis not what you think," Marcus said quickly. "My lord told his knights of your circumstances, that you ran from your home fearing retribution from the king. I simply wanted you to know you may trust me. I am loyal to Gareth . . . and to you. As I am sworn to my lord's protection, so I am to yours. 'Tis the same for all of his knights."

Gillian was touched beyond measure. "Thank you, Marcus," she said softly. "That truly means a great deal to me." She smiled up at him in gratitude.

Marcus smiled, displaying two deep dimples. "Excellent," he murmured, and now his eyes were sparkling. "Now, 'twill not do that you look so sober, my lady . . ." He dipped her so that her eyes flew wide and she had to clutch at his shoulder, and then suddenly she was laughing . . .

Watching the pair from across the hall, Gareth straightened in his chair. Why, the little vixen! He wanted to grind his teeth in sheer frustration, march over and pry Marcus's fingers from the narrow span of her waist. God's blood, but he had not foreseen this side of her, never dreamed it might exist! The chit was flirting with Marcus — and Marcus appeared to be quite receptive to it and, indeed, quite admiring of her!

Not that he could blame him. With her hair upswept, it revealed the long, graceful arch of her throat, the fragile-looking sweep of her nape. All the while she'd sat beside him, he longed to reach out and caress the soft, baby-fine hairs that curled on her nape. As irresistibly tempting as it was, as flattering as the regal coronet atop her crown was, Gareth preferred it down, an ebony curtain tumbling about her shoulders in wanton disarray, much like the morning when each had gazed in startled surprise at the other. He longed to comb his fingers through the silken mass, tug her close and bring her mouth into his.

Her skirts swirled high, revealing a tantalizing glimpse of trim ankles. Even from here, Gareth discerned the worn fabric of her gown, the tattered hem. He frowned. Her wardrobe was pitifully limited. He would have to see that it was remedied, for he couldn't have his wife looking like a waif. And he needed to fatten her up a bit . . .

The dance ended. But Marcus had barely stepped back when another man took his place; before long, still another and another. Gareth fumed. Leeches, every one of them! A smoldering anger reared its head, anger fostered by her indifference to him — and her attentiveness to his men!

But she belonged solely to him now. He was the only man who had the right to claim this beauty, he reminded himself. And claim her he would . . .

And very soon now.

Her maiden state might prove a slight hindrance, but it pleased him mightily. He would see to it that she had little pain. He would ease the way with melting kisses and molten caresses. It was a heady sensation, knowing she was innocent of all men but him. He'd felt for himself the frail, delicate barrier of her maidenhead — her heat and tightness — and they had not been apart but for last night. Though she knew it not, he'd posted a guard at her door. Oh, aye, knowing she was a virgin — that she'd been bedded by no other man — made him burn inside. His blood began to simmer and his loins began to heat.

He craved the feel of her against him, small and soft and delicate, lithe and firm. The night spent apart from her had only sharpened his desire a hundredfold. Erotic images of the night ahead danced in his mind. She would be naked this time, as naked as he . . . But his mouth turned down as he discovered the object of his thoughts bestowing a charming smile upon Sir Bentley, ever the clown — but nearly as handsome as Sir Marcus.

"You do seem to enjoy the company of my knights," he remarked pleasantly.

Gillian resumed her seat. "You told me to make merry with your people, so I did." A tiny little smile flirted at the corner of her lips. "But I must admit, I did enjoy the company of your knights — no doubt because I've had so little company for so many months."

Gareth swore beneath his breath. She'd just deliberately dismissed him, as if their time together had never happened.

He quirked a brow. "You wound me, lady," he stated mildly. "Do you not recall that we spent every hour of the day — and night — together these many weeks? You cried upon my chest. You slept with your cheek nestled against my shoulder, the curve of your breast against my side." He shook his head. "A pity it's now *your* memory which fails you. Indeed, 'tis just as I told the king. You came willingly into my arms every night while I healed." His eyes bored into hers. "Or am I mistaken?"

Gillian glowered at him. Oh, but he was so damnably smug! And why shouldn't he be? He was home, reunited with his son . . . while hers had been burned to the ground. She wanted nothing more than to snatch the pitcher of wine from the table and toss it into his lap — to see him toppled from his lofty perch. Perhaps that would dampen his intentions!

She would not dignify him with an answer. Instead she said levelly, "I've done what you asked. May I be excused?"

She had already started to rise. A steely hand clamped about her wrist. "You may not."

If the chilliness of his features were anything to go by, his pleasantness had been deceptive.

She sat down again, so hard her teeth hurt. Gareth had already leaned back in the chair. His pose was indolent, almost lazy as his unhurried gaze surveyed the swarm of people. A fresh surge of outrage shot through her. Oh, but he looked every inch the master of the castle!

"You appear to be feeling rather proud of yourself."

His eyes flickered to her, but did not

251

linger. "Why shouldn't I? I am home, and I have my son back."

"And you also have a wife."

His hand moved, trapping hers where it rested upon the arm of the chair. His fingers moved, his fingers tracing hers from the tips of her fingers to her knuckles.

"Do not fear, Gillian. You'll not be slighted."

His tone was almost one of silky menace. To those who might have chanced to look upon them, it might have appeared a tender caress between lovers. But Gillian knew better. It was but a way to goad her. It was not banter, but war — and he played the game far better and with far more subtlety than she.

She wrenched her hand from beneath his. "This marriage is a travesty!" she hissed.

"Nonetheless, it is a valid marriage," he observed coolly. "We are bound as one, and I look forward to the birth of our first child. Indeed, it's good of you to remind me . . . I do have a duty to discharge this night if we are to beget that child."

Oh, the lout! "Perhaps you shouldn't have lied," she shot back.

"If I hadn't lied, you wouldn't have lived. Indeed, your gratitude overwhelms me." His lip curled. His eyes hardened to green chips of ice. "And now, I do believe it's time to begin."

There was no time to contemplate the comment, no time to rally anew. In one fluid move, he hauled her to her feet and heaved her over his shoulder, like a sack of wheat. Gillian gasped as the world turned topsy-turvy. Loud guffaws and bawdy jests were immediately tossed their way. Gareth staggered in great exaggeration, as if his wife's slight weight were more than he could withstand.

Oh, the brute! Gillian shrieked in protest, demanding that he release her, but he kept an iron-thewed arm doggedly banded around the back of her legs. With a cocky grin, they left the hall behind. With unflagging steps he carried her up a long, narrow flight of steps and into a room.

Gillian was still sputtering when he closed the door with the heel of his boot and placed her on her feet. She instinctively scrambled away, not stopping until she backed into something — a chest at the end of the bed. Her gaze darted to the arched door beyond his back, then to every corner. Dozens of candles set into the walls revealed the immensity of the chamber. But it was not big enough to hide her, she thought vaguely. Indeed, the kingdom had not been big enough to hide in.

Gareth strode toward the fireplace. A small round table stood before it; upon it was an artfully arranged array of fruit, a decanter of wine, and two goblets.

His manner was relaxed, as if he had all the time in the world. Gillian, on the other hand, felt as if the world were spinning away, out of control and beyond her grasp.

He regarded her with the veriest lift of black brows. "Something to eat?" he inquired politely.

Gillian shook her head.

"Wine, perhaps."

Again her wordless denial.

He shrugged. "As you wish, then." He poured himself a generous portion of wine and lifted it to his mouth.

The muscles of his throat worked as he swallowed. But it was his hands that held her spellbound. Curled loosely around the goblet, they had always held a secret, almost forbidden fascination for her, and never more so than now. His fingers were long and lean, bronzed and starkly masculine. Her thoughts were a mad jumble. Would those hands be gentle? Hurtful? Panic lodged in her throat. Would he have a care that this was her first time? Would it even matter? Would it be quick? Nay, she thought with a shiver, for he was a man who would savor his conquest.

And these were the hands that might have easily stolen her life's breath from her . . . and still could. She could not forget that he was the man who would have murdered her without a second thought.

Her eyes squeezed shut. God, she could not bear it!

"Gillian."

Her eyes opened. A smile lurked upon his lips, a smile that sent a spiral of dread clear to her very soul. His gaze pinned hers.

Uneasy with his prolonged stare, her tongue came out to moisten her lips. "What? What is it?"

Very deliberately he set aside the wine. That arrogant smile widened ever so slightly. "It has just now occurred to me," he said softly, "that our wedding day is almost over . . . and I've yet to kiss my bride."

14

For the span of a heartbeat, Gillian was incapable of movement. Of thought.

There was a protracted silence, as if a tempest brewed within them both. Gillian was the first to let loose of it.

The angle of her chin conveyed her contempt. "You're a fool if you expect me to fall into your arms," she said recklessly. "You have no shame. No conscience. What you want you must take, for I will yield to force and naught else!"

Her righteous scorn made him laugh outright. Such fire. Such spirit. He had only to channel it, to make her passion flame as brightly as his.

"You will yield to me, lass — and I promise you, there will be no need of force."

Oh, the swaggering oaf! His laughter — his certainty — but fueled her determination to resist him. "Oh, I knew it. I perceived your arrogance even before you awoke at the cottage — and I was right!"

His laughter waned. He studied her for a long moment, his expression screened behind his eyes. "So you remember that, do you? Well, I have the feeling you forget what else happened at the cottage." His gaze fell meaningfully to her lips.

The muscles in her belly contracted. Her heart tripped over itself. "I forget nothing, my lord." Haughtily she contested his statement. In truth, she had not. In truth, she had only to look upon him to relive every second of the searing heat of his mouth upon hers, the treacherous warmth of his hand upon her body.

"Oh, but you do." His eyes bored into hers. "You knew it would come to this, Gillian."

"I knew nothing of the kind!"

"You lie. There was a restless stirring and clamoring inside . . . the yearning to touch and be touched. I saw it in your eyes. I felt it with every beat of your heart. Regardless of the falsehood you speak now, you felt the same desire that I felt."

A little shock went through her, for it was as if he saw deep inside her. She drew herself up proudly. "Lust was all you felt!"

A fleeting amusement crossed his features. "Well, perchance a bit of that," he murmured. "Indeed, that day near the beach, had I persisted — had I chosen to — the issue of your maidenhead would have been dispensed with then and there. Aye," he said again, "you knew it would come to this, and I had already decided it would."

Gillian went hot inside. It was true she had wondered what it would be like to experience his hand plying her breasts, taunting and teasing her nipples as he had the night of his dream. Her breasts felt heavy and swollen. She very nearly pressed her palms against them, for they had begun to tingle and ache just as before. But her imaginings — or perhaps her innocence — had never allowed her to wonder what it would be like to . . . to actually lie with him.

But his self-assured pronouncement made her see a fiery haze of crimson. She refused to pander to his ego — he was too full of it.

Hotly she contested his claim. "Had you chosen to, you might have tried, my lord, but you would never have succeeded! Indeed, I allowed you to kiss me only because I'd not yet discovered what a fiend you really are. And if indeed I felt anything, it was because I was lonely!" The words might come back to haunt her, but she would not recant a single one.

His eyes hardened. "A word of warning —" his voice was as smooth as the finest wine from across the Channel — "this is a battle of your choosing, Gillian, and one you cannot win. Perhaps you should bear this in mind — and retreat before it is too late."

"Only a coward would retreat," she said feelingly. "Only a coward would surrender."

Gareth's temper had begun to smolder. He was torn between the need to shake her and tame her reckless pride. "You begin to try my patience, Gillian."

"Patience?" she cried. She lashed out furiously. "You dare to speak of patience, when you stood before the king and boasted . . . What was it you said? Ah, yes. You said you touched me as you pleased, did you not? You said I came willingly into your arms. You had me — but you will never have me! And I promise you, my lord, you're about to discover just how *un*willingly I come to your bed, to your arms! I have a mind of my own. A will of my own. And you will indeed have to keep me under lock and key if you wish to *control* me." In truth, it was a desperate bid to delay the inevitable, but by the Cross, she would not repent of her outburst — nor meekly submit to his lust!

His smile was anything but pleasant. "I would not be averse to that. If it proves to be necessary, I promise I will keep you well occupied." His expression was almost a jeer. Hands on his hips, his eyes journeyed boldly down her slim form, his evaluation no less than a brazen insult.

"Is that why you wed me? In order to bed me?" Her nails dug into her palms. Her eyes flashed fire. "Tell me, Gareth. Are you so atrocious in bed that no woman will have you? That no woman wants you? That you must trap one into marriage to ease your lust?"

Even as the taunt spilled forth, in the back of her mind, Gillian realized she'd gone too far. It was a foolish thing to say, for she'd just dealt an arch blow to his manhood.

There was an inflexible cast to the thrust of his jaw. A storm brewed within him. She sensed it with every fiber of her being.

Gareth shook his head. "Ah, Gillian," he said softly. "Lady, that was not wise — not wise at all." A slow smile crept across his lips — a smile that shivered her to her very bones. "I would have been happy to show you that surrender need not be defeat. But now you add insult to denial, so you leave me no choice but to prove you wrong . . . for I do believe the way to woo and win a lady is something I've not forgotten."

A single step carried him forward.

Filled with trepidation, Gillian edged back. Something hit the back of her knees — the chest at the end of the bed. A band of tightness crept around her chest.

Her mind was racing, along with her heart. It was just as he'd said . . . too late to retreat. Too late to turn back, too late to take back the angry exchange that had passed between them this night.

Nor could she lie to herself. Nothing could change all that had happened, all he had done — all that he was. And nothing could change the way she felt about him, even if they were able to come full circle and start anew.

Yet she couldn't just give up. She couldn't just give in!

'Ere the notion revealed itself, Gillian bolted for the door. Her fear lent her an urgent strength, but she hadn't a prayer. With pitiable ease, he hooked her with one arm and swung her around to face him.

Strong hands clamped down on her shoulders. She could feel their heat burning through the cloth of her gown. She was caught squarely in the vise of his gaze — and alas, his arms!

His eyes glittered down at her, burning like fire, glowing like emeralds in the dark. "Resign yourself to this. Resign yourself to me."

Her chest rose raggedly. "I can't! I can't!"

"You can, lady. We shared a bed many a night. 'Tis time we shared our bodies as well."

Everything within her cried out. Couldn't he see? It wasn't just her body. It was her heart. Her soul. She was not a woman to give herself lightly. She had spent her entire life believing that there should be a bond of love; that to share her body in this way was an intimacy that should only be shared in love . . .

It was not like this in her dreams.

Nonetheless, Gareth was the first to kiss you, needled a voice inside. *He is your husband. You are his wife. 'Tis only right that he should be the one to take you to the marriage bed.*

But not in love, argued another. *Never in love.*

For alas, she was right. She had led a sheltered life at Westerbrook, but she had no trouble discerning the lust that flared in his eyes.

And then there was no more thought as his mouth trapped hers. For one perilous moment, she sensed in him a hot, consuming demand that was overwhelming. He took possession of her lips with an insistence that left no room for denial. His kiss was not brutal . . . but brutally thorough.

She inhaled sharply, and as she did, her lips parted, and he pressed home his advantage. In some distant place far, far away, Gillian was aware that he had not lied — he hadn't forgotten how to please a woman. For against all will, against all odds, she felt everything inside go weak.

With no hesitation he staked his claim, seeking entrance to her mouth. With bold, sweeping strokes, he tasted the hot, honeyed interior with a smooth, seductive rhythm that made reality fall away. She felt as if she'd been pitched into the center of a storm that tossed and raged, much like the storm that had brought him to her.

Lost in a void of insidious, unexpected pleasure, she was only hazily aware as his hands briefly settled on her shoulders. In one fluid move, he pushed her gown and shift from her shoulders, down past her hips.

A strangled sound caught in her throat. She tore her mouth free. The scoundrel! Her gown now lay puddled about her feet.

With a cry she started to reach down and drag it up that she might shield her nakedness. But Gareth gleaned her intent and caught her about the wrists, trapping her hands at her sides.

His gaze stroked slowly over her, taking in

every detail at his leisure — and aye, he took his time about it! There was no part of her left untouched. She felt stripped to the bone. A sound of mute frustration escaped. She knew why he did this. He meant to punish her for daring to oppose him, for her ringing condemnation. By the time he'd finished, her entire body flooded scarlet with the heat of her embarrassment. Awash with humiliation, she railed inside at her helplessness, for he allowed no chance to shield herself.

But he was not done. A hard arm clamped about her back, bringing her up against his frame. The tips of his fingers slid across her nape, a wispy caress that sent a shiver all through her. Then his fingers were sliding up and into the silken tresses. A few tugs and the long, heavy mass spilled down her back. His head lowered. His mouth against the side of her neck sent a shaft of lightning all through her.

His palm coursed along her side, climbing relentlessly upward, tracing the ladder of her ribs. It did not stop until it reached the underside of her breast. For a timeless moment, he hovered there . . .

Was it to prolong the torment? Would he touch there . . . or not? A flurry of panic traced along her spine. Her gaze slipped inevitably down, even as he dared to cup the fullness of one breast. Her skin was white against the brand of his fingers, splayed wide now to encompass the jutting fullness.

The sight of her own creamy flesh was jarring. 'Twas as if those twin mounds ripened before her very eyes, the disks of her nipples pouting and thrusting toward him, a wanton offering. And they felt so strange, all tingly and tight, especially there at the very tips. In truth, *she* felt so strange, as if another had slipped into her body.

With a fingertip, he traced a feathery circle around and around one roseate peak. On the second pass, his thumb raked across the very peak. Her nipple sprang taut against his palm. A thousand currents leaped from that very spot. To her horror, the other grew pebbled and hard, as if in anticipation of that very same caress.

"Come. Do tell me, Gillian." Her name was a rush of sound across her ear. "Is this to your liking?" As he spoke, the caress came again, and yet again.

His mockery escaped her. Her breath snagged in her throat. Never had she thought to experience such unbearable sweetness. She dipped her head low, afraid her answer was starkly visible in the depths of her eyes.

He lifted his head, gazed down to gauge his victory. A soft laugh betrayed his triumph. "Oh, Gillian, I not only see it, I can feel it."

And indeed, Gareth had already glimpsed her pleasure, reluctant though it was. No matter that she decried him to the ends of the earth. Her body betrayed her. Her body bespoke a far different message than the strident oaths hurled at him from lips that still glistened from the damp heat of his tongue.

With a ragged breath, Gillian tried to raise a hand to push him away. He thwarted her, trapping it back against her side.

She was suddenly frightened of the way she felt. As if she had no control over herself, as if she didn't know herself and her emotions were flying all about with no hope of recapture. Why did she feel this way? She had no wish to give what he would take, as if it were his due.

She pushed aside the inner voice that whispered what she did not wish to hear. That it was indeed his right — his due — for he was her husband.

"Stop!" she cried.

If he heard, he ignored her. His mouth captured hers once more, holding her against him, dragging her tight against him

— even into the cradle of his thighs! — so that she was aware of every long, powerful inch of him. Something hard as stone jutted the hollow of her belly. She could feel it stirring, as if restless. Growing . . . Her heart leaped into a frenzy. This was the part of him that was so different from her own softness — the part of him that would become a part of her. But it felt nothing like what she'd seen at the cottage.

His kiss was starkly sensual, blatantly bold. His tongue traced the outline of her mouth, then dipped along the seam, a silent demand for entrance to her mouth. Her lips opened. The plunging of his tongue erotically mimicked the act that was soon to follow. She should have been frightened, should have protested anew, but a languorous warmth had slipped over her. Her pulse clamored and her insides melted. When he swept her high into his arms, she caught at his shoulders instinctively.

The coverlet was soft and smooth against her skin. Yet when Gareth suddenly loomed over her, the reality of what was about to happen swamped all through her.

Very deliberately he placed his hands near her face, his knees alongside her narrow hips, straddling her. That smile she'd begun to despise crept across his lips, as though to tout his mastery over her. She hated that she was the king's pawn . . . and now his.

Everything within her rebelled. All at once Gillian refused to submit meekly. Nay, she would not bow to him as if she possessed neither wit nor will. Everything within her demanded resistance, futile though it was. This was not Gareth, the man who had very nearly stolen her heart in the cottage. This was Gareth, lord of Sommerfield. Arrogant. Presumptuous.

Wildly she said, "Is this the bed where you took your wife's virginity?"

Gareth froze. His jaw locked tight. The very air around him sizzled and cracked. His visage grew black. His features were suddenly a mask of pure granite, his eyes like ice.

His lips curled. "Aye," he said heartlessly. "The very one where I'll take yours."

His mouth devoured hers, taking her lips with scalding passion. There was no evading him. No stopping him. He clamped his fingers against her scalp and held her lips captive to the punishing furor of his kiss. His chest was an oppressive weight that cut off her breath. His lips left hers; openmouthed, he dragged his lips down the arch of her throat, clear to the valley between her breasts. Gillian filled her lungs with air, for she could scarcely breathe.

He was seething. She could feel it in every pore of his body. She sensed in him a ruthless determination. His patience had fled, his gentleness with it. Nay, there was no tenderness in him. She knew the difference now. She could feel it in the constriction of his muscles, the clench of his jaw, the brittleness of his features.

Straightening upright, he tore off his tunic and threw it aside. When he turned back, he was naked to the waist, clad only in his hose. Gillian's mouth grew dry. She couldn't look away. She'd seen him without benefit of clothes before, to be sure. But alas, this, too, was different. Her heart lurched. Her mouth grew dry as bone, for he exuded an aura of latent strength and vitality that could not be dismissed.

A dense, curling mat of hair covered his chest and belly, disappearing into his chausses. His arms were lean and knotted with muscle. The candlelight flickered, revealing the clearly visible outline of thick, turgid flesh beneath.

A shudder ripped through her. She pressed her lips together to keep them from trembling. Strong male hands closed over the pale white flesh of her thighs, parting them wide. She hated her vulnerability, her feminine secrets lying open and exposed to his gaze. There was no mercy in him, for he had no mercy to give! Nor would she beg or plead. Nay, she thought brokenly. Whatever might follow, she would not cry out.

Nor would she bestow on him the victory he sought. Though he would bend her to his will, he would not break her. Her conviction thus avowed, when he lowered his head, seeking her mouth, she jerked her head aside.

It was a vehement denial. A flagrant refusal of his kiss . . . and him.

Such sacrifice did not come without cost.

Sheer fury splintered through him. Blast her hide for spurning him so! With a growl, steely fingers bracketed her cheeks; by God, she would see him when he took her!

But what he found brought a vivid curse to his lips. He snatched a candle from the bedside table and held it above her.

"Don't!" She dragged her elbow across her eyes, wiping away the evidence that still lingered on his fingertips. "Don't look at me!" Her cry was half-angry, half-defiant . . . and wobbled pitifully.

For Gareth had already glimpsed the trickle of tears leaking from her eyes. Silent tears she'd held inside, that he would not know.

For one thundering moment, her tears did not erode the pounding in his brain, the red-hot haze of desire that churned within him and swelled his rod to stiff, painful erectness. Desire commanded his body, a desire that eclipsed all thought. All reason. All he could do was feel . . . and what he felt was a fire in his soul, the craving need to quench the hunger in his loins . . . to tear away his chausses and drive deep into her tight, virginal flesh until he exploded in ecstasy.

Should he stop? He didn't want to. Sweet Christ, he didn't think he could. Not with her lying beautifully naked and open beneath him. The temptation was almost more than a man could bear — than *he* could bear. Passion had taken root and would not be banished so easily.

A battle warred deep in his being — a battle no longer waged between the two of them, but solely within his soul.

It was a battle such as he had never fought.

He almost hated her then. For the tears that cracked his heart and left it open, deterring his plan. For rousing a pang of guilt he didn't want to feel. For defying him and daring to accuse him. He wanted to tame her, to smother her impudent tongue with the fever of his kiss.

In a heartbeat he was on his feet. "Dry your tears," he said harshly. "I'll not bed a bride so reluctant." He stared at her, his eyes blistering, his temper barely in check. "But bear in mind, Gillian, the king can count — and will no doubt be eagerly counting the days until you deliver a child. If you do not, we'll both pay the consequence."

Snatching up his tunic, he left her alone.

Gillian's lips still throbbed from the fierceness of his possession. Suddenly cold as death, she crawled beneath the covers, uncaring that she was naked. Despair wrapped around her like a shroud.

Perhaps it was the strain and uncertainty, the tumult of the day, but the tide of emotion inside her erupted in a torrent of tears.

Before long, there was a silvery flash of light outside the shutters. The crash of thunder in the distance reached her ears. She turned her back to the window and hugged a pillow to her chest, but there was naught she could do to shut out the sound.

It came to her then. She had done naught but exchange one place of storms for another . . . and a patient for a jailor. Aye, she thought with bitter rancor, she had surrendered herself . . . to her executioner.

15

Gillian woke the next morning feeling totally drained. For the longest time, she stared at the ceiling with burning eyes, feeling as if she'd been sucked dry. As if all emotion had been leeched from her. She could scarcely summon the will to crawl from the bed. Though she willed it not, memories of the night before crowded her brain . . . but no, she would not succumb. She would not think of *him!*

For sometime during the night, Gillian had sworn a vow to herself. Never again would she allow Gareth to bring her to tears. He already controlled her life. She refused to let him rule her feelings. Brother Baldric had said she was strong, and so she must be, no matter how difficult it proved.

With a sigh that seemed pulled from the very bottom of her being, she slipped from the bed. Her gaze chanced to alight on her

273

clothing, lying in a heap on the floor. Hurriedly she gathered it up and draped it over the chair. It was then a knock sounded on the door.

Gillian dove for the bed and curled the covers up under her chin. Was it Gareth? Her heart was suddenly pounding. But no, she thought with a sniff, *he* wouldn't have bothered to knock!

"Yes?" she called.

" 'Tis Lynette, my lady. Your bath water is ready. May I come in?"

Gillian let go a pent-up sigh of release. "Of course," she responded.

Lynette entered, a trail of maids with buckets of steaming water behind her. When they'd finished pulling out the wooden tub and filling it with water, the maids departed. Lynette remained.

" 'Tis late, Lynette, is it not?"

Two bright spots of pink appeared on the girl's plump cheeks. "My lord said you would be tired this morning, my lady." She flashed a shy, dimpled smile. "And that we should not wake you too early."

It was apparent from Lynette's smile that she was under the impression Gareth had spent the night in his bed — even clearer that she was convinced he'd spent it with her.

It embarrassed her beyond words to crawl naked from the bed, knowing that Lynette believed her lord and his new lady had spent the night indulging in fleshly pursuits, when in truth they'd spent it apart. Oh, the devil take her vows! Where *had* Gareth slept?

One thing was for certain. She would not ask him, or any of his people. To do so would humiliate both of them. She winced inside. The prospect of facing him again was one she did not relish, especially in light of the way he'd stormed away last night.

After her bath, Gillian sat down to partake of the tray of food Lynette had left. It was simple fare, bread, ale and smooth, creamy cheese. She ate heartily, having eaten little the night before. Brushing the crumbs from her skirts, she heard a rustle near the door, which stood ajar. Thinking it was Lynette come to collect the tray, she called out, "I've finished, Lynette."

But Lynette did not enter. Gillian glanced over with a frown, for she was certain she'd heard someone.

All that was visible were eight small fingers curled around the frame of the door. Before she could say a word, a blond head and a pair of impish green eyes followed.

Gillian blinked in surprise. She advanced closer, but not so near that she would frighten him. "Hello, there," she said with a smile. "Would you like to come in?"

By then he'd presented himself in his entirety. He ambled several steps within, then stopped and regarded her curiously.

Gillian tipped her head to the side. "Are you lost, Robbie?"

He shook his head.

She suspected as much, for he looked neither lost nor forlorn. "Are you looking for Nurse?"

He shook his head.

"Have you run away from Nurse?"

Again a shake of his head.

"Well, then, let me have one more guess. Are you hiding from Nurse?"

He giggled, and bobbed his head up and down. Those incredibly green eyes sparkled. His impish smile was surely contagious, for despite her best efforts, one tugged at her own lips.

"She will wonder where you are, Robbie." Gillian tried to sound stern and failed. "Surely she will be worried."

"But you said I could come in," he said promptly.

Gillian bit her lip. "I did, didn't I?" She didn't want to go back on her word. It would not set a good example for the boy. "Well, perhaps just for a bit. Then we'll have to go in search of Nurse and let her know you are safe." She moved to the bed and patted the coverlet. "Would you like to come sit with me?"

She'd barely spoke when he darted across the room toward the bed. It was set high off the floor and he could not manage it without assistance. With no hesitation, he lifted his arms for her to swing him up.

Gillian placed her hands on his waist and lifted. "Oh, good heavens!" she said when she'd deposited him next to her. "What have you been eating? You are heavy as a stump of fallen oak in the forest." She spoke only half in jest, for he was surprisingly solid. All at once, pictured in her mind's eye was the way Gareth had lifted the lad into his arms as if the boy weighed no more than goose feathers.

The image faded. "How do you know my name?" he asked.

"Well," she said lightly, "I saw you ride in with King John and his party yesterday. 'Twas then I learned your name was Robbie."

His lower lip pushed out. His brows puckered over his little nose in a frown. "I do not like King John," he announced.

Gillian lowered her head and beckoned him close with a finger. "I'll tell you a secret," she whispered. "Nor do I. But it must be a secret," she cautioned. "What do you say? Can you keep a secret?"

"A secret," he breathed, then clapped his hands together. "I have a secret!" he chortled.

Gillian smothered a laugh. Faith, but it didn't seem possible — to laugh when speaking of the king! She pressed a finger to the middle of her lips. "*We* have a secret."

With a giggle, Robbie did the same.

Gillian felt her heart catch. Lord, but he was a beautiful little lad. His cheeks were plump, his skin so fair. His hair was silky and gold, with a few curls at his nape. Lynette had said the boy greatly resembled his mother Celeste.

And all at once she couldn't help but think of her own dear brother. Not nearly so young as Robbie, but still just a boy, hardly ready to be on his own . . . *Clifton*. A rending ache pierced her heart. *Oh, Clifton, where are you?*

But a moment later the boy's sparkling green eyes searched her face. Then: "Are you my papa's wife?"

Some of the smile deserted her heart. "I am," she confirmed.

He appeared to consider. "If you are my papa's wife," he said slowly, "then you must be my mother." He peered at her more closely. "*Are* you my mother?"

He was so earnest, his expression so hopeful. Gillian's heart twisted. Indeed, she almost hated to disappoint him.

"Nay," she said gently. "I am Gillian. Sometimes, you see, when a man's wife dies, he may choose to take another wife, a second wife. That is what your papa did, and I" — she stumbled a little — "I am your papa's second wife. Your mother, Celeste, was your papa's first wife. She's gone to live with our Lord in Heaven." She hesitated, suddenly a little uncertain what to tell him about Celeste — what he knew, or what he'd been told. It was strange, to speak of a woman she'd never known.

But not just any woman. Gareth's *wife*.

Just as strange, to realize that while she spoke of this child's mother, she — Gillian — would likely be the only mother Robbie would ever know. But that was too much for a child of his age to grasp just now. Indeed, she thought faintly, almost too much for *her* to grasp.

Unable to stop herself, she asked, "Do you remember your mother, Robbie?"

"No. Do you?"

For an instant Gillian was taken aback. But it was a logical question, she realized.

This time it was she who shook her head. "I never knew your mother, since I've only just now come to live at Sommerfield," she explained. "But do you know what?"

"Nay. What?"

"I'm rather lonely, Robbie, and . . . I am in great need of a friend."

Chubby fingers slipped within hers. "I shall be your friend, Gillian," he said gravely.

Gillian's heart melted. "Would you?" Lord, but he was sweet! "That would make me very happy, Robbie."

The lad beamed up at her.

"But now, my young sir, I do believe we should find Nurse." She rose and held out her arms. "Shall we?"

It was odd, Gillian reflected later, for it was Robbie who gave her the courage to brave the day . . . and the lord of Sommerfield.

Nonetheless, she was rather relieved when she heard one of the men mention that Gareth had ridden out to inspect his lands. Lynette spied her in the hall and hurried over. When she offered to show her the castle and grounds, Gillian readily accepted. It felt good to stretch her legs, and no trace of stormy skies remained. Though the air was bracingly cold, sunshine peeked through fleecy white clouds.

There had been little time to explore yesterday. Once again, Gillian was left in awe. The castle sprawled high atop a hill, surrounded by the deep waters of the moat. To all appearances, it had been well kept in Gareth's absence. They walked about at leisure, clear to the soaring battlements atop the castle walls. The river snaked through the valley. Not so far to the north were the wilds of Scotland.

Gillian was grateful for Lynette's company, and she was an excellent guide. She relayed how the castle had been built by Gareth's Norman forebear, Lord Robert, who had been granted the land by the Conqueror in reward for his assistance.

"Was Robbie named for him, then?"

"I expect so," Lynette replied.

Gillian tugged her mantle more tightly about her shoulders, for the breeze that whipped here on the battlements was decidedly cold. A pang swept through her. There was so much she longed to know about Gareth's marriage to Celeste . . . or was she better off not knowing?

Lynette left her, but Gillian lingered a while. Despite the whistle and chill of the wind, she liked it here. Below in the courtyard, figures moved briskly to and fro.

Laughter and shouts drifted upward, borne by the wind. She'd hated the solitude of the cottage, the feeling of being so alone. And — oh, but a part of her would be loath to admit it to Gareth — it felt good to be a part of something again.

It was midafternoon when she descended the long stairway to the ground. She made her way across the courtyard, nodding to some of the servants, calling a few by name. Lynette had introduced her to many, and her head still buzzed with all the names and faces. It would take her a while to know all of them.

She skirted a cart sitting in front of a narrow doorway, but suddenly a sack topped from the end of the cart to her feet. Gillian started to lift it back, but all at once a woman darted from the doorway.

"Nay, my lady, let me! A woman in your state dare not lift such things!"

The woman wrestled with the sack, then dropped it back into the cart. Wiping her hands, she turned toward Gillian with a broad smile. "My lord made the announcement to all of the servants about the babe, my lady." Before Gillian could utter a word, the woman seized her hand and rushed ahead.

"Oh, I am glad for you, my lady. My 'usband and I 'ave six wee ones, and there is no blessing like a child. We wish you much joy, my lady." With a curtsey, the woman ducked through the doorway.

Gillian was mortified. Dear God, she had wandered blithely among these people the entire day. And all of them believed . . . Oh, God, how would she ever be able to hold her head up again?

A shadow fell over her. Gillian knew, even before she turned around, who stood behind her. Without a word he took her elbow and led her to where no one stood near.

Gillian yanked herself away the instant he stopped.

Gareth tipped his head. "I trust you have something to say, wife."

She squared her shoulders and looked him straight in the eye. In all her days, she didn't know when she'd been so furious. "You heard?" she asked tightly.

"Aye." Hands behind his back, he was totally nonplused.

Gillian's gaze traveled from his black hair, tousled by the wind, to the tip of his dusty boots. "Well," she stated bitingly, "your opinion of yourself never wanes, does it? 'Twould seem you are a man above all other men to announce to all that we expect a child — especially when you've yet to plant the seed."

"And I must point out that in order to conceive a child a woman must lay with a man."

Gillian's eyes were snapping. "I need no reminder!"

A black brow quirked. "Why so distressed? The king believes you are. What if he should return and mention it? Would you have everyone agog? He might easily guess the truth then, that you did not conceive before we were wed. And the king's men will know as well."

Gillian shivered. The king's men, Stephen and Alexander, stood near the guardhouse, burly and bearded, their thumbs hooked into their swordbelts.

As always, Gareth had an answer ready at the fore. She cursed the glibness of his tongue, yet in truth, she must concede the point. But all at once her heart leaped . . .

"And what if I am barren?" The question emerged with difficulty.

Gareth's regard sharpened. He could almost see the invasion of fear. In truth, it was something he'd neglected to consider.

Uncertain how to answer, he feigned a nonchalance he was suddenly far from feeling. "Then we will both be damned to hell. But take comfort — at least we will be there together, husband and wife."

That, at least, brought her chin aloft. Deliberately he changed the subject. He was pleased when he arrived back at Sommerfield to hear that she'd spent the day mingling with the servants in order to learn their names and duties. His first glimpse of her came in the courtyard, walking idly across the yard, smiling at those who called out in greeting.

"I would like to present you with the keys to the household." A brow arose. "You do know how to run a household?"

"Of course I do. After my mother died, my father left such things in my hands."

"Ah," he said softly. "And I'm sure we shall find that they are capable hands, indeed."

Gillian flushed. Her guard went up like a shield, for the smile that flirted on his lips made her heart pound. She had the uneasy sensation he meant something else entirely, for though it was her hands he referred to, his eyes had dropped to her lips . . . and it was there they now dwelled.

Reaching for her hand, he uncurled her fingers and placed a set of keys in her hand. With his own, he closed her fingers around the keys. When it was done, he didn't release it for the longest time. Aware of the way his hand completely enveloped hers, an odd tumult began to rage in her breast.

"I shall see you at dinner."

With a long, slow look, he left her standing there, her heart in her throat.

The conversation weighed heavy on her mind as she returned to the bedchamber. Ah, but she was a fool! she acknowledged despairingly. Gareth was right. She could hardly beget a child herself.

She had no choice but to reconcile herself to the inevitable . . .

She must lie with him.

Tonight.

At dinner, he greeted her, cut her meat, and kept her cup filled. Much of his attention was claimed by his knights as they discussed the events of the day.

Nonetheless, Gillian wasn't nearly as composed as she wished. It was disconcerting to sit beside him. Every so often his thigh nudged hers. For Gillian, it was a potent reminder of all that had passed between them last night. She hadn't forgotten the way he'd looked, his chest wide and imposing, so unmistakably virile and masculine. Nay, she need not be near him, even see him, to remember what he looked like. But alas, she *was* near him, and all at once she couldn't forget the way he'd wrenched her thighs apart, the ruthlessness of his kiss as he tumbled her down upon the bed. Though she had sidestepped the thought throughout the day, she was still stunned that he had stopped. That he chose not to take her as he had promised.

Aye, he had stopped. He had not hurt her . . .

What if he was not so generous tonight?

Her nerves were screaming and her head had begun to ache. She raised a hand to rub the hollow between her brows, unaware of Gareth's scrutiny.

He turned his head. "Would you like to retire now?"

There was a definite coolness in his tone. Gillian felt as if she'd been caught in a web from which there was no escape. She smothered an hysterical laugh. Should she say yea or nay? Indeed, what did it matter?

Either way, the outcome was the same.

To prolong this torture must surely be harder than to bear it, she decided bitterly.

The veriest tremor went through her. "Aye," she said woodenly.

"Then I give you leave to do so."

Gillian quickly rose. She'd not gone more than a step when his voice stopped her.

"You may wish to wait for me." A deliberate pause. "I'll not be long."

Their eyes collided. A trace of panic shot through her, for his features were set in implacable lines. Within his eyes shone a determined resolve. And Gillian knew . . .

It was a warning.

She lowered her lashes and fled. But Gareth had glimpsed her bruised, wounded expression. He caught up with her near the entrance to the stairs, swinging her around to face him.

"Why do you look like that?" he demanded.

"You know why." Her eyes grazed his, then slipped away.

His features darkened. She stood with her arms huddled over her chest, her narrow shoulders hunched together, her gaze averted. It was a pose of abject misery, of defenseless hurt — a pose that made him feel as if he'd crushed her like he would a bug beneath his heel. A sliver of remorse shot through him, but he refused to give in to it.

She'd dealt him a substantial blow to his ego that he'd not soon forget — or forgive, for that matter! He'd spent a hellishly uncomfortable night, curled up against an outer wall, that no one would know he'd been spurned by his wife on their wedding night! In the cottage, he'd known the feel of her even before he'd known *her*. He missed the feel of her in his arms. He missed her warm, sleepy scent, the warm trickle of her breath against his skin. He felt . . . bereft without her softness warming his side. He had no wish to douse her spirit, but she was his, and she must come to terms with it.

A thumb beneath her chin dictated she meet his gaze. "You make me out to be a monster," he said, his jaw tense. "But I am not a man without compassion, without mercy. I did what I had to do to guard my son's life — just as I did what I had to in order to save yours."

Gillian regarded him with eyes both pleading and accusing. "Please" — with the tip of her tongue, she moistened her lips — "if you could only give me time."

His breath hissed in. His gaze stabbed into hers, as he would stab into her, she thought wildly. "There is no time," he cut in abruptly. "Now make yourself ready. I will be up shortly."

On that note, he left her alone. Gillian made her way to his chamber — she could not think of it as theirs. It was too soon, if indeed she ever would . . .

She would accept that she must get with child. But she did not have to like it, she thought with a sniff.

As before, the chamber glowed with candlelight. Again, there was a decanter of wine and two goblets on the table near the hearth. It was there that Gillian directed her steps. She poured herself a generous portion of wine, and sank down on the rug before the fire, the goblet next to her.

Holding her hands to the fire, she stared into the crackling blaze, then reached for the wine. 'Twas a fine wine, indeed, and she sipped again. Smoother than any she'd ever consumed, she decided, as the beaten silver touched her lips once more.

The first glass, along with the blaze crackling in the hearth, made her all toasty and warm, both inside and out. The second made her rather blurry and fuzzy — and lent her courage. The prospect of the night ahead no longer seemed so daunting. She was hardly the first woman to lie with a man; 'twas silly to dread it so.

At length, she pillowed her arms on the upraised hearth, and lay down her head. Fatigue settled in. She was suddenly so exhausted she could not move. She would rest, she decided, for just a moment . . .

It was longer than Gareth expected before he was able to excuse himself and take his leave. At least a dozen urgent matters were left in limbo, but they had waited this long;

they could surely wait until the morrow. He was too impatient to concentrate anyway. The day had been long and tiring. There had been little sleep the night before.

He pushed himself away from the table with feigned reluctance, not wanting to appear too eager. But of a certainty it was not the matter of the night's rest that filled his mind as he announced his intention to seek his bed.

It was the lady who was in it.

His knights cast knowing glances and grins between themselves. A few were frankly envious. They well knew just why their lord was so eager to say good night and retire.

Ah, but what would he find? Gareth wondered. A spitting, defiant she-devil? Was this but one more chance to refuse him? Such was the turning of his mind as he mounted the stairs that would take him to his chamber; he was afraid the answer would hardly be to his liking. With a stab of black humor, he advised himself that he'd best be ready to duck when he opened the door — she would heave whatever was in reach to keep him out.

Cautiously he opened the door a crack, then stepped within. The chamber was dim but not completely dark. A few candles still sputtered.

As he closed the door, his heart skidded to a halt. His narrowed gaze riveted to the bed. It was empty, by God! He was ready to explode. Christ, where the devil had the wench gone? Mayhap he should have kept her under lock and key after all!

Embers from the fire burned, aglow with a miserly heat, for the fire needed to be replenished. It was then he spied her, there before the fireplace. Her head was propped on her arms. Her legs were tucked beneath her, her skirts swirled all about her. Her hair was a wild, ebony waterfall around her, spilling rich and thick and swirling upon the floor.

There was a half-empty goblet near her hand.

Four steps took him to the table near the hearth. Lifting it, his brows shot high. He glanced from the decanter, to Gillian, and back again. Slowly he lowered it to the table. *Hmm.* She had partaken freely of it, it seemed, *very* freely.

His mind was suddenly circling. Bedamned! he swore darkly. What was this that she must fortify herself with spirits in order to lie with him?

He disliked the notion. Disliked it intensely.

What do you expect? The voice of admonishment echoed in his brain. *You hardly played the tender lover. Would you bring her unto you with harshness and fear between you? 'Tis no way to begin a marriage.*

He very nearly had . . . He cursed himself roundly. Alas! No wonder she'd felt the need for wine, he admitted slowly. His mood had been stormy last eve.

Stormy? chided the voice. *'Twas a veritable tempest!*

But she had surprised him. Oh, aye, she had surprised him indeed . . .

Gareth had felt badly that there had been little time to speak with Robbie, to tell him of his new life. What with his wedding yesterday, the king's arrival, and everyone clamoring for his attentions, there had barely been time to think. And last eve before the celebration, when he went to Robbie's room, the lad was already fast asleep — thus, he'd searched out the boy this afternoon after he'd returned from inspecting his lands.

He'd felt rather sheepish when Robbie informed him that he already knew of his wife — that he had already met Gillian, as he called her. Robbie spoke of her with shining eyes. Then later, he'd seen Gillian sitting with him near the hearth. Her arm slid about the boy's shoulders, and Robbie had laughed up at her. It seemed there was a bond between them already, and for that, he was vastly relieved, his concerns nearly banished.

For he knew how she felt about him. She resented him fiercely, and he hadn't been entirely sure how she would feel about his son. He'd been foolish to worry, he decided. For despite her tumultuous emotions about him now, she had tended his wounds with the utmost gentleness and attentiveness. He'd sensed her capacity for love and caring long ago, felt in her gentle touch when he lay ill. Such a woman could hardly turn aside his son. And if the pair held each other in affection already, 'twas surely a good sign that all would be well by the time the babe came along.

Ah, yes, the babe . . . the babe that had yet to be conceived.

Aye, he was pleased with her. But if only there were more time to gain her trust.

He drew a slow, deep breath. *Time,* he thought. She had asked for more time last night. He'd countered that there was none to give — and how he suddenly regretted that there was not! For then he might have gained her trust . . .

Dear God, he could never have killed her. *Never.* And what of her brother? What of Clifton? That part of his memories still eluded him. When all had settled, Gareth decided, he would send several men in search of the boy. But he would keep this to himself, for he could not bear to give rise to Gillian's hopes, only to see them dashed yet again.

He crossed to the fireplace and sat down upon his haunches, very near but not touching her. A strong wrist dangled from one knee as he looked at her for the longest time. Her beauty struck him like the butt of a sword, low in the belly, robbing him of both his breath and his senses.

Dark, silky lashes, the color of smoke, rested upon her cheeks. The wine had stained her mouth a lush, deep crimson; a drop still lingered, there upon the swell of her lower lip, catching the flame of the fire and turning the ruby bead translucent. They were parted now, her breath deep and rhythmic. Almost reverently, he traced the delicate plane of her cheek. With the pad of his thumb, he blotted the drop of wine and carried it to his lips.

Her eyes fluttered open, still hazed with the blur of sleep — and wine.

She stirred. "Gareth?" she murmured.

"Aye," he said huskily.

Dainty fingertips touched his mouth — a startling caress that made him reel.

"I fed you," she whispered.

"Gillian —" He spoke her name with an uncharacteristic hesitation.

Her gaze roamed his features, as if she saw him for the very first time. His pulse began to pound, for he glimpsed neither fear nor resentment.

"When you were ill, I fed you" — her voice was but a wisp — "like this."

Before he could utter a sound — before he gleaned her intention — she filled her mouth with wine from the goblet.

A hand upon his chest, she pushed him back to his elbows. She leaned over him, her hair cocooning them in a curtain of silk. When her lips met his, he needed no urging to part his own. When he did, a warm drizzle of wine trickled from her mouth to his.

Comprehension dawned in a flash. Gareth was shocked. Humbled that she had gone to such lengths to save his life.

It might have been a dream. Sweet Christ, some wanton, erotic dream. Desire churned his gut and he smothered a groan. It was the wine, he knew, that was responsible. It had wiped away her inhibitions. Yet at the same time, something in him soared giddily.

His hands tightened almost convulsively a dozen times. He had to fight to keep them from closing around her and fusing her mouth to his in a boundless kiss. But he sustained the impulse, and didn't withdraw. He swung to the heavens, then plunged back to earth. The urge to take what she offered so freely was strong in him.

For there was fire in her, the same fire he'd felt when first they kissed. Oh, she could pretend resistance. She could spout her outrage until the end of the earth. But she'd unwittingly given him a glimpse of the heat beneath the icy cold facade.

She kissed him until there was no more wine to give. Only then did she slowly relinquish the sizzling contact of their lips. Leaning back, she reached anew for the goblet. Gareth quickly set it aside.

"Oh, no," he said with an uneven laugh. "You've had enough wine for tonight, Gillian."

Rosy lips pouted up at him. A faint disappointment puckered her brow.

He lifted her to her feet. She swayed unsteadily, and he caught her. An arm beneath her knees, he swung her into his arms and carried her to the bed. She slipped an arm around his neck with a sigh. For a moment, Gareth stood unmoving at the bedside, selfishly reluctant to free her.

At last he eased her down. Her head

turned into the pillow. Her lashes fanned across her cheeks. He stared. She was asleep once more!

So much for his dreams of a night well-pleasured.

He divested her of her gown and slippers, tossing them aside, heedless of where they landed. A slow curl of heat unfurled in his belly as he stared down at her with undisguised yearning. Moonlight gilded her limbs, smooth and gleaming and ivory. He longed to wake with her slender legs deliciously entwined with his. Coral-hued nipples stood out against the cool night air; they begged to be kissed and sucked. He wanted to bend low and take those luscious peaks into his mouth, feel them grow hard and erect against the glide of his tongue.

She shifted. She angled one knee away from her body. 'Twas a pose that left the font of her womanhood open and unguarded, vulnerable to his boldly seeking gaze. He knew that, were he to reach out and explore those soft, pink folds, her internal heat would cling damply to his fingertips.

He had to force himself to look away, a stream of low, vivid curses on his lips. His head was pounding; an answering pulse throbbed heavily in his loins. Ah, but he was a fool, to torment himself so! She was here, naked and bare, with a sensual allure that beckoned to everything that was primitively male within. Before God, she was his wife . . .

But she was not yet his.

His laugh held a trace of self-derision. She tempted him beyond measure, almost past bearing. But he dismissed the scalding rush of desire that flamed in his veins, testing his willpower to the limit.

Oh, aye, her stubbornness taunted him. Her beauty of face and form held a fascination too strong to resist — nor did he wish to.

But he would not take her, not like this. He wanted her fully awake and aware. He wanted to make her moan into his mouth and feel her body cling to his, the velvet clasp of her secret cove clasped tight about his rigid member.

So it was that he shed his clothes and climbed into bed beside her. It was like their time in the cottage, only now they were naked. And she was his wife. Gathering her close against his side, he twined his fingers into her hair and tipped her face to his. He had to have just one more sampling of her lips . . .

In her sleep, she kissed him back. In her

sleep, she surrendered what she would not have in the cold light of day.

In time, he drew back. He was far from sated. But for now, this would do.

16

Gillian woke to the feel of swords clanging inside her skull and an incredible thirst. Trying to think was like slogging through a marsh. Lord, but she felt dreadful. And her mind was all amuddle. The events of last evening were vague. She remembered supper in the hall, coming upstairs and pouring wine . . . dear God, it was the wine!

Still half-asleep, she brought her hands up beneath the pillow and eased to her side. Though she was careful, pain shot through her forehead like a lance. She moaned and dragged her eyelids open.

She beheld the last thing in the world she wanted to find — her husband stretched out beside her.

Words were impossible to come by. They were lying face-to-face. Lazy amusement glimmered in those sea green depths.

301

"And how is milady feeling this morning?" he inquired.

His knowing smile was infuriating. He knew well indeed precisely how she felt, the goat.

"Your head aches abominably, does it not?"

"Aye." She fixed him with a venomous eye. She suspected he was enjoying this, and she thoroughly detested him! She had a sudden urge to deliver a blow to his nose and bloody it with her fist, as youths were wont to do when they were raucous and anxious to prove their mettle. Indeed, she told herself, she would have if she had the strength. He'd not be so smug then! Yet in the very next instant she was appalled. She was neither a youth nor raucous nor intent on proving anything. Never in her life had she been compelled to do anyone bodily harm as she had with him. Oh, but he was making a madwoman of her!

"Does your belly feel like a ship on a storm-tossed sea?"

"Nay," she muttered crossly. "Now go away." Her eyes closed. She didn't want to think, didn't want to deal with him when he chose to be difficult.

"Certainly," he said in all pleasantness.

He left the bed, hauling the sheet and coverlet with him as he rose. Even as his nudity struck her, chill wintry air washed over her like the brine of the sea.

She glanced down, then stared in horror as her gleaming flesh confronted her. 'Twas a calculated move, she realized, for she wore not a stitch. In her misery, her comprehension was muddled and slowed by several degrees.

She dove for the coverlet. Alarm flooded her. Her gaze swung to Gareth, who still stood at the side of the bed. Judging from his expression, he was awaiting her reaction.

Gillian balked. Cold fingers latched onto the fur coverlet. "Dear God," she said faintly. "Did you . . . did we . . ." Her heart was hammering. She couldn't go on, but she searched frantically through her string of memories of the night gone by. If they had . . . wouldn't she have remembered?

"Nay," he said softly. "I would have you an active participant, sweet."

Gillian gulped. "Then why am I . . ."

"Naked?"

She was right. He *was* enjoying this. That he had taken her clothing from her was obvious — and vastly disturbing. Save these past two nights, she'd never slept unclothed before in her life.

"Aye," she quavered.

Those green eyes gleamed. "My castle. My bed —" his smile was utterly wicked — "my way."

Gillian eyed him warily. She didn't like the sound of that.

"What do you mean?" she asked nervously.

The mattress dipped as he sat, nearly tugging the fur from her desperate grip. "Only that from now on you will sleep without benefit of clothing in this bed, as will I. In a word . . . naked. Indeed, perhaps we should leave our clothing outside the door."

Gillian gaped. Surely he wasn't serious!

His laugh was hearty and deep — and so very, very different from the fierce and formidable man who had been so bent on taking her virginity the night they wed. Hearing it, Gillian felt something catch at her heart.

"Rest easy, wife," he stated brashly. "Only in bed must we be naked — unless you choose otherwise, of course." That cursed fingertip now trespassed along her collarbone, running back and forth. "The winters here at Sommerfield can be cold," he said mildly, then winked. " 'Twill be warmer, I promise you."

Gillian stared at him leerily. The turnabout in his mood was disturbing. What was behind his sudden good humor?

"And speaking of clothes, up with you, milady," he went on. "I've grown tired of seeing you in that detestable gown — that and the other. We're going to the market fair in a nearby village to buy some cloth for you today."

Heedless of his state of undress, he strode to the shutters and threw them wide. Gillian pulled her arm over her eyes to evade the light. The dull pounding in her head wouldn't go away. She didn't want to rise, so she swatted at him in annoyance when he dragged the covers away once more, but it was no use.

And indeed, she did feel more ready to face the world after a bath. Together they descended the stairs to the hall. There were a few other latecomers there to break their fast, as they were. Robbie and his nurse were among them.

The boy's eyes lit up when he saw them. He jumped up and darted toward them as fast as his little legs would allow. "Papa," he cried.

Strong arms caught him high in the air. Robbie planted a wet, sloppy kiss on his father's lips. Gareth chuckled and leaned his forehead against the boy's, his expression incredibly soft.

An odd feeling crept around her chest. Watching him — watching *them* — she began to gain a glimmer of true understanding. His was a fiercely protective urge to shelter his child, to shield him from any and all harm, no matter the cost. He had, she thought with a painful twist of her heart, done the king's bidding for one reason and one reason alone.

His son.

He was a good father, a gentle father. The truth was there before her. Witnessing the tenderness between father and son, a pang shot through her. All at once Gillian couldn't help but feel the outsider.

She owed him . . . a great deal. She owed him her very life, though God help her, she wasn't entirely sure she could trust him! And, indeed, when his seed took root inside her, what would happen then? For it *would* happen, and the certainty made her tremble inside.

Her cheeks heated, and she excused herself, moving to the table before he could see.

It was decided that Robbie and his nurse would accompany them to the market. Gareth rode a prancing white stallion, with his son perched on the saddle before him. Gillian was given a gray palfrey with soft brown eyes that reminded her of a doe in the forest. Nurse trailed behind on a nag.

Gillian glanced at Gareth as they rode through an open field. "I thought perhaps you might ride the fine chestnut steed that carried us back to Sommerfield," she observed.

Gareth was not fooled by her comment. "Ah, but the chestnut is no longer in my possession," he said smoothly. "I sent one of my men to return him to the inn where we found him — and with ample recompense, as I promised."

Gillian made no reply, but she was pleased.

In the next village, they left their horses at a stable near the town square. Once they were outside again, Robbie slipped his hand into his father's, then gave it a tug.

"Papa."

"What is it, son?" Gareth stopped and looked down.

"Gillian is lonely," he said earnestly. "She needs a friend. Will you be her friend, Papa?"

Gillian blinked. *Oh, no,* she thought in horror, heartily embarrassed. She couldn't look at Gareth . . . yet she couldn't *not* look either . . .

His eyes were alight. "Ah, but I would be

delighted to be Gillian's friend." There was just the faintest emphasis on his last word. Robbie was too young to notice his suggestiveness, but Gillian did. She felt her cheeks go scarlet.

Once again she wondered at the change in his mood. If she was suspicious, she couldn't help it. He was up to something, something that did not bode well for her, she was certain.

"Then you must take her hand," Robbie directed earnestly.

"Gladly," Gareth murmured, his smile purely devilish. His hand caught hers. Lean brown fingers threaded through hers. His skin was like fire. Gillian longed to snatch it back, but she couldn't refuse the contact without hurting the little boy's feelings.

Robbie beamed.

They started down the street, Robbie on his right, Gillian on his left. Nurse and a guard were behind them.

The market fair was lively and bustling. Merchants called out for them to come inspect their wares, growing louder as they vied for the attentions of those who strolled by their stalls. Robbie stopped and stared in rapt absorption at the jugglers. A musician let him pluck the strings of his lute. He laughed delightedly, and Gareth tossed him a coin.

They found several stalls with fabric, side by side. Gillian picked out several sturdy ells of wool, and linen for a chemise. While Gareth paid for them, she wandered to the second. A lovely blue silk caught her eye. Gillian ran an admiring hand over it, marveling at its softness. It would make a stunning gown, but she shook her head, for the price the merchant wanted was ridiculously expensive.

"Do you like it?" Gareth's low voice rushed past her ear.

"Oh, aye, but —"

"Then 'tis yours."

He turned to the merchant, who grinned ear-to-ear when they left, for Gareth bought several more expensive ells as well.

Robbie soon grew tired, so Gareth sent him home with Nurse and the guard, along with the fabric they'd purchased. Once they were alone, she couldn't help but notice Gareth no longer held her hand. Not that it mattered, Gillian assured herself hastily. Indeed, she was glad to be rid of his touch.

Gareth had stopped to inspect a finely made leather saddle, and was now engaged in haggling with the merchant. Growing bored with the discussion, Gillian wandered away, idly looking over the wares on display.

Where the idea came from, Gillian was

never quite certain. Her mind began to turn. They were outside the castle. There were no guards, no sentries at the watch-tower . . .

The stable was very near.

She moved to the next merchant's stall, then glanced at Gareth.

He never even noticed.

Still another . . . and he had yet to look about for her.

She had reached the stable. Holding her breath, she bolted inside and found her palfrey's stall. The animal looked up lazily, munching a mouthful of hay. Gillian grabbed for the reins, but they slipped from her grasp.

"Gillian?"

Blessed be, it was him! If she stayed where she was, she would surely be discovered, for this was the first place he'd look — that was her one and only thought as she hurtled herself into the next stall, occupied by a spotted gelding. She ducked beneath its belly to the far corner. It was a large animal, large enough, she prayed, to hide her. . . .

And large enough to have expelled a con-siderable amount of waste . . . the scent of which arose all around her, choking her, making her eyes water.

She held her breath, afraid to move, to

make a sound, trying desperately not to gag. Her eyes flew wide as a pair of booted feet appeared. They paused and she squeezed her eyes shut, as if willing them to disappear.

"Come out, Gillian."

Gillian's heart plummeted. Her eyes opened. She smothered a moan, for her prayers had been for naught. Those boots were now squarely before her, braced slightly apart.

"I will not repeat myself. Come out now, Gillian."

It was the stench that drove her from her hiding place, not his imperious command. Her gaze started with his dusty boots, then climbed almost painstakingly to his features. He towered above her, dark and imposing and exuding such power and masculinity that she was sorely tempted to dive back into the stall. He was unsmiling, utterly formidable. Without a word, hard fingers closed around her arm, an iron manacle. She felt herself plucked upright.

A groom had suddenly appeared with both horses, but Gillian was not allowed to ride her palfrey. Instead, she was placed on his stallion in such a way that she nearly tumbled off. She had to clutch the animal's silky mane to right herself.

The entire way home, she could feel his rigid seat behind her. His arms bracketed her waist, but his forearms did not touch her.

Not a single word passed between them.

In the courtyard, he swung her down from his mount and set her jarringly upon her feet. A hand digging into her back, he marched her into the hall and up the stairs. He tossed something over his shoulder to a servant, but Gillian did not hear.

The reigning silence continued in his bedchamber. A cloying sensation clogged her throat. Gillian moved to stand near the fireplace.

Gareth didn't move at all.

He did not chastise her, nor condemn her. He merely looked at her, his lips ominously thin. His silence was more frightening than if he'd shouted and raged; it dispelled any inclination she might have had to defend herself, to explain. Yet what was there to say? She could provide no excuse — and she would not make one, she decided proudly.

There was a knock at the door. He opened it and a stream of servants walked in, each carrying a bucket of steaming water. One of them dragged out the wooden tub. The others emptied their buckets, then quickly withdrew. Stupidly, all Gillian could think was that the afternoon was an odd time for a bath.

The door closed. Still wearing that damnable mantle of silence, he approached. Lowering his eyes, his fingers went to the shoulder of her gown. Gillian batted at his hands. "I can do it," she cried.

He was undaunted. He raised neither his hands nor his gaze. Ignoring her, he dragged the gown from her shoulders. Gillian recoiled as a steely arm snaked around her waist, lifting her free of the ground. But he only lifted her away from the garment, then bent to pull off her slippers. When he was done, he scooped everything from the floor, strode to the shutters and pitched them out the window.

Her arms crossed over her breasts. Her jaw fell open. "What are you doing?"

"Your clothing has acquired a rather noxious odor, my love — and so have you."

"But now I have only one gown left!"

"A pity you didn't think of that before you crawled in the muck. At any rate, you will soon have an abundance of gowns" — his smile was but a parody — "as long as you sew quickly."

By now he'd reached her again. She was swept off her feet, then dumped without ceremony into the tub. Her head went under. She came up gasping, clawing the streaming hair from her eyes.

What she saw made her heart lurch. Piece by piece, Gareth's clothing dropped to the floor. Water sloshed as he proceeded to climb in. To her dismay, it was big enough for two, having been fashioned for a man's large frame. Leaning back, arms along the sides of the tub, he boldly met her shock with something akin to a leer.

Her nerves were wound so tautly she could have screamed. But she'd not allow him to know how disconcerted she was. He would only gloat. "Get out!" she shrilled.

He paid no heed, but angled his head and regarded her. "What would it take," he mused, "for you to welcome me as your husband?"

Her eyes blazed. "What would it take for me to be rid of you as a husband? Now leave me to bathe in peace, Gareth!"

"I think not, sweet. Indeed, you may recall I told you once that people not only bathe together" — those hard lips curled into a dangerous little smile — "but they bathe each other."

Gillian drew a sharp breath. Her face burned. Surely he wasn't serious. Yet she was very much afraid his deadly calm masked a will of iron. The edge in his tone was just as unnerving.

She tried to stand, to climb from the tub. An arm about her knees made her slip. She landed with a spray of water, horrified to find herself atop him! Her breasts were crushed against the hard wall of his chest. Her nipples abraded the dense dark fur that grew there. Her body was squarely between the vee of his legs; her loins nested intimately against his. She could feel the thickening swell of his sex there between her thighs.

With a gasp she scrambled back against the opposite side of the tub. But she didn't try to rise again.

His eyes had darkened. "Wash me," he said in a low, taut voice.

Gillian's eyes locked helplessly on his face. Her heart slammed against the walls of her chest.

"Gillian."

That dangerous smile had yet to leave his lips. She sensed his unwavering intent with all of her being. Her head was buzzing. There would be no reprieve, she realized dimly, and this . . . this was but a prelude.

A small square of cloth was pressed into her hands. She lathered it with soap, then jerkily made a swipe across his chest.

Lean fingers banded her wrist, stopping

her. Confused, Gillian looked up at him. "Slower," he said, gazing directly into her eyes. It was almost as if he dared her to go through with it.

The incline of her chin climbed, but inside she was quaking. Her first tentative touch on his shoulders almost made her snatch her hand back. He was so hot! It was impossible to wash him . . . and not touch him. Impossible not to look at him. Her fingertips encountered the bulging contours of his shoulders and arms, hard and solid. They skidded over the curling forest on his chest; it was slightly coarse, abrading her sensitive fingertips. She swallowed, for the task was not abhorrent to her at all. The water made the dense mat curl into little whorls. Indeed, 'twas almost mesmerizing. One last draw down his chest to his belly . . .

For the space of a heartbeat, she hovered uncertainly. Was she to bathe the part of him she couldn't see?

"Finish, sweet."

'Twas a challenge, pure and simple. Judging from the hard glitter in his gaze, she was well aware he'd not back down. Nay, he would allow her no quarter. His only desire now was to impose his will over hers.

Gillian swallowed. Water swirled around the ridge of his hips. His belly was flat and hard, covered with the same dark hair that grew so thickly on his chest. The prospect of cleansing him *there*, below the water line made her entire body go hot. She braved a quick, hasty glance; her eyes widened and her breath caught.

Despite the haze of bathwater, his maleness was clearly visible. His manhood was forged of iron . . . as he was forged of iron. It jutted out from between his thighs, a spear of bold, turgid flesh.

A paralyzing sensation closed her throat. The cloth dropped from nerveless fingers.

It was Gareth who rescued it. "Turn around," he said harshly.

Gillian obliged, unwilling to make further argument. But it was not to her satisfaction, for he pulled her back against him. She froze. She could feel him, every inch of him. The hard, hairy length of his legs were a vise around her own. Her buttocks . . . a fiery blush surely suffused the whole of her body, for she dare not even think where they were.

But his touch was almost impersonal as he twisted her hair into a long rope, and pushed it over her shoulder.

The cloth dipped into the water, and then he was soaping the slender length of her back, in slow, monotonous circles, then over the slope of her shoulder.

Now he had moved around to the front. Gillian was horrified to discover he'd discarded the cloth. She wanted to protest, but for the moment, speech seemed a skill she could not master. Slick with soap, his bare hands glided over her belly, unabashedly brazen, then up to her breasts. Time hung suspended while he hovered there, almost touching — but not quite — the aching tips that seemed to quiver and swell. Her heart took refuge in her throat. She was shocked to discover she wanted him to touch her there. She wanted to clamp his hands against her . . .

In perfect tempo, his fingertips grazed the swollen tips. Gillian couldn't look away as lean, brown fingers indulged in a tauntingly provocative rhythm. A jolt of pleasure shot through her, centered there in those hard pink buds, now straining toward his palms. The muscles in her belly tightened. Gareth's mouth was on her nape now. She shivered when his tongue raked across the very top of her spine. All at once she was aware of the pulsing of his rod against her buttocks.

Nay, she thought hazily. It was wrong. Surely he would not take her in the daylight. Not in the bath . . .

Indeed, Gareth was fast in the midst of a struggle of his own. Her shoulders were damp and glistening. The urge to turn her in his arms, to bind her hips in his hands and plunge her down upon his rod was almost more than he could bear. Sheer effort of will was all that stopped him. Reluctantly he disregarded the notion, for he knew that if he did, it would shock his lovely, innocent bride to her very core.

And it was no way to take a maid. But someday, he promised himself. Someday he would show her that there were many sides — and many ways — for a man and woman to make love.

But he had to have her. If he didn't, he would surely die in an agony of longing.

In a heartbeat he was on his feet, and her along with him. A linen towel whisked the dampness from them both. Catching firm, lush buttocks in his hands, he brought her high and tight against the vise of his thighs for one breathless moment, claiming her mouth in a blazing kiss, gritting his teeth against a pleasure so intense he almost spilled himself in that instant.

Gillian could feel the hunger in his kiss — along with the rise of her own traitorous longing. When he swept her high in his arms and laid her on the bed, she clung to his shoulders.

He stretched out beside her. His eyes were

no longer cold, but heated and searing. His fingers at her chin, he turned her mouth up to his. Over and over he kissed her, turning her blood to molten fire.

A hand coursed over the mounds of her breasts, leaving flames wherever he touched. His mouth followed the path his hands had taken, clear to the summit of one breast. Her pale flesh contrasted sharply with the bronze of his hand. Gillian couldn't look away as he cupped her burgeoning fullness in his head and took stark, wanton possession of one straining peak. His mouth closed around one dark coral center; the curl of his tongue traced it stiffly erect. Then he took it into his mouth and sucked strongly. She inhaled sharply, for she'd never experienced sensation so intense. Her hands came up to catch the back of his head, holding him there as he licked and teased and sucked first one and then the other, all the while playing with the other in the same evocative play, grazing and circling with the tips of his fingers.

She nearly cried out when he left her breasts to plant a kiss in the trough of her belly, taking up tiny droplets of water with his tongue.

Her breath rushed from her lungs. She felt so strange, so unlike herself. There was a heartbeat low in her belly, a questing rest-lessness there in the forbidden place between her thighs. She wanted . . . something. She knew not what . . .

But Gareth did. His fingers grazed over the hollow of her belly. She gasped, a sound of confusion, as his fingers slid with unerring intent through the thatch of dense, curling hairs that crowned the top of her thighs. Boldly his hand clamped possessively over her woman's mound.

"Gareth —" His name was a soft sound of confusion. She sought to tighten her thighs against his encroachment, but he would not be dissuaded.

Above her, he gave an odd little laugh. His breath hastened past her ear. "Stay with me, sweet. I promise I won't lead you astray."

Shockingly intimate, his fingers delved further, skimming her secret cleft, tracing the furrows of pink, pliant flesh that seemed to flower 'neath his ministrations. A single finger extended the exploration still further, searching out and finding a hidden nub of flesh she'd never known existed. His finger circled and rubbed, dipped and flirted — oh, a wanton, wicked torture she almost wished would never end.

Her breath was shallow and quick. Suddenly there was a sharp stab in her belly. Her head came off the pillow and she cried out.

Gareth raised his head. A faint sheen of sweat glimmered above his upper lip. Belatedly it occurred to him. . . . Before the haze of pleasure cleared her eyes, he grabbed the towel and slipped it beneath her hips.

"There can be no blood," he muttered. "Otherwise all will know there is no child yet."

He heard her breath catch, and then he was rising to his knees, guiding the head of his rod through damp, ebony fleece. Fleetingly he registered the frail barrier of her maidenhead, then he was shearing through it. At last he was fully inside her, his lance embraced, encompassed, enclosed by a tight, clinging sheath of velvet heat.

She felt it then. The power. The heat. The size of him. Felt the splitting resistance of her own body, parting beneath his rigid thickness with a stab of pain. But alas, his shaft was lodged deep in her body — a part of her now, she thought wildly.

She pushed at his shoulders, seeking desperately to twist away. A strangled cry broke from her throat. "No!" she cried. "No!"

Gareth didn't move. Dear God, he couldn't. His heart was hammering, his passion barely in check. Her squirming but made it the harder, for he could feel his passion searing his veins, setting his blood afire.

"Hush, sweet," he said hoarsely. "The pain will last but a moment, I swear." Reaching up, he laced her fingers with his. With his lips he smothered hers, kissing her until he felt her lips soften, the eddy of her breath swirling with his.

She trembled, suddenly afraid of the way she felt . . . afraid of the way he made her feel, so uncertain of herself. She'd been so certain she didn't want this — would never want it.

"Gareth, no. No . . ."

"Yes," he whispered against her mouth. "God, yes . . ." He could hold back no longer. He'd waited too long for this moment. Wanted her too much — and too long — to deny himself. Drawing back, he left her completely. Then he was breeching her anew, parting her anew, trapped to the hilt in the hot, velvet prison between her thighs.

Gillian's lips parted, but no sound emerged. His power was awesome, his heat scalding. She had deemed it impossible that she could ever hold his massive length without being torn in two, for she'd caught a glimpse of his staff, thick and rigid and straining. Yet this time she felt her body give way, closing tight around his turgid flesh as if she'd been made for him. Did she only imagine it . . . or could she feel the pulsing throb of his heart there, there where his rod lay rooted deep within her, so tight she could not breathe without being searingly aware of the way he possessed her so thoroughly.

"Look at me."

His dark whisper compelled compliance. Gareth's features were twisted in a grimace of tightly leashed restraint. His eyes were all a-glitter. The cords of his neck stood out. Only then did Gillian realize the strain he was under, the extent of his desire, the way he held back.

He lowered his head. "Don't fight me, Gillian. I won't hurt you. Just . . . don't fight me, for I cannot stop. God help me, I cannot . . ."

There was a ragged harshness to his voice. Hearing it, something gave way inside her. Imprisoned in the dark web of his burning gaze, her lips parted and her mouth was filled with the sweeping stroke of his tongue.

That first tearing pain had ebbed. She caught her breath when next she felt his rigid strength slide slowly inside her. Again, and yet again.

His hands swept down to catch her buttocks in his hands, lifting her, binding her to him in the place where their bodies enjoined. The driving rhythm of his hips quickened. A flame caught fire inside her. She felt possessed. Enflamed. Consumed. His fluid grace, the churning thrust of his body . . . she was engulfed in a raging inferno. Her mind encumbered by sensation, she twisted her fingers in the dark hair on his nape and arched her back . . . seeking . . .

A shudder ripped through him. The feel of her fingers scaling his back, her in-drawn breath at each carefully measured plunge of his body into hers, the sweet offering of her mouth . . . it was too much. There was a storm building inside him. He drove mindlessly deep, hard and wild, again and again, penetrating deeper and deeper with every thrust. Her moan sent him spinning over the edge. His seed spewed hotly forth. He exploded again and again, fire at the entrance to her womb.

In the aftermath, she hid her face in the hollow of his shoulder. Gareth's chest expanded in a laugh, the sound low and resonant. Whether she would admit it or not — and he strongly suspected she would not — her body told the truth. He knew he'd pleased her . . .

Gillian was galled that he made her go down for the evening meal. She was certain his absence had been duly noted; that everyone was aware they'd spent the afternoon in his bedchamber. Indeed, he had only to touch her and she'd melted in his arms. She was suddenly reminded of what he'd said the night they were wed . . .

Surrender need not be defeat.

Yet Gillian was not so certain. She had yielded so easily, and now despaired her body's weakness. She hated being a pawn. And perhaps it was wrong, but she salvaged what little remained of her pride by telling herself there was no way to battle such a man and win. He'd robbed her of what choice she might have had.

But in so doing, he'd saved her life.

After supper was served, Robbie crawled up in his father's lap. His green eyes agleam, the boy beamed at her before tugging at Gareth's tunic.

"I have a secret," he confided.

Gareth lowered his wine to the table. His eyes softened. "Do you now," he murmured. "Would you like to tell me your secret?"

Gillian cringed inside. Oh, no! Would he announce her disparagement of the king? For all that Marcus claimed Gareth's knights were loyal to him, the prospect made her uneasy.

Robbie crossed his arms over his small

chest and glowered. "No. If I tell you, it won't be a secret." He was plainly displeased. "And you should not ask, Papa."

Gareth's brows shot high, but then he nodded his agreement. "You are right, lad," he said gravely. "I should not have asked, but your answer pleases me. A man of honor would not reveal a secret he'd sworn to uphold — and I would teach you to be a man of honor, a man of true heart. I would teach you to be a man who will not lie, nor cheat, nor do harm to those who are weaker than you."

Ah, but was *he* a man of true heart? *Do not do harm to those who are weaker than you.* So he said. Yet did his deeds match the words? For he would have done harm to her — and to Clifton, a boy older than his son yet still a boy. An aching tightness settled around her heart. She couldn't bear the thought that Clifton had died at his hand. He claimed no knowledge of such a foul deed. Had he changed so much, then? Or had he changed not at all?

Perhaps the better question to ponder was this: What kind of man was he now?

It wasn't long before he arose, pulling Gillian with him to the entrance to the hall. "I am to relieve the guard tonight on the east tower."

Gillian frowned. "Why?" she queried.

"Have you a shortage of men?"

"Nay," he replied. "But now that I have returned, I will do my part alongside those of my men." He paused. "Perhaps before you retire you would be so good as to bring me something that I may eat later in the night."

She should have refused, she thought later, making her way up the drafty tower stairs with food in hand. A fierce wind billowed her mantle around her slender form and struck her full in the face as she stepped onto the narrow enclosure. Yet she couldn't help but admire his willingness to work beside his knights. His earlier words to Robbie echoed through her mind; she found herself conceding that such consideration revealed much about the man.

And she wondered anew if he was a man of true heart.

His shoulders broad beneath the heavy wool of his mantle, Gareth stood near an embrasure, gazing out into the night. The heavens were but a vast sea of gloomy, endless midnight. There was neither moon nor stars to light the sky. A wind-whipped fog curled eerily about the tower, and a heavy drizzle had begun to fall.

He turned at the sound of her slippers on the stairs. "Ah," he said lightly, "I'd begun to fear you'd forgotten me."

Gillian matched his tone. "And I fear I was not so lucky." She passed him the food and ale. Their fingers brushed. She felt his heat like a bolt of lightning, and started to quickly turn aside.

"What, wife? Will you not stay?"

" 'Tis raining," she complained.

His teeth flashed white in the darkness. He swept his cloak wide. "I would be only too happy to warm you."

"And I fear I must refuse." A smile twitched at her lips, a smile she couldn't withhold.

"Ah, later then . . . when I join you in our bed."

Gillian's smile vanished. Drat the man — and just when she was tempted to soften toward him.

She marched toward the stairs, her shoulders stiff.

"What, do you leave me already?"

Gillian compressed her lips. Oh, but he was so smug! Before God, she'd not grace him with a reply.

" 'Tis cold and damp," he called after her. "Do you not worry that I shall molder?"

She whirled and fixed him with a glare. "Oh, that I should be so blessed!" she snapped.

His hearty burst of laughter followed her all the way down the stairs.

17

The rains that plagued the latter half of January soon gave way to a frigid blast of winter that swept down from the north. There were many at Sommerfield who gave thanks that they had thus been spared a long, ferocious winter. But for nearly a month, snows blanketed the countryside and brought everyone crowding round the fire or huddled together in groups, seeking warmth wherever they could.

But these past days had seen a gradual lifting of the freeze and clearer skies. On this fine afternoon, the sun's rays had vanquished the morn's gauzy layer of clouds to gild the world below. After being confined indoors for so long, many of the castle residents ambled outside to enjoy the sunshine.

A host of knights and squires, among them Sir Marcus and Sir Bentley sat outside the armory, polishing the blades of their broadswords. Sunlight glinted off steel as they turned them this way and that. But they all leaped to their feet when Gillian passed by.

"What, good sirs! Would you do battle with me?" A hand fluttered to her chest; her eyes opened wide and she feigned great fear. "I must plead mercy, for I am but a defenseless woman."

Knights and squires alike caught their breath at the breathtaking smile the lady of the manor sent forth their way. Bareheaded, a cascade of ebony skeins spilling over the hood of her mantle, she was quite the loveliest picture the knights had laid eyes on this day.

"My lady," someone called. "Will you stay and watch us practice?"

Gillian hesitated, tempted to politely refuse. But then she chanced to catch a glimpse of Gareth, at the far end of the courtyard. He conversed with one of the masons, but every so often he glanced over at her. Even from this distance, she could see his scowl of displeasure; it but kindled the urge to prolong it. Did he think to control her every move, like the falcons in the mews who must remain leashed until they were trained — and then returned to their master, never to be free again?

She swept them a low curtsy. "I shall be happy to oblige, gentlemen."

Sir Bentley cocked a brow at Sir Marcus. "We shall go first," Bentley declared.

Sir Marcus swung his sword in a deft circle, a roguish smile on his lips. "I accept your challenge." He turned to Gillian. "You declare the victor, my lady."

Someone ran to fetch a stool for Gillian.

Together they took the field. A brief salute to her and the pair raised their weapons and shields aloft. Then the contest was on, each man eager to prove their strength and ability. They circled each other, then parried and thrust, forward and back, side to side, all the while gauging the other's weakness. But both were evenly matched in skill, height and breadth, and so the fight went on and on. Crouched low to the ground, Marcus spun fully around in a lightning-quick movement. Silver flashed through the air as he struck out. Bentley leaped high to avoid the blade. Gillian could stand it no longer.

"Oh, enough, please!" she cried. Her hands were pressed to rose-tinted cheeks. "Men may enjoy such sport, but I vow my heart stops every time your swords cross!"

"They but play like boys," shouted someone from the back. "If you want to see *real* swordplay, my lady, you should watch his lordship!"

Marcus and Bentley had ceased, stabbing the point of their swords in the frosty ground. They eyed each other, pretending affront toward the heckler. "And who do you think taught us what we know?" Marcus tossed back with a grin. "Why, we were his most proficient pupils."

"Aye," chimed in Bentley. "Why, we've been taught by the best!"

Gillian caught a flicker of movement at the corner of her eye. Someone else had joined the ring of knights. She stole a quick glance far afield. Gareth was absent from the spot where he'd been moments ago — and she had a very good idea where he'd gone.

Rising from the stool, she crossed to where Marcus and Bentley stood. There was just enough space for her to step between them. Slanting them a warm smile, she inclined her head and extended her hands, placing her fingers daintily in their gloved hands. "I commend you both on a job well done and declare you both victorious. And you are gracious indeed, both of you, to praise your lord's skill above your own. But surely you exaggerate my husband's prowess with the sword."

"Nay, lady!" someone protested. "Do you not know how he acquired much of his wealth?"

"I believe from his father and his father's father before him."

"Well, there is that," said Sir Godfrey with a chuckle. He stroked his beard. "But our lord also made his way from tournament to tournament. Oh, the purses he won, the ransoms he gained! There was no one like him, save William Marshal himself in his younger days!"

"Why, he could take on a dozen armed men all at once and fell them all before a minute was gone!" said another.

Slender black brows climbed high. "Indeed. That must account for his arrogance."

With that, Gareth strode toward her with long, lithe strides. "Nay, not arrogance, lady," he called. "I prefer to call it confidence."

Their eyes tangled. The soft line of her lips compressed. She could make no argument, for of a certainty he possessed an abundance of that trait as well!

He presented himself before her. Turning to his men, he raised a hand. "In all fairness, I fear some of those deeds still elude my mind. So no more tales of my illustrious deeds, lads, else my wife will decide she's wed to a god and not a man." He extended an elbow, "Shall we, my love?"

He missed nary a step as he escorted her from the field and into the great hall. Gillian quickened her pace as she sought to keep up with him; she took two for every one of his. They did not stop there, but continued up the stairs to the bedchamber.

He ushered her inside, then closed the door. Gillian shook off her mantle and laid it over a chair. She could feel his gaze digging like the prick of a dagger into her back. Determinedly she pretended to brush something off her bodice. With a swish of her skirts, she turned, as if she'd only become aware of his presence behind her. He stood with his arms crossed, the fingers of one hand drumming on one woolen covered bicep.

Pretending innocence, she tilted her head. "Is something wrong, my lord?"

No reply. But those lean brown fingers kept drumming . . . drumming . . .

"Well, my lord? Did you wish to speak to me?"

Still he said nothing, but he had yet to relieve her of his unbending gaze.

"Speak if you must, sir." Beneath the lightness of her tone was a faint gibe. "I lend rapturous ear to your every word."

His disapproval was evident. "I think you know very well what is wrong, my lady. You distract two of my finest knights with the sweet coercion of your smile, batting your lashes and lavishing them with your compliments." He snorted. "Preening like peacocks, the both of them!"

In all truth, Gillian knew not what came over her. "I was but passing by them on my way to the great hall," she demurred. "I merely stopped to speak with them; I stayed to admire their skill with the sword. Though I must say, there is much else to admire."

A pause, just for effect. "Sir Marcus is quite handsome, is he not? Ah, and Bentley has such a disarming smile. I confess, I know not which one I fancy more."

Gareth's eyes glinted. "There had best be no other man that captures your fancy, sweet."

This was beginning to prove rather enjoyable, Gillian decided. "You told me it would be in my best interest to get myself with child," she stated daringly. "You did not say it must be *your* child."

Gareth swore beneath his breath. Why, the little vixen! That she graced Marcus and Bentley with the seductive warmth of her smile incited something inside that could only be jealousy. With them, she laughed.

She flirted. But not with him, and it was like a thorn beneath his skin. She avoided him. It grated that she had yet to touch him of her own accord. He longed to feel the stroke of her hand upon his flesh, her mouth hot on the naked skin of his chest. Sliding across his belly. Tasting and exploring the velvet head of his rod with her small, wet tongue . . .

He cursed inside, for his thoughts had taken a direction he hadn't foreseen — and aye, was having a profound effect on that very part of him! He shifted uncomfortably, aware of the heavy heat of arousal straining his clothing. Aye, he thought darkly. He ached for her to offer her lips freely, without need of coaxing the heat he knew lurked beneath her cool exterior. Just once he longed for her to come to him.

Nay, not just once. Forever.

His thoughts grew stormy. By day she avoided him. By night she held herself aloof. She did not spurn him outright — yet she spurned him just the same! Many a time she pretended to be asleep. He would gather her close and she would hold herself stiffly. But he had only to toy with the tips of her breasts until they stood quiveringly hard and erect, for she was acutely responsive there . . . or caress the furrowed cleft between her thighs until his fingers were wet with the evidence of her arousal. And even when he was seated so deep inside her that every breath was his own, she battled her own pleasure, biting back her cries until her lips were almost raw . . . only to sleep nestled in his arms like a warm kitten the rest of the night.

Were it not for the dilemma with King John, he wouldn't have cared how soon his seed took hold in her womb — for now, 'twas an excuse to bed her and bed her often.

Still, Gareth was a prideful man.

"Some men are wont to share wives," he informed her curtly. "This one does not."

Gillian savored her victory, small though it was. A tiny smile curved her lips. "Could it be you are jealous, my lord?"

"Not in the least," he lied smoothly — and so convincingly her good humor vanished. "But while I am not jealous, I am a possessive man. And did I think you had thus betrayed me —"

"And what makes you think that I have not? Both Sir Marcus and Sir Bentley are very handsome and gallant."

This time it was he who smiled. "That is true. Yet despite that, I don't believe you would betray your husband."

Oh, that he was so certain! Still, the

sudden glint in his eyes gave her pause.

"And why not?" she asked coolly.

"Because I know you, wife —"

"Oh!" she cried. "You do not —"

"Oh, but I do." His vexation had given way to a leisurely air. "You are a woman who saved a man who was helpless. You gave him sustenance with your own lips . . ."

Gillian was aghast. How was it possible he knew when he'd been delirious with fever! "You — you knave!" she sputtered. "How can you know that?"

He threw back his head and laughed like the rogue he was! "It was you who told me, Gillian. It was you who showed me" — his eyes snared hers. That devilish smile widened — "the night you were sotted, my love."

Her cheeks flamed. Her entire body flamed. Never again, she vowed, would she imbibe so freely!

He advanced toward her, a predatory air about him. Gillian backed away, only to encounter the wall alongside the bed. She damned herself a fool, for she had done naught but aid him!

With precise deliberation he settled his palms flat against the wall, alongside her head. Gillian's heart bounded. She was trapped, she realized. The weight of his chest held her pinned to the wall. The entire length of her legs were trapped squarely between his.

"It occurs to me that perchance I'm neglecting you, that you should relish the company of my knights so — in particular Marcus and Bentley."

She drew a sharp, wary breath. "Gareth —"

His mouth hovered but a breath above hers. "Marcus and Bentley may long for you in their beds, but only I will have you, sweet. Only me . . ."

His mouth closed over hers. Yet even as a part of her was outraged at such presumption, 'twas a kiss that left her weak at the knees . . .

He dragged his mouth away, breathing hard. "Undress me."

"Nay!" She could never be so bold . . . or could she?

His gaze roved intently over her features. "You stripped me of my clothes once before. Why will you not do so now?"

She pushed ineffectually at his chest. "That was different. You were helpless."

A gleam appeared in those emerald eyes. "You could bind me," he suggested wickedly. "Then I would be helpless."

Gillian swallowed. His scent swirled all around — leather and wool and the musky male scent that was uniquely his own. A near painful heat collected deep within her, spreading to her limbs, to every part of her. He had only to look at her and the sizzling awareness she always felt with him raced to the surface.

But to take his clothes from him. Strip him, letting her hands drift over the contours of muscles hewn by long hours of swordplay and at the tiltyard. Oh, aye, she was tempted, so very tempted! But she possessed not the courage to show such boldness.

Something leaped in his eyes, something that made her tremble inside. Whenever he claimed her body, she could have sworn it was not a duty but rather more like a . . . a hunger. Was it lust? Her heart cried no. But it was as if he could not get enough of her . . .

There was no dissuading him. She had learned that. Never had she dreamed she might partake of such pleasure at a man's hands . . . at *his* hands. Yet always it was so. Like a drug. Seductive. Persuasive. Addictive.

Her fists curled against his chest, as if she were uncertain. As if she could not make up her mind . . . as if she were torn, as indeed she was. She longed to put aside the restlessness that burned within her at the sight of him. He'd married her only to rescue her from the king's clutches, she reminded herself. Or perhaps out of guilt. Even gratitude for saving his life.

There was an aching twinge in her breast. 'Twas not because of any tender feelings he harbored for her. And God above, she was afraid to want him so. Afraid this yearning inside would give way to something far deeper. How could she risk it, when he might never feel the same? How could she endure such hurt? To love . . . yet never be loved in return. She could not bear it, for it would truly be the end of all the hopes and dreams she'd cherished for so long. Oh, aye, she must shelter her heart closely.

Lowering her lashes, she turned her head aside. The move only bared the side of her neck, long and graceful. He wasted no time, but feasted there on the vulnerable hollow just behind her jaw, his lips a torment.

"Gareth," she said weakly. "Gareth, please."

He raised his head. His hands closed around the narrow curve of her waist, hard and warm. "Aye," he said, his eyes darkening. "That is what I would do, lady. Please you."

The next thing she knew, she'd been borne to the bed, divested of her clothing.

His boots dropped heavily to the floor. His tunic was ripped over his head and fell atop his boots.

Oh, that she was so bold, to stare at him so in the bright light of the day. Yet no matter . . . she couldn't tear her gaze away.

Her throat was suddenly parched. His was a warrior's body. Strong . . . Magnificent . . . Finely chiseled, his arms and shoulders cleanly sculpted, powerful and burnished. His shaft sprang free and untethered as he yanked away his hose . . . standing proudly erect, gloriously aroused, growing still more beneath her widening eyes. The very sight of it made her heart begin to pound.

Then she was caught fast in his embrace, his lips upon hers, fused in a hot, devouring kiss that leeched from her what little resistance remained. With hot, melting kisses he praised her, a steely thigh riding between her own.

With his hands he squeezed her breasts together. Her nipples thrust high and pink and round, irresistible fruit just waiting to be plucked. The contrast between deepening pink centers and pale ivory flesh delectably enticing. He whisked across each summit, relishing the way she gasped for the pure delight it evoked.

She heard his voice, a low, vibrant

whisper. "You have glorious breasts, sweet. The blush of a morning sunrise" — with his tongue he slowly polished the bud of one nipple, leaving it wantonly swollen, shiny and glistening with dampness — "I've never seen anything so beautiful."

Her fingers were on his nape. "Perhaps none that you remember," she said breathlessly.

"None come to mind. None but you."

His words gave her an undeniable thrill. Oh, she knew there had no doubt been other women in his life. He was older than she by half a score. His was a striking presence, arresting and powerful. Many a woman's head would be turned by just such a man. A treacherous little pain curled around her heart. Oh, not so much at the thought of Gareth with other women . . .

But with Celeste.

Even that thought was blotted from her mind as his mouth closed over first one stiffening peak, then the other. The sight of his mouth on her breasts was wildly sensuous. He suckled hard and long, a tugging she felt all the way to the center of her being.

But he was not yet done. His fingers twined intimately in the triangle of ebony fleece on her mound. With his lips he trailed a path down the silken hollow of her belly.

All at once he shifted. He was there between her knees; the breadth of his shoulders parted her wide. Her heart tripped over itself. What was this? she wondered dazedly. Her buttocks filled his palms, lifting her . . . Her mind reeled. Her eyes flew wide at the sight of his dark head poised at the juncture of her thighs.

Her fingers wound into his hair. She tugged desperately. "Gareth —"

Her cry caught halfway up her throat. Nay, she thought frantically. 'Twas impossible . . . unbelievable . . . that he would kiss her *there* . . .

He did far more than just kiss her.

His thumbs pulled wide the petals that enclosed her silken core. The first glance of his tongue was shattering. A bolt of lightning sheared through her.

The second was rawly intense.

Blistering flames shot through her. There was no stopping him. She clutched at his head, the golden skin of his shoulders. He was insistent. Commanding. The bold lick of his tongue darted between slick, dewy folds, brazenly torrid, a starkly erotic plundering that danced and swirled around the budding pearl hidden within . . . Grazing. Circling. Teasing. Almost . . . yet never quite there.

A moan broke from her lips. The sound only seemed to incite him further.

She could feel her hips rising. Questing. Desperate for an end to the elusive torture.

And when it came, there was a starburst of ecstasy, exploding from the inside out. Liquid heat spilled from her body. Dimly she heard herself cry out, again and again.

Gareth's blood was boiling. Desire pumped through him, a thrumming heartbeat in his loins as he stretched his length beside hers. Lean fingers tangled in her hair, tilting her face to his. Her eyes opened, glazed and smoky.

His head was roaring, his whisper almost fierce. "Did you enjoy that, sweet? Did I please you?"

Small fingertips came to rest on the raspy hardness of his cheek. "Aye," she said unsteadily, and then again, "Aye!"

When she realized what she'd said, her eyes flew wide. She would have ducked her head in shyness, if not for his fingers in her hair.

There was no room for shyness. Not now. The words, his closeness were almost more than he could bear. For this was how he'd dreamed of seeing her.

His hand captured hers — and so did his gaze. One by one, he curled her fingers around his shaft with the urging of his own. Her hand engulfed beneath his, he heard her ragged inhalation.

But when his hand left hers, she didn't withdraw.

His eyes squeezed shut. His belly clenched. The feel of her hand clasped tight around his rod was everything he'd known it would be. A jolt shot through him as dainty fingertips feathered over the velvet head, lingering for a heartstopping moment as she discovered the tiny cleft there at the surging tip. Inflamed almost past reason, his hands fisted at his side as he battled the need to tangle his hands in her hair. To guide her head down . . . down . . . to feel her silken tresses caressing his thighs, to feel his rising crown trapped in the hot, wet cave of her mouth . . .

His eyes flicked open. They sheared directly into hers. "Touch me," he said thickly. "Feel me . . ."

'Twas odd, how that low, vibrating plea lent her such boldness . . . how the feel of him there lent her such courage. Her heart beating high in her throat, she fitted her palm even more tightly around his flesh. He was so brazenly full, so stunningly aroused he stole her breath; not even if her other hand joined the first, she noted with a shiver of awe, could she have thus confined all of him . . .

His flesh was searing, so hot her skin felt scorched. Then she was squeezing, exploring his steely-ridged length, slowly gliding her hand up, then down. Guided by some erotic sense she didn't fully understand, spurred on by fever-bright green eyes, the rhythm of her hand began to quicken . . .

"Sweet Christ," he muttered, dragging her hand from his burning rod long, tortuous moments later. "Where did you learn that? Must I be jealous of Marcus and Bentley after all?"

Even as he spoke, he was above her. She could feel the hair-matted friction of his chest against her breasts, the way his muscled limbs widened and parted her own.

Gillian gasped, for she could feel the fiery probe of his lance demanding entrance. His eyes cleaved into hers . . . and so did his body.

She cried out as she felt herself stretched . . . impaled . . . filled with his swollen flesh until she could take no more.

He braced himself above her, his arms and shoulders flexed with strain, his eyes simmering with molten desire. "God help me, I cannot be slow and easy" — the pitch

of his voice was low and raggedly harsh —
"for you are a temptress, love. An irresistible temptress . . ."

His words ignited a fire within her. A
cramping excitement raced through her,
that she could arouse him so. Awash with
pleasure, Gillian could hold back no more
than he. Was it wicked, this floodtide of ecstasy churning inside her? Wanton? She
knew not. She cared not. For in that moment she cared naught about Celeste;
naught about the king or the world beyond
this chamber. All that mattered was him.
Gareth. The fever-pitch of hunger questing
within her; the fervent need to be with him
in this most intimate of ways . . .

Her fingers slid down the knotted tension
of his arms. With a moan she caught his
head, bringing his mouth to hers, churning
her hips against his in wordless, wanton
abandon. And he gave her what she sought.
Again and again, his thickened spear
plunged deep into her honeyed vessel, the
power of his thrusts such that she clutched
at his shoulders.

With every driving thrust, she climbed
closer to the heavens. Higher. Ever higher . . .

Her head fell back on the pillow. She was
wholly unconscious that the tiny little
whimpers filling the air were her own.

His mouth on the hollow of her throat, he gritted his teeth. His thrusts were wild. Torrid. The thunder of his heart pounded a drumming echo of hers. He tried to slow himself, to rein in the thunder that pulsed in his loins, to savor and prolong the exquisite pleasure of burying himself deep in the prison of her flesh.

He sought desperately to delay the climax building inside him, but blindly primeval urges had taken control. The grinding undulation of her hips — the splendor he knew awaited him — beckoned him near. Ever nearer. His breath grew harsh and rasping. Sweet Christ, he was steaming inside. Close . . . so very close.

"Gareth," she moaned. "Gareth . . . *Gareth!*"

He felt it then — the clinging spasms of her channel around his burning flesh. But it was her unbridled chanting of his name that sent him plummeting over the edge. He exploded with a scalding rush, again and again.

When it was over, he rolled to his back, bringing her close against his side. Spent, trembling, 'twas a very, very long time before either of them were able to move.

It was Gillian who stirred first. "Gareth?" she said timidly.

He kissed her palm and brought it to rest on the dark fur of his chest. "What, sweet?"

Her cheeks were scarlet. She could hardly bring herself to say it. "Was that . . . lust?"

He chuckled, the sound low and husky. She could feel the sound vibrate deep in his chest. Though she didn't want to, he made her look at him.

The veriest smile hovered on his lips. His eyes were sparkling, so very green her heart turned over.

"That, my dear Gillian, is a question you must judge for yourself. What might be lust for one . . . might well be something far different for another."

He kissed the tip of her nose before ambling from the bed. Gillian frowned, reaching to draw the covers over her body. She smothered a yawn, not inclined to leave the comfort of the bed so soon despite the hour.

His answer was really no help at all.

For if it was lust, she decided vaguely, she was likely destined to spend the afterlife in hell . . .

For God help her . . . it had surely been heaven.

18

In the weeks that passed since she'd first come to Sommerfield, Gillian had grown very attached to Robbie. From that very first day, when he'd peeped into her room, he'd captured a piece of her heart.

As the days passed, he often spent more time with Gillian than he did his nurse. Many a time he trailed behind her as she attended to the household needs. Sometimes in the afternoon, when she and Lynette were in the solar sewing or embroidering, he played contentedly at their feet. When they walked together, his chubby hand was nearly always in hers.

He was a beautiful child, with long-lashed emerald eyes and a shining cap of golden hair. When he grinned up at her, his eyes aglow, it never failed that something inside her melted. He loved it when Gillian took him in her lap and told him stories about the days of old — just as she'd once dreamed of telling her own sweet little girl — just as she prayed she someday would. And Gillian loved it too, for it was a feeling unlike anything she'd ever experienced — the coziness of his small, warm body snuggled against her own, seeking a tender hand, her warmth and comfort and care. He listened raptly, and sometimes he would fall asleep, but she rarely put him from her. She rocked him and sang to him . . . just as she'd dreamed of rocking her own sweet child. Indeed, these were the times she treasured most.

For despite everything, at times the uncertainty of her fate made dread coil tight in her middle. She was unable to banish all her misgivings. To all appearances, Gareth was a man of honor and valor.

As he'd once said to Robbie, a man of true heart . . .

Yet the shadowy apprehension within could not be wholly silenced . . . Gareth had once agreed to search her out and murder her — and Clifton.

'Twas at those times she couldn't extinguish a flicker of fear. To completely yield her trust as she had done . . . Did he protect her? Or was she a fool?

For the memory of the king's vengeance could never be fully put aside. It was an ever-present, ominous fear hidden deep inside. God, but she hated him! Would she ever be free of him?

She feared not.

The thought was as terrifying as ever.

Winter had begun its thaw. Warmer rains and days revived life to the frost-encrusted earth. All around the castle, shoots pushed through the ground. No longer was it brown and brittle. The world had begun to grow lush and green once more.

There was a small bench 'neath the window of the bedchamber. One day she chanced to see Gareth stride into the courtyard. Robbie was there with his nurse. When he spied Gareth, his little legs pumped furiously as he ran toward his father. Gareth scooped him high in his arms; one big hand gently cupped the back of Robbie's head as he said something to the boy. It was a silent, telling affirmation that bespoke his love for his son more clearly than words. All at once an aching band of tightness crept around Gillian's chest. When he looked at the lad, did he see Celeste in the boy? Was his longing for Celeste kindled anew?

Gareth had lowered the boy to his feet. Robbie picked up a long thin branch, brandishing it as if it were a sword, whipping it through the air. A wispy smile curled her lips as she remembered the day on the beach — faith, but it seemed so long ago! — when Gareth had done much the same. Robbie pretended to strike a blow at Gareth, poking at his thigh. The stick broke; Gareth slipped to the ground, sprawling on his back as if he were gravely wounded.

Even from here, she could see Robbie's grin. The boy moved close, but Gareth lay unmoving, utterly still. Finally he prodded him in the chest with a finger. All at once Gareth seized him and brought him down upon his chest. She could almost hear his squeal of delight.

A memory whispered in on tiptoe, black and bittersweet. She saw Clifton and her father outside the walls of Westerbrook, engaged in much the same, teasing play, that of two knights engaged in battle.

Moisture glazed her eyes. Her heart began to bleed. The memory wrenched at her. Father and son. Son and father. Never again would the two be reunited. As an awful dread twisted her insides, she was very much afraid that never again would *she* be reunited with her brother. . . .

Hugging her legs to her breast, she laid her head on her knees and wept. She knew not why, but her emotions lay perilously close to the surface these days.

It was in the midst of this heavy-hearted mood that Gareth returned to the chamber. Sharp green eyes immediately noted her unhappy pose, the startled way she jerked her head up, quick to brush the dampness from her cheeks.

It was too late. Gareth had already surmised her unhappiness. He crossed to her. His knuckles beneath her chin, he took in her red, swollen eyes, the tremor of her lips. Oh, she tried to hide it, but he knew.

"Why do you weep, Gillian?"

Her eyes grazed his. "I was thinking about Clifton," she said quietly.

Without a word, Gareth pulled her to her feet and into his arms. For the longest time, he simply held her, stroking her hair with his hand, his own eyes shadowed. Yet for Gillian, his comfort — his tenderness — unloosed all the tremulous fear locked deep inside.

The breath she drew was jagged. "Sometimes I think I cannot bear it," she confided, her voice half-stifled against his neck. "Not knowing where he is . . . if he is well . . . if he is even alive . . ."

The break in her voice tore at him. More than anything, he wished he could reassure her.

Alas, he could not.

His big hand stilled on her hair. "Gillian," he murmured, "It may sound cruel, but Clifton could be anywhere. Your father's man may have met with foul play. For your sake, I pray it is not true. But you should prepare yourself for the worst, that we may never know his fate —"

"Don't say that!" Eyes blazing, she wrenched herself away. His words splintered her heart, the depths of her being. "Perhaps you don't have the courage to tell me straight out that you —"

Gareth's jaw thrust out. He moved like silent lightning, seizing her shoulders and giving her a little shake. "Stop it, Gillian," he ordered tightly. "By God, cease, for I will hear no more!"

He released her so suddenly she stumbled a little.

Stalking to the fireplace, he presented her with his back. Strong hands linked behind his back, he gazed unblinkingly into the flames, the set of his shoulders stiff and proud. But his profile was tight and drawn, his rugged mouth a grim, straight line. She could almost see the bitter agitation that churned inside him.

A spasm of guilt and shame seeped through her. Ah, little wonder that he was frustrated with her! She was ever suspicious, ever doubting of him . . . ever accusing.

But the truth was now her own to confront. Had she ever truly feared him? Feared him as she did the king?

Perhaps for the fleeting spin of one breath to the next, such had crossed her mind . . . but in truth the answer was nay.

Had he ever harmed her?

Never, came the fervent echo in her heart.

Oh, aye, he could be fiercely compelling and demanding — as in the day he'd made her wed him! And aye, many a time he'd been angry with her — and her with him! But the emotions between them had always been strong — turbulent and stormy. Even the sizzling pull between them had rarely been peaceful or placid.

But it wasn't *him.* 'Twas the turmoil into which they'd been plunged.

Her feet carried her to his side 'ere she knew it. Lifting a tentative hand, her fingertips came to rest on the broad sweep of one shoulder. She could feel the tautness that gripped his body. She nearly cried out, for at her touch, he tensed further, as if in protest.

Her voice, when at last she found herself able to summon it, was pitched very low. "I'm sorry, Gareth. 'Tis just that . . . I feel so helpless." She swallowed, hating the way her voice wobbled. "He is so young and I fear you may be right. What if something happened and Alwin can no longer protect him? I know not what to do . . . yet to do nothing tears me apart inside. Waiting. Wondering. Sometimes I think I should ride out and try to find him myself —"

Gareth turned abruptly, his eyes flaming. "By God, I think not! Do you truly think me so callous and uncaring of my wife? 'Tis far too dangerous — and hardly a task for a woman."

His protectiveness startled her — and sent an odd thrill through her. Before Gillian could say a word, however, he was already speaking.

"Besides, there is no need. I have already done so."

Had she heard aright? She had girded herself against something far different . . . "What?" she said faintly. "You dispatched one of your men to search for Clifton?"

"Two."

Her lips parted. "Why didn't you tell me?"

"Because I didn't wish for you to stew and fret and worry even more," he said gruffly. " 'Tis risky, Gillian, so say nothing of this to anyone. King John has left well enough

359

alone thus far. But if he discovers we still search for Clifton, it may well revive his thirst for revenge."

A dire prediction, that. Gillian felt herself pale. He must have gleaned her distress for he gave an impatient explanation and pulled her roughly into his embrace.

Gillian's fingers curled into the fabric of his tunic. He could feel their icy coldness. As she clung to him, he felt her shudder; he was keenly aware of her grappling for composure, struggling against tears.

Gathering her more tightly against him, he rested his chin against dark, ebony curls. He would not speak aloud the bleakness that bled through him. She had weathered these past months with a strength and fortitude that many a man could not have endured. Yet he would not burden her more. Not now. She seemed so small, so defenseless.

In truth, he harbored but feeble hope of finding Clifton.

Less still of finding him alive.

As usual the next few days, Gillian spent the mornings with Robbie. On this particular morn, however, she felt as if she were a limp rag as she crawled from the bed. Robbie begged to walk outside, and she didn't have the heart to refuse his plea. They ended up near the rose garden on the other side of the chapel. Together they stooped low. Not a month past, the two had inspected the rows of thorny, barren stems. Robbie had bemoaned their loss. Gillian had laughed, and told him that in spite of winter's bite, they would bloom again, filling the air with sweet perfume. Before she could warn him, he'd extended a chubby hand and promptly pricked himself. As he howled, Gillian had gathered him against her breast and soothed him.

Now Gillian pointed out the stems that Robbie was convinced had no hope of life.

"There, Robbie. Look there." Her hands on her thighs, she nodded toward one of the bushes. "See the tiny new leaves? Before long, you shall be able to see the buds."

Green eyes widened in amazement; he nearly landed on his noggin twisting this way and that to stare at them. With a chuckle, Gillian reached out to steady him. His interest soon wandered elsewhere, and he scampered off to play in the grass nearby.

A wispy smile on her lips, she surveyed him for a moment. But as she started to rise, something strange happened. Blackness flashed before her. A vile, bitter taste burned her throat. She swayed, landing hard on her bottom. She felt so strange — hot, yet at the same time clammy and cold. Her heart was thudding as if she'd run up and down the tower stairs a dozen times.

She was hazily aware of Robbie's return. She could feel the damp earth beneath her side, but couldn't recall how she got there.

"Gillian?"

Gillian did not answer; she couldn't. Sun and sky veered crazily. She tried to reassure him, but she couldn't seem to speak or move.

"Gillian!" he cried.

She could not see him, for a foggy world of gray had enclosed her. But she could hear the fright in his voice. God, what was wrong, that she was so dizzy and weak? Gritting her teeth, she sought to rise once more.

"Get up, Gillian!" Robbie tugged at her, clearly aware that all was not right. "Gillian, please! Get up!"

God, she felt as if she were going to be sick. Her hand fluttered to the ground. "Robbie," she said faintly. "I'll be all right. Just wait . . ."

But the boy was already gone.

Moments later he tugged ferociously at his father's tunic. "Papa!" he cried. "Papa, come!"

Gareth was in the midst of a discussion

with the guards at the gatehouse. "Just a moment, son." He gestured at the boy distractedly. In the back of his mind, he told himself to remember to tell the lad it was rude to interrupt another's conversation.

"Now, Papa!" he screamed. "Come now!"

Gareth glanced down. His sharp rebuke withered on his lips. Tears were streaming from the boy's eyes.

He dropped to one knee. "Robbie!" he exclaimed. "What is it, lad?"

Robbie was sobbing so hard Gareth had difficulty understanding him. "She won't get up, Papa. She won't get up!"

"Who, Robbie? Gillian?" Comprehension dawned even as the boy's head bobbed furiously. He recalled seeing the boy and Gillian earlier.

His heart skipped a beat. "Show me, lad. Show me where she is."

Robbie took off at a dead run toward the chapel. Gareth was right behind him.

He swore when he saw her slumped on the ground in the rose garden. She lay curled on her side, her legs drawn up to her chest. Her face was ashen.

"Gillian," he said urgently. "Gillian!"

Gillian's eyes fluttered open. She struggled to focus. Gareth's image wavered before her, his rugged features dark, his expression almost wild. His voice came to her as if through layers of mist.

"Gillian. Can you hear me?"

She felt his hands on her and pushed them away. "I'm all right," she muttered. "Stop fussing over me."

Gareth's mouth compressed, but he withdrew his hands. "Can you rise?"

She nodded, hauling in a deep breath. Gareth helped her up, then released her. To her dismay, once she was upright, blackness surfaced once more. Her legs buckled beneath her.

Gareth reached out and caught her as she fell. Enough of her foolish stubbornness! Robbie's nurse had appeared, and he nodded for her to take him.

Gillian had no recollection of being carried inside. The next thing she knew, she was snug in Gareth's arms and he was moving through the door of the bedchamber. He closed it with his boot, then crossed to the bed.

He started to lower her, but all at once her stomach began to heave and roll violently. She clamped a hand to her belly. "I'm going to be sick!" she moaned.

And aye, she was, sitting in a most unladylike position on the floor, her back propped against the bed. Her skirts slid back on her thighs, for Gareth had thrust the chamberpot between her legs just in time.

She was spent and shaking when he lifted her onto the bed. He pressed a cup to her lips and ordered her to rinse and spit into a basin. Gillian obeyed, then sagged back, utterly drained. Gareth did not leave, but took a place beside her, wiping her face with a cool cloth. When he finished, he set it aside.

As always, she felt the pull of his gaze. She turned her head on the pillow to gaze at him. Why, he was smiling, the wretch! Never had she been so miserable in her life — and he would make light of it!

"Oh!" she gasped. "Do you enjoy seeing me like this?"

His knuckles skimmed down her cheek, resting there. "Don't you know why you're ill?"

Aye, she knew. Deep in her heart, she knew. But she had been afraid to believe it. Afraid to acknowledge it to Gareth. Afraid he would gloat . . .

As it appeared he did now, for he still wore that abominable smile.

"Gillian," he said softly, " 'tis the babe you carry."

Her bewildered astonishment made him want to chuckle. He suspected he didn't dare.

"I know," she said testily. "But how do *you* know?"

"You've not had your courses since we've been here at Sommerfield," he said calmly. "I know. I watched for it."

His bluntness shocked her to the core.

"My guess is that you quickened almost at once." A light danced in his eyes. "Perhaps even the very first time we lay together." He laid his hand on her belly. "I suspect you're nearly three months gone."

"Three months!" She tried her best to glare at him.

"There have been changes in you," he said simply. "Have you not noticed?"

"Changes?" Her heart was beating madly. Somewhere inside her, she knew he was right.

"I fear there is no delicate way to put this." He paused deliberately. A brow climbed aloft. "Your breasts, love. They have grown quite . . . ample." His lips twitched. "They strain the fabric of your gowns . . . but quite enticingly, I might add."

Gillian colored hotly and dragged her arms across her chest. She *had* noticed. For a time, she'd thought she was merely growing fat. Indeed, she'd let out the seams in several gowns lest they burst. But she'd had no idea that *he* noticed. And if he had, had anyone else?

Lean fingers wound around her wrists and pulled them away. He bent low, his aim unerring. Through the cloth of her gown, his tongue ringed the very peak of first one ripe mound, then the other. When he raised his head, his grin was purely wicked.

"And there, my love . . . I've noticed you feel quite plump and full in my mouth . . . and are you not more acutely sensitive there as well?"

Gillian sputtered. It was true, her nipples had been more sensitive — oh, for a long time now! Sometimes her breasts had even ached in a way that had never happened before. She hadn't known such things went hand-in-hand with pregnancy. Perhaps she should have, but she hadn't.

"Do not look at me like that, you swaggering oaf! You boast to the king that I am with child when my womb is empty yet now I am three months gone! . . . Why must everything come so easily for you? And how is it you know so much about a woman with child?"

"It does not come easily. I've lost half my life, lady, for I remember but half." He tapped his head. "As for knowing such things about women . . ." He stopped. All at once his smile faded.

Gillian stared. "Aye, I suppose you

367

would," she said weakly. "This is not new to you. You were with Celeste when she carried Robbie —"

"Nay," he said, his tone oddly strained. "Not just Robbie."

Her gaze sharpened. His expression was strange. A half-formed suspicion winged through her.

"What, Gareth? Was there another babe?"

Holding her breath, she sat up slowly. He never even noticed. His gaze was fixed on a point beyond her shoulder. 'Twas as if he were in another place . . . another time.

"Aye," he said slowly. "Celeste was with child when she died."

Gillian caught her breath. "Dear God! Gareth, I'm sorry. I-I didn't know."

"How could you?" His tone was very low, almost hoarse. "I've only just remembered myself."

She looked at him sharply. A horrible thought clutched at her. "Did she die in childbirth?"

"Nay." He seemed to speak with difficulty. "She was like you, I think . . . several months gone. It was winter. She had been ill, I think. I remember . . . a pall hanging thick in the room. The smell of sickness. Being with her at the last. Hands clasped feebly within my own . . ."

368

A flicker of pain sped across his features — she was certain of it. His eyes closed, then opened. Whatever she had seen was gone.

He shook his head, "There is no more."

Gillian's chest ached. Oh, God. How sad. Her throat closed, raw with tears unshed. Both for his loss . . .

And her own.

"Did you love her?" she asked in a voice that ground her very heart.

His silence cleaved her cleanly in two.

She looked away, a suffocating heaviness in her breast. "I'm sorry," she said haltingly. "I should not have asked such a thing —"

"I don't know," he said softly.

Her gaze swung back to his. "What?"

"I cannot say that I loved her." His tone was very quiet, his expression somber. "I cannot say that I did not. If you had not told me I dreamed of a woman with golden hair — if I'd not been told that Robbie has the same pale hair, I would not know. I have tried to recall her, but I can summon neither face nor form. When I think of her, there is naught but a void."

He paused. "At times it happens just as it did at the cottage — a blink of an eye . . . and I recall with absolute certainty. At other times, 'tis as if a door has been left ajar, and the memories creep in, little by little. But

369

with Celeste, there has been naught to revive my days with her," he said again. For the longest time, he said nothing.

"What will come . . . will come," he said at last. "I have accepted that there are many things from my past I may never recall — and so should you, sweet."

Pierced by a bittersweet pang, Gillian regarded him. Did he lie? Did he seek to spare her? Yet what reason was there? It wasn't as if he loved her . . .

Suddenly it was all rushing out. "I know what you would say, Gareth . . . and yet, something inside tells me it must be awful for you, being here at Sommerfield without her."

"Why?" he said.

"You know why," she said painfully. The breath she drew scalded her lungs. "Your wife —"

With the press of blunted fingers on the swell of her lips, he halted her outburst. "Is you," he finished. "You are my wife, Gillian." He caught her in his arms and brought her against him, once again the commanding lord.

"Now come here, wife . . ."

Gillian clung to him — to his powerful strength — burying her head against his neck and stifling a jagged half-sob. He must have sensed the ragged tumult that crashed inside her, for he cradled her against him, easing down beside her on the bed. He stayed with her for a long while, in time tucking one arm beneath his head. His free hand idly sifted through her hair, occasionally catching a wayward lock and bringing it to his lips.

She must have dozed, for when she awoke, the sunlight was leeched from the sky. Shadows steeped the corners of the chamber.

Gareth was gone.

He did not make love to her that night. Gillian suffered the loss keenly, hating the doubt which crowded her breast. For she could not help but wonder . . .

. . . if the reason was Celeste.

19

In stark contrast to the loveliness of the previous day, the next was cloudy, the wind raw. Gareth had risen at dawn to begin the labors of the day. Gillian rose cautiously several hours later. As the day progressed, no more sickness plagued her, and for that she was glad.

It was early evening when the blare of a horn sounded. She glanced toward the gatehouse, thinking it was a group returned from the hunt. She was about to turn away as the body of men dismounted. But then two men disengaged themselves from the others and walked toward the hall.

Her heart lurched. Unless she was mistaken, the two were Lord Geoffrey Covington and Lord Roger Seymour.

Within the hour she knew for certain when Gareth strode into the room. "We have visitors," he announced. "Covington and Seymour."

"So I saw." Dark, slender brows arose. "Will they be staying the night?"

"Aye." Booted feet wide apart, he paused before her, an imposing figure garbed in shirt, leather vest, and tight hose that outlined the tautly muscled length of his legs.

Her chin came up. He was so tall she had to angle her neck to glimpse his face. Her hands knotted in her skirts. "I confess I'm curious. Is it me they seek, or you?"

Her gaze met his with a boldness that surpassed even her own expectation.

"I've been summoned by the king," he said curtly. "I ride with them in the morning to join him at Winchester for further detail."

Winchester was the royal castle where John's father, Henry, had shut away his wife Eleanor for sixteen long years. The shiver that went through Gillian was swiftly suppressed. In its stead was a stinging, heated resentment.

"Well," she stated coolly, "I wonder who it is he would have you murder this time."

Strong hands seized her shoulders, hauling her upright so suddenly she was robbed of breath.

Green eyes glittered as he cursed baldly. "Dammit, Gillian, but you are willful and stubborn. I begin to think you are not worth the trouble I've taken with you!"

Her feelings lay scattered to the winds. A part of her longed to throw herself into his arms and feel them close about her with the warmth and protectiveness that only he could give. But another part longed to pummel her fists against his chest and scream her outrage that he had invited the king's men to stay beneath this very roof.

It was that which won out. Her icy disdain pricked his temper and fired her own.

"Let me go, Gareth!"

He held her fast. Stormy green eyes flickered over her. "Not until we understand each other, milady. Now. Our supper awaits in the hall. We will go down together —"

"I will not sit at table with the king's men!"

The smile he offered was tight. "You will sit at table with the devil himself if I so decree, lady."

Their eyes locked. Her lips opened. A narrowed look from those green eyes squelched her retort, but not her rebellion.

He scowled. "Be civil," he growled. "That is all I ask."

With that he hooked his fingers into her elbows and pulled her from the room. Gillian simmered all the way down to the hall. He was right, she decided heatedly. Indeed, she *would* sit with the devil — all three of them!

Both men rose when they entered the room. Gillian greeted them politely.

Roger Seymour looked her boldly up and down. "You hide your child, well, madam. When do you expect it?"

Gillian stiffened. It was a trap. She knew it, as surely as she knew the man was a scoundrel of the highest degree — little wonder that he served King John.

Beside her, she felt Gareth's tautness. From the corner of her eye, she saw he was about to speak. But her answer was surprisingly ready at the fore. "The middle of September," she said smoothly. In truth, if Gareth was right, 'twould be nearly a month later . . .

Supper was a tense, strained affair. An icy knot coiled heavy in the pit of her stomach, so that she was scarcely able to eat.

During the meal, Geoffrey Covington leaned close. "My lady," he said, "why do I have the feeling we've met before?"

Gillian's gaze veered sharply to his face. He was a handsome man, with russet hair and steady brown eyes. She encountered no hint of either malice nor trickery in the manner of his gaze. It was Covington, she recalled, who had urged the king to stay his punishment. She would never have trusted him — after all, he served the king! But if Geoffrey Covington had been the only one present, she'd not have been quite so wary.

"I cannot say, sir," she said with a shake of her head. "I've never been to court. Indeed, I-I'd never even laid eyes on the king until his arrival here at Sommerfield."

"Ah," he said. "Then it seems I'm mistaken."

He spoke to her several other times throughout the long meal. Gillian was not the sort to be swayed by a handsome face and a winsome smile, but with his quietly engaging manner, somehow it wasn't as difficult to be gracious to him.

As for Roger Seymour . . . she disliked him. He frightened her. His black eyes put her in mind of a wild dog, mean and vicious, darting all around. At Westerbrook, she'd seen such a dog attack a peasant once. It took two men with swords to halt the dog's attack. The man had been covered in blood, his arm badly mangled.

Gareth touched her repeatedly during the meal, sliding a hand along the back of her chair, toying with a lock of hair that curled on her shoulder. He even pulled her hand onto his thigh and weaved his fingers through her own. Gillian clenched her teeth;

she'd not forgotten their bitter exchange upstairs. Not only that, but it was a daringly intimate gesture before others. Was it to needle her? Or for Covington and Seymour's benefit? No doubt 'twas a little of both. Outwardly she smiled; inwardly she smoldered.

By the time the last tray was served, her nerves were wound so tightly she wanted to scream. Her head ached horribly. She longed for nothing more than to escape to her room. Robbie had been present throughout the meal as well. When those at the table began to disperse, she murmured her intention to put the boy to bed; his nurse had been given leave to retire for the night.

His hand in hers, they made their way into the passageway off the hall. But she stopped short when she spied the silhouette of two figures a few footsteps away — a man and a woman. The angle was such that she couldn't make out his face. He had a woman pinned to the wall, his hand up her skirts, his mouth fastened greedily on hers.

Gillian glanced down at Robbie, who had yet to notice the pair. "Come," she said hastily. "Let us go the other way." It was in her mind to turn and tiptoe away, back to the hall. But then she heard a low moan.

It was not a moan of pleasure.

"Nay," the woman pleaded raggedly. Her voice was laden heavy with tears. "Please, nay!"

Gillian's gaze swung back over her shoulder. Her eyes widened. Why, it was Lynette . . .

Lynette had spied her. "My lady," she cried.

She did not stop to think, she simply acted. Springing forward, she grabbed a handful of the man's hair and yanked as hard as she could. His head snapped back and he yowled.

It was Seymour. As he whirled around to behold his attacker, his elbow came up and swung wide. It caught Gillian in the chest, sending her tumbling to the cold floor.

There was a blur. Robbie lunged forward, sinking his teeth into Seymour's thigh. Seymour grunted. The way his eyes widened in shock at the sight of his small assailant was immensely gratifying. But in the very next instant, he grabbed Robbie by the neck of his tunic and gave him a shove. The boy landed in a heap near Gillian. Gillian snatched him against her, enclosing him in her embrace, turning his body into hers, shielding him. Fire blazed in her eyes as she heaved herself upright. Flinging up her head, she bravely faced down Seymour's wrath.

Menace contorted his features. His lips drew back over his teeth in a snarl, just like the wild dog she'd likened him to.

"By Jesus Christ, I'll teach you, bitch," he swore. A meaty hand clenched into a fist, he drew back his hand.

His arm was caught and twisted behind his back. A hand like a vise wound around his wrist, the grip so merciless that his eyes bulged in pain.

"You've been offered the hospitality of my home, Seymour. But if you dare to lay a hand on my wife or my son — aye, even my wife's maid — it will be withdrawn. And I do believe I will have to kill you."

Sir Marcus and Covington stood near Gareth. He delivered his ultimatum calmly, yet there was something utterly forbidding about him just now.

Seymour was released. Gillian sensed that were Seymour to make one false move, Gareth would make good on his prediction.

Lynette had yet to move. She stood frozen, her palms flat against the wall, still gasping in fright. Marcus stepped forward. He took Robbie from Gillian's arms, then gently took Lynette's elbow and pulled her away.

It was Geoffrey who broke the tense, expectant silence with an uneasy laugh. "Well,

Seymour, 'twould seem you met your match in those two."

Seymour glared at him, then transferred his regard to Gareth. He nodded at Gillian, still rubbing his wrist.

"You ride with us on the morrow 'neath the king's banner, so I will defer to you in this, Sommerfield. Indeed, I doubt the wench is worth it!" He hitched his chin toward Lynette with a sneer. "As for your wife, I vow she is as treacherous as her father, the traitor! Since you are one of us, I'm surprised you've survived so many weeks with her — that she hasn't slit your throat in the dead of night!"

Gareth greeted this with a lazily observant smile. "I have no regrets, Seymour. I daresay she is a wife well pleased, as I am a husband well pleased." He reached for Gillian and brought her to his side. "Mayhap you should take note that you may find such a woman for yourself."

Gillian bristled, slightly indignant. Well pleased, was she? Well, she was that, but still . . .

Gareth inclined his head with a thin smile. "I bid you both good night, gentlemen, and I will see you in the morn."

With that Gillian found herself hustled toward the bedchamber. Gareth paused only to order that two sentries be posted outside Seymour's door.

In the bedchamber, she raised her brows. "Sentries, my lord, and two of them. Could it be you do not trust him?"

"Nay," he said curtly. He frowned, his gaze sliding over her. "Did he harm you?"

"Oh, so now he thinks to ask! As much as you will leave with him in the morn, would it matter if he did?"

His eyes narrowed. "Tell me, Gillian."

"Nay." It was her turn to be curt.

Folding his arms across his broad chest, he gave her a long, measuring look. "Will you see me off in the morning?"

"See you off? With the king's men at your side?" She turned away, unable to withhold her brittle condemnation.

Without a word Gareth pulled her around to face him, his displeasure unconcealed.

"Do you think I'm in league with the king?"

"I know that you are!" she said bitterly. "You are one of them! 'Tis just as Seymour stated — you will ride beneath his banner!"

"What would you have me do?" he demanded. "Deny him and bring his wrath down upon us both?"

"You have a point," she conceded stiffly. "Yet I wonder if you will ever remain his humble servant." It was unfair of her. Deep in her soul, Gillian knew it. But the bluster of emotions inside her would not be quieted. "It would seem as much as Seymour and Sommerfield, you are the king's pupp—"

"Do not say it," he warned through his teeth. "By God, Gillian, do not dare —"

She dared. "You are!" she flung at him recklessly. "You are the king's —"

His mouth crushed hers. Hot, demanding lips smothered the scathing denouncement 'ere she could finish. A sense of weightlessness assailed her as she felt herself lifted and borne to the bed. His big body followed her down.

With a gasp Gillian twisted her head away. His mouth slid down the slender column of her neck, dwelling with lingering awareness on the throbbing pulse at the base of her throat. Then his mouth was on hers again, reclaiming with stark possessiveness the kiss she would have withheld, boldly consuming. She made a sound of mute despair. Why was it always thus with him? He had only to touch her to make her his own — to make the world fall away and ignite a blistering heat that raced through her veins like wildfire. And he knew . . . *he knew!* For only when he felt the answering tremor of her lips beneath his did he raise his head.

He stared at her with burning eyes. She inhaled, the sound deep and jagged. "Why do you do this?" she asked with quavering voice and quivering heart. "You've accomplished what you set out to do — what had to be done. Your seed flourishes in my womb. I carry your child, Gareth, yours! So now there is no need for you to —"

His eyes darkened. "Need, she says. Why, she asks." His tone was utterly fierce. "Fever once raged throughout my body, Gillian. But now that fever is *you*. It blazes inside me, alight in my very soul. I would stay if I could, but I cannot. Do not deny me, for I would have this moment to carry in my heart those long, lonely nights away from you."

The fiery hold of his gaze trapped her as surely as the taut, powerful arms that engulfed her slender form. The timbre of his voice sent a shiver along the length of her spine. 'Twas not arrogance, not determination, but a questing, fiery desire that seared his eyes to emerald fire.

Gillian was helpless against it. Against him. Against her own desperate yearning. With a half-strangled cry of surrender, slender arms locked around his neck. Her angry hurt was forgotten. Everything was forgotten — the king and his men — everything but the desperate need that surged like a rising tide within her. She reveled in the way he crushed her against him, the wild, consuming way he kissed her. Her clothing was dispensed with, and then his own.

He rose above her. The sight of him made her weak inside. She was achingly aware of everything about him. He was darkly magnificent, all sleek, powerful grace. Her palms slid over the tight, gleaming contours of his shoulders, thrilling to the sleek, knotted strength of his arms and shoulders, fluid and tight beneath smooth, binding flesh. Unbidden, her small hand swept down . . . down to the steel lance that jutted between his thighs.

Heat stormed through her at the feel of him. Above her, he inhaled sharply and squeezed his eyes shut. She felt the thunder of his heart pounding against hers. Caught up in the same passionate frenzy she sensed in him, she watched as he splayed her legs wide.

His forehead rested against hers. "Take me inside you," he said raggedly. "Take my flesh within you . . ."

It was a heated, searing whisper. She could not deny him. She could not deny herself. Holding her breath, stunned by her boldness, small fingers curled around him and guided the velvet head of his shaft through damp, ebony curls.

Neither could look away as he came inside her. The sight was wanton. Erotic. The friction of her hot, silken sheath gripping tight around his swollen member drove them both half-mad. She felt the shudder that racked him, the grimace of pleasure that twisted his features as he buried himself deep with a single stroke. He pulled out, his spear wet and glistening with her honeyed dew, only to plunge again . . . and again.

His whisper touched her cheek. "Remember this, sweet. Remember *me* . . ."

She moaned as he thrust inside her, plunging again and again, the driving tempo of his thrusts shattering, as if he would pierce her very soul. Her nails carved into his shoulders as she held tight, afire in a crimson haze of passion.

"Gareth," she heard herself whisper, and then it was a cry: "Gareth!"

A cascade of rapture burst inside her, through her, a rapture so intense she cried out again and again. Above her, Gareth's entire body went taut. A groan erupted from his chest. The pulsing stream of his essence flooded her with liquid fire.

But that was not the end of the night.

'Twas just the beginning . . .

Near dawn she drifted into an exhausted slumber. It seemed she'd just closed her eyes when the sounds of movement filled the room. Struck by the awareness that Gareth's presence was glaringly absent, her eyes fluttered open.

He stood near the fire, towering and strong, dressed for travel. As he strapped his sword to his side, he glanced over and discovered her eyes wide open and upon him.

Half a dozen steps brought him to the bedside. His features revealed nothing of his thoughts. He gazed down at her, his manner distant.

"I must go," was all he said.

She sensed his impatience to be off. A wave of desolation swept over her. An oppressive heaviness settled on her chest. Bitterness bled through her like slow poison. If it was Celeste who still lay in his bed, would he have been so aloof and dispassionate? Nay. He'd have gathered her close and tight, lingered as long as he could.

The breath that filled her lungs was torture. "Begone then!" she cried. "The king awaits." She pressed her cheek into the pillow . . . and away from him.

His features tightened. He swore. "Dammit, Gillian!" Lean fingers gripped her chin and tipped it to his.

She tried to bat his hand away, but he held firm. The iron clench of his jaw bespoke his anger, that and the simmer of his eyes. A scalding rush of tears closed her throat, tears that lay perilously close to the surface. She swallowed them back, lest he see them. Lest he see inside her, lest he glimpse the tangled web of emotions that roiled within her.

Her tremulous control was fast eroding. He was so close she could feel the heat of his body warming her own. She longed to wrap her arms around him and cling, pleading that he stay.

"Leave," she choked out. "Please, Gareth . . . just leave!"

Something smoldered in his eyes, something she couldn't put a name to. The furs were brushed aside. She felt her mouth seared by the branding possession . . . and a fleeting kiss brushed on the smoothness of her belly.

"Look after yourself — and my babe."

The jangle of spurs came to her ears, the sharpness of booted heels across the floor . . . the click of the door.

It was her undoing.

Pain like a clamp grabbed hold, squeezing her very heart. What had she done? she thought brokenly. A scalding tear slipped down her cheek. All at once she was sobbing wildly, the sound raw and heartbroken.

Too late she despaired her reckless folly — her foolish, foolish pride. Throwing on her gown, heedless of the startled glances and the sleep-tumbled darkness of her hair, she sped to the courtyard . . .

Alas, her husband was already gone.

20

"Did Gareth love Celeste?"

Gillian and Lynette sat on the bench beneath the window in the bedchamber. It was several weeks after Gareth's departure that Gillian posed the question to her maid. For it was a question that was ever on her mind . . . as he was ever on her mind.

She put aside her embroidery to regard her maid.

Lynette was startled. Gillian witnessed the faint wariness that crept into Lynette's wide brown eyes. She hesitated. "My lady," she said awkwardly, "is that not a question that would best be answered by his lordship?"

Gillian folded her hands in her lap. "He is not here, Lynette. And he does not remember his feelings for her." She could be no less than honest with her maid. "But you know, don't you, Lynette?"

Lynette bit her lip, clearly in a quandary.

Gillian laid a hand on her shoulder. "Please tell me, Lynette, for I must know."

"Aye," Lynette said slowly. "He did love her — and she loved him."

Gillian's tone was very low. "Did love come before or after the marriage?"

Lynette's eyes were wide. "My lady —"

"Just tell me, Lynette. Please."

Lynette's eyes flitted away, then returned. "It came before." There was a pause. "Lady Celeste's father was on the verge of announcing her betrothal to another man when they met. They wed within the month."

A pang pierced Gillian's breast. No matter that she had girded herself for the answer — that somehow she'd known it all along — to hear it spoken aloud made her ache inside.

"Gareth recalled once that she was ill when she died," Gillian said quietly. "That she was with child."

A shadow darkened Lynette's expression. "Aye," she said softly. "It was nearly two winters past that she and Robbie took sick. They were both so ill, so pale. Wheezing and coughing . . . Lady Celeste was so afraid that Robbie would die, for he was so young. Yet in the end it was she who perished, along with the babe."

Gillian was quiet for a moment. "And Gareth?"

"He was not ill."

Did Lynette deliberately misunderstand? Did she seek to spare her feelings? Ah, but were her own so obvious then?

"Not that," Gillian said quickly. Through stringent effort she kept her voice even. "How was he after Lady Celeste's death?" She hesitated. "When King John was here, he said Gareth had grown harsh and cruel after the death of his wife."

Lynette was adamant. "Nay. Not harsh and cruel. Bitter, perhaps, at times impatient. Yet never was he cruel. And . . . oh, I do not mean to hurt you, but we all knew how deeply he mourned. His eyes were so empty, except when he was with Robbie."

Gillian smiled wistfully. "She was quite lovely, wasn't she?"

"That she was, my lady. Lovely in face and form, and loving in spirit as well. All who knew her loved her. She was kind and gentle and sweet" — all at once Lynette dropped to her knees before her — "as you are kind and sweet and gentle. The people of Sommerfield have come to love you just as they did the Lady Celeste, and-and so has my lord."

Gillian felt her eyes glaze over. "Oh, Lynette," she said with a faint catch in her voice, "you cannot know how it pleases me to hear you say so." Impulsively she reached out and hugged her maid. Lynette's eyes were suspiciously a-shimmer, too, when they drew back. They both laughed shakily and went on to other matters.

But even as her heart filled to overflowing, she felt like weeping. The depths of despair dragged at her. She could not bear to disappoint Lynette, and so she said nothing.

For what Lynette had said about Gareth was not true. Gareth had not come to love her. Indeed, she feared he never would . . .

Her mood that night was pensive. When she combed her hair that night, she picked up a long raven lock and let it trail across her palm. It was shiny and gleaming, soft and full of life as ever, for her pregnancy had not made her pale and wan, but for those few days before Gareth's departure.

But all at once a painful ache constricted her throat. She recalled the wild, desperate way he'd made love to her the night before he left, the fervent, passionate whisper breathed in her ear.

Do not deny me, he had said, *for I would have this moment to carry in my heart those long, lonely nights away from you. Remember this. Remember* me . . .

But did he? she wondered helplessly. He had loved Celeste, loved her with all his heart. He had loved Celeste, as he did not love *her*. And she couldn't stop herself from wondering afresh what would happen if he remembered his life with Celeste.

She tried to pretend it didn't matter, but it did. Was it wrong to envy Celeste, Celeste with her golden tresses and loving nature? Gillian could not delude herself — would not. Gareth had every reason to love Celeste.

Raw anguish spilled through her. He had given her his body. His seed. It might well be that his heart was locked away forever, along with his memory of Celeste.

And with that heartrending thought came another, one that was like a thorn being ground into her breast. Would he love her child less than he loved his son, his child with Celeste? Robbie had been a child created out of love.

And theirs had been created out of necessity.

The next morn, her pillow was still wet with tears.

The days of summer turned long and warm, yet still Gareth did not return. With every breath, she yearned to see her husband again. She began each day and ended each night by praying for his safety, for she trusted neither John nor his men.

In truth, it was Robbie who made the separation bearable, who claimed much of her time and energy. His exuberant laugh never failed to make her spirits climb. Indeed, it was Robbie with whom she shared the babe's first movements in her womb, for the child within her flourished, thickening her waist, swelling her belly and breasts.

Robbie had been playing with clay balls upon the floor, but soon climbed up beside her on the window seat. Gillian brought him close; he snuggled against her side. His chubby hand beneath hers, she shaped his palm to her womb. As if the babe knew exactly what she wanted, there was a fluttering movement there beneath that very spot. It came again, stronger this time.

Feeling it, Robbie gasped and snatched his hand back in alarm.

"Don't be afraid," she said with a soft laugh.

He sat up. With mingled curiosity and suspicion, he eyed her belly. "What is in there?"

"A babe grows inside me," she told him, "a babe that is your brother or sister."

"Is that why you grow fat?"

Gillian chuckled, for she knew he meant neither affront nor disrespect. "Aye, I suppose it is. But he must grow even more before he is born."

Robbie cocked his head to the side. "But how will he get out?"

Lynette was in the room as well. For an instant she was too shocked to say a word. She looked at Lynette blankly, whose eyes had gone as wide as hers. But then Lynette's shoulders began to heave in silent laughter.

Robbie was still waiting for an answer. "How will the babe get out?" he said again.

Gillian bit her lip. "Robbie . . ."

"Does Papa know?"

Gillian glanced at Lynette, whose eyes were sparkling. Lynette's brows arose, as if she, too, awaited an answer.

"Aye," she said weakly.

Robbie gazed at her calmly. "Perhaps he will tell me when he returns." All at once his childish lips puckered thoughtfully. "But wait. How did the babe get *in* your belly?"

Gillian was utterly mortified. She was certain her face was crimson, and she heartily wished she'd never broached the subject!

"Did he crawl?"

Gillian longed to sink through the floor. "Robbie, I-I cannot say. But I think you are right. 'Tis a good question between father and son."

"You seem much perplexed." Robbie crossed his arms over his small chest and nodded. "Perhaps you should ask Papa, too."

"Perhaps I should," she said faintly.

"Perhaps he will even *show* you."

Gillian didn't know whether to laugh or cry. *Indeed,* she thought vaguely, *he already had . . .*

"He showed me how to ride my pony, you know," Robbie boasted.

She gulped. "Your father is . . . a man of great knowledge and . . . and many abilities."

Lynette's shoulders were still shaking with barely restrained mirth as she exited the room. One thing was certain, Gillian decided. She would most assuredly *not* linger should Robbie pose such questions of Gareth in her presence.

One night a few days later, there came a knock on her door at midnight. She opened it to find Robbie's nurse standing there, with Robbie at her side.

"Forgive the intrusion, my lady," the woman said quickly, "but the little one here is fretting and refuses to sleep until he sees you. I'm sorry to be a bother, but he's most insistent."

Gillian had already opened the door wide. "It's no bother, Nurse. Robbie can spend the rest of the night with me." She glanced at Robbie. "Would you like that, my little lord?"

There was no need for an answer. Robbie was already inside, hiding his face against her legs and clutching her bedgown.

She bid his nurse good night, then closed the door. She lifted him into the bed, giving an exaggerated groan.

"My, but you're heavy. Why, you've grown so I daresay your papa will hardly recognize you."

The glimmer of a smile chased across his lips, but then it was gone. His eyes were red-rimmed and swollen — she could see he'd been crying. She climbed into bed and tugged the covers over them both. Something was wrong, she knew, but perhaps it would be best if he told her of his own accord.

She gathered him close, pressing a light kiss on his brow. He nestled against her side, his cheek plumped against her arm, his fist curled against the mound of her belly.

She hadn't long to wait. "Gillian," he whispered. "How long will you stay at Sommerfield?"

Taken aback by his question, Gillian went

still. Once she and Gareth were wed, once she was with child, she had always assumed that she would remain here after the babe's birth — indeed, the rest of her life. Yet for an instant, a flurry of panic assailed her. When the danger of King John was no more — she could not bear to think it might never be so! — what would happen then? Would Gareth want her gone? Her and the babe?

No. *No.* It was an answer pulled deep from the reaches of her soul. Aye, she hated that Gareth served the king, yet she could not fault him for it. In setting out after her and Clifton so many months ago, he sought only to protect his son. In marrying her, he sought only to protect her.

She would never know the man he had been. In all truth, *he* might never know the man he had been, for he might never recapture his past.

But she knew him for the man he was now. With every deed, with every word, with every touch, he had revealed himself as a man of honor and respect. A man of depth and feeling, of care and consideration.

Aye, it was duty that first brought him to her. Duty that bound him to her, the duty of a husband and father. He might never love her as he had loved Celeste, but Gareth would not abandon her.

He was not a man to forsake his duty.

And she could never leave him. For in this matter of trust that she had battled almost from the moment she'd tended him back in the cottage, there was suddenly no more doubt. She had yielded her life into his hands, and he had guarded it well.

He was her husband. Her heart. And if only someday he would come to love her. Love her the way he had loved Celeste . . .

Love her as she loved him.

But Robbie still awaited an answer. She smoothed his hair from his forehead.

"Always," she whispered. She blinked away a stinging rush of tears before Robbie could see. "I will be here always, Robbie."

"You won't leave me like my mother did?" His voice was small and quavering.

Her fingers stilled. "Robbie, why do you ask such a thing? Did someone say something?"

"Aye," he admitted woefully.

"Who?"

"Cedric, the wainwright's son. I told him . . . what you told me. That my mother was Lady Celeste, that she had gone to live with Our Lord in Heaven. But he laughed at me. He said my mother left me because she did not like me."

"Robbie, that is not true." She sat up,

twisting slightly so she faced him. She hunted for the right words, and prayed they would come. That it was a concept he was not too young to grasp. "Cedric is wrong. Your mother was indeed the Lady Celeste. She carried you here —" she pressed his little hand against her belly — "as I carry this babe. Your mother was your father's *first* wife. I told you that, too. Do you remember?"

Those woebegone eyes never left her face as he nodded.

"Your mother did not abandon you." Her conviction rang out. "She did not desert you. She was very ill and-and she died. She did not *choose* to leave you. And you need not tell Cedric, for I shall tell him myself."

She'd thought to reassure him, to convince him. But he remained utterly forlorn.

Her hands cradled his shoulders. "Robbie. Robbie, do you understand?"

"Aye," he said.

"Then what is wrong, love?"

With the back of his hand he scrubbed away the tear that splashed onto his cheek. "I still don't have a mother," he said in a wobbly little voice. "Unless . . . you will be my mother." He eased closer. Huge blue eyes searched her features. "*Will* you be my

400

mother?" he whispered. "And . . . may I call you Mama?"

Gillian stared down into his upturned face. *Robbie,* she thought shakily. *My dear, sweet boy. . . .*

She remembered the day he'd first come to her room, asking if she was his mother, and something inside her came undone. Nay, he was not a child of her flesh. She had not felt him move and kick and stir beneath her breast, as the child in her womb moved now.

Yet she couldn't have loved him more.

She loved him for his laughter and sweet nature, for the sheer delight she felt in holding him close . . . for the bounding joy he brought into her life. She loved him because he was Gareth's son . . .

And hers as well.

Shame pricked her soul then. All at once her jealousy of Celeste seemed so petty and small, for Celeste would never hold his small, sturdy body snug against her own. There was so much that Celeste had already missed. The way he played at swordplay with Gareth, a sight that never failed to make her smile. The way he grew straight and tall, even now.

Her heart twisted and tears spilled down her cheeks. She reached for him, gathering him tight against her breast. Her knuckles tenderly stroked his face. "Robbie," she said unsteadily, "are you sure that's what you want? To call me Mama?" She drew back to look at him.

"I do," he said promptly.

There was a glow inside her, spreading to every part of her. "I would like that very much, Robbie. So if it pleases you, it most certainly pleases me!" She hugged him long and hard, burying her chin in the golden cloud of his hair.

Finally she drew back. "Now, young sir" — she wagged a finger in mock admonishment — "I do believe it's time you slept."

His eyes had begun to sparkle anew. "Very well . . . Mama." With a mischievous giggle he dove across the bed.

Gillian snared him and gave a watery laugh. He snuggled against her, warm and content.

They both slept quite late the next morn.

"Papa is home!"

Less than a sennight later, Robbie whooped the announcement and charged from the hall into the courtyard.

Gillian had just come up from the storerooms where she had stowed away the spices the cook had used for the evening meal. Her eyes widened in dismay. Her hands flew to her cheeks.

"Tell me quickly, Lynette," she cried. "Is there dirt on my face? My chin?" She'd tied a ribbon around her hair to keep it from her face. No doubt she looked like a child! "My hair," she fretted. "I must comb my hair." She glanced down at her skirt and gasped. "Oh, heavens, I'm filthy! I must bathe —"

Lynette laughed at her. She stepped forward and briskly brushed away a cobweb from her skirts and straightened. "You look fine, my lady. Truly you do." Her lips twitched. "Besides, there is no time." With a lift of her brows and a nod, she gave a silent signal that someone had joined them.

Gillian swung about. The beat of her heart grew still.

Gareth stood in the doorway, holding Robbie. Hearty. Whole. So devastatingly handsome he made her quiver both inside and out.

Their eyes caught and held — endlessly, it seemed. Slowly he lowered Robbie to the floor and advanced toward her. The hold of his gaze had yet to release hers.

Nor could Gillian tear her eyes from his. The rush of feeling that swamped her made her feel liquid and weak. The world could have crumbled beneath her, and it would have been just the two of them. She couldn't have moved if red-hot flames had licked beneath her slippers.

And then he was before her. Close enough to reach out and touch. And oh, how she wanted to! She wanted to run her fingertips over the pleasantly abrasive roughness of his beard-stubbled jaw, the smoothness of his lips.

"You've gained some flesh," she blurted, eyeing his tall, powerful form. The width of his shoulders and depth of his chest strained the fabric of his tunic so there was nary a wrinkle.

A corner of his mouth turned up. He looked her up and down. "So have you, sweet."

She blushed hotly. "In different places, methinks." Her hand fluttered to her middle. Nearly three months had passed since they had seen each other. She knew she looked much different than when he'd left. "Robbie says I am fat."

"Hardly that," he scoffed. "You're more beautiful than ever." His gaze roved her face avidly — almost hungrily — sending her spirits aloft.

His gaze settled on her mouth, no doubt deepening her blush to a deep pink . . . and doubling the rhythm of her pulse.

Together they withdrew to the table, her hand nestled intimately into the crook of his arm, tucked there by strong, lean fingers.

His knights had already begun to file inside. Meat and ale were brought to the table while they spoke about all that had transpired in his absence. His men were eager to hear news of the outside world. When one of his knights queried him about the doings of the king, a light seemed to go out inside him. He was all at once very somber.

A hush went over the table as every eye turned upon him.

"The winds of unrest blow across the land, more strongly than ever. I fear for England," he said softly. "I fear for Sommerfield. I sought not to choose sides, not to rally behind the king, nor aid the rebels who fought against him. And now I am forced to wonder . . . was I wrong?"

"You did what you had to," Sir Godfrey said. "Ye gods, man, he had your son! You could not have stopped him from taking young Robbie hostage! His troops would have burned Sommerfield to the ground!"

Gareth raised a hand. "It pleases me to hear you say that, for once again, the king put me to the test. These many weeks, I do believe I've traveled every hill and valley of our land at least thrice. The king, you see, sought to have me curry favor with the barons in an attempt to win them back to his side, or so he claims."

Gareth's smile held no mirth. "Not an easy task, I assure you. In truth, many a time I was lucky to escape with my head, for there are some who still regard me with suspicion because I was not present at Running-Mead.

"Perhaps I should have been. Indeed, there are many who abandoned the cause when the Great Charter failed. But now the rest of the rebels rail against the king, and I fear they will tear this kingdom apart. They cannot rally themselves together as they should. Even now they still bicker and fight amongst themselves. And now there has come yet another threat to England."

"From France," Sir Marcus said quietly.

"Aye," Gareth said heavily. "The king regained the pope's good graces by promising that when the troubles with his barons has ended, he will lead an army to the Holy Land. Now the rebels are in disfavor with the Church. In fighting against John, they made an enemy of the pope. They are fools," he stated flatly, "all of them, and in their foolishness they appealed to Prince Louis of France to help defeat King John. But Louis's only intent is to seize England for himself! Indeed, he already controls a corner of the southeast. But the castles he took were not returned to the barons who requested his assistance. They were turned over to Louis's own men!"

A murmur of protest went up among the men. They glanced at each other and murmured their astonishment — and outrage.

"I must be honest. The king is capricious and unpredictable. He had entrusted much of his wealth to monasteries across the land. But now he travels with his gold and jewels as part of his procession." He paused a moment, then glanced around the table. "If John triumphs over the barons and Prince Louis, we all lose. Yet if Prince Louis prevails, we still lose.

"I do not pretend to have made all the right decisions. But we have choices to make, all of us, and I have made mine." His voice revealed his conviction. "I will not leave Sommerfield again. I have been gone far too long already. The king has laid seize to the castles of many of the rebels and I will not aid him in this. 'Tis every man for himself now. I will not surrender Sommerfield to King John, nor to Louis of France, nor to anyone. I will do whatever it takes to defend my home, my lands, my family and my people. I will not stop you, nor condemn you, should you decide to join the king's cause, or that of the rebels. Whatever your choice, you are free to leave."

For one long, perilous moment, there was a protracted silence. Gillian held her breath.

Marcus first arose, then Godfrey, and Bentley at almost the same instant. Within seconds, every knight was on his feet, his sword raised high. There came a bold, hearty cry.

"We stand behind you, milord!"

"Our loyalty is to you, milord — you and no other!"

It was a rousing, stirring display. Tears stung her eyes, tears of pride. What courage it must have taken, for Gareth to humble himself so before his own men!

Together, they put Robbie to bed a short while later, then climbed the stairs to the bedchamber. There, Gareth crossed to the hearth. He stood there for a long time, saying nothing, his back to her. Gillian frowned, for she sensed there was an air of guarded tension about him. She remained where she was, near the oaken door.

"Gareth," she said finally, "what is it?"

His shoulders hunched, then came stiffly down. He turned to face her, a pained reluctance reflected in the depths of his eyes.

There were deep lines of strain etched beside his mouth.

"I was in Cornwall," he said quietly, "near the coast. I stopped at the church to pay my respects at Brother Baldric's grave."

"And did you?" She dreaded what he would say next, though she tried not to.

"Nay. There was no grave, Gillian."

"What?" she said, stunned.

Gareth shook his head. "I spoke to Father Aidan. He said Brother Baldric's condition worsened after we left. He was on his deathbed. He administered last rites one night, and Brother Baldric asked him to leave. Father Aidan honored his request and left him alone." He paused. "The next morning, Brother Baldric was gone."

Gillian was puzzled. "So why is there no grave —"

"Nay, Gillian. He was *gone*. Sometime during the night he left the church. The next morning a man from the village found a trail down to the beach . . . not far from the cottage."

Numbly she regarded him. For a moment it was too much to comprehend . . . that Brother Baldric had cast himself into the waves. Or had he lain there until death — and the tide — carried him out to sea?

"Likely we'll never know why," Gareth

said softly. "Father Aidan did not understand it."

"He went out to die alone," she whispered. "He didn't want to be a burden." Yet all at once another thought occurred. Could it have been another reason, perhaps? Her mind veered straight to her father. Because Ellis of Westerbrook had taken his life, had Brother Baldric felt that he must as well?

But Gareth was right, she reflected achingly. They would never know why. Not now.

A tear escaped, then another and another. Gareth took a step forward, but she gave a quick shake of her head.

"Nay." Her voice caught, but did not break. " 'Tis hard at this moment, yet in my heart I've known he was dead all along. I will be all right. Truly."

He watched as she wiped away the tears. "There is more," he said finally.

Gillian stared. Something in his expression gave him away. Her heart began to hammer. Everything inside her wound into a coil.

"It has to do with the king, doesn't it?"

"Aye. He-he is mad, I think. Throughout his life he has flaunted God and the Church, yet now he fears Him. He knows he has sinned and wears the relics of saints about his neck, with the prayer that God will spare him. He fears he's being poisoned. He will not eat until his food and drink is tasted by one of his men. One moment he suspects everyone around him of plotting to seize the crown. The next he's convinced the assassin who escaped still seeks to kill him. Gillian, he has renewed his vow to capture the man who conspired with your father . . . and for Clifton."

Gillian paled. Her breath was painfully shallow. "And what of me?" she whispered.

"He said naught of you, Gillian. And by the bones of Christ, I vow you will come to no harm by the king or any of his men."

Gillian said nothing.

In unbroken silence Gareth's eyes captured hers. "Harken to me," he said into the quiet.

She didn't want to. Inside, she felt as if she were flying apart. But there was something in his tone that commanded she obey.

On shaky legs, she moved across the floor.

"Gillian" — he caught her hand, imprisoning both within his own. They were strong and masculine, those hands, and all at once she wanted to cry once more — "did you hear me, sweet?"

"Aye," she said woodenly.

"But you do not believe me."

She swallowed. " 'Tis not that," she said, her voice scarcely audible.

She tried to pull away. His grip tightened. "What then?"

Courage flagged, while fear climbed aloft. She could scarcely force a sound past the lump in her throat.

"Promise me," she said haltingly. "Promise me that if something happens to me that you will take care of our babe."

He swore. "Do not look like that. Nothing will happen to you, I swear."

Her eyes grazed his, then slid away.

He swore beneath his breath. A hard arm swept her close.

"Look at me, sweet."

Shimmering sapphire eyes lifted to his.

His eyes darkened. "Know that I am your husband. Know that I am yours." The timbre of his voice plunged to a whisper. "Know that I will never betray you."

21

Know that I am your husband.
Know that I am yours.
Know that I will never betray you.
Her heart squeezed. His vow vibrated all through her, making her tremble all over again. With a strangled sob, she buried her face in the hollow of his shoulder. Gareth tangled his fingers in her hair and tipped her head to his.

Her arms twined about his neck and clung. She raised tremulous lips to his in wordless offering. Gareth's eyes blazed fiercely. He made a sound low in his throat and then his mouth closed over hers. He was kissing her as she'd dreamed he would, with tender fierceness, with molten possessiveness. Drawn into the dark velvet world of desire, passion flooded through her and drowned her senses to all but the need that simmered inside her.

A lean, dark hand fell to her belly. His fingers splayed wide, so big it nearly encompassed the rounded swell where their babe curled within. Then before she knew what he was about, he was down on his knees before her, pushing her gown up and away, renewing his claim on her belly with both palms.

Gillian gasped, pushing at his shoulders. "Gareth, stop!"

He caught her hands and brought them to her sides. "Don't be shy, love. I've dreamed of seeing you like this."

Gillian was aghast. "Not quite like this, methinks!" She'd still been slim and narrow of waist when he left, but now she was round and plump.

"Ah, that's where you're wrong." His laugh was low and husky. His hands coursed boldly over the hard swell of her belly. "I've been starved for the sight of you. The taste of you." He kissed her belly. "You're beautiful," he whispered. "Beautiful and desirable and — Lord, how I've missed you!"

A sentiment she echoed with wholehearted fervor, she thought, and suddenly he was on his feet, bearing her high in his arms.

Small fingers rested on the abrasive squareness of his jaw. She smiled, feeling joy pour through her like sunlight blazing through a mist. "I've missed you, too, milord," she confided shyly, uncaring in that moment if he saw deep into her soul.

Gareth laughed, his eyes tender. "Methinks we should discuss this further, then." He laid her on the bed, impatiently shucking off his clothes.

Whatever embarrassment she had about him seeing her thus fluttered away beneath a torrent of scorching kisses and flaming caresses. Perhaps it was her pregnancy — perhaps the separation of time and distance between them — but she felt every touch to the bottom of her soul. She cried aloud at the instant he came inside her. His breath filled her mouth. His shaft filled her body, even as his child filled her womb.

The emptiness in her soul was no more.

Twice she spiraled to the heavens before his shuddering release came. She floated back slowly. Fingers that were immensely gentle brushed away the damp raven tendrils at her temples. He kissed her mouth with lingering sweetness, then cradled her close to his side.

It was before the evening meal a few days later, Robbie pouted when his nurse came to fetch him for bed. He pleaded and cajoled, but Gareth was firm. Finally Robbie frowned up at him from between his boots.

"A kiss and I shall go, Papa," he announced.

As always, Gareth's gaze as it rested on his son reflected the depth of his love. He leaned forward indulgently and planted a kiss on pursed red lips.

His hand very dark against the boy's fairness, he pinched his cheek. "Away with you, lad," he said in mock sternness.

Robbie's eyes gleamed impishly. "Nay," he said with a wrinkle of his nose. "Now a kiss from Mama."

Looking on, Gillian had been shaking her head and smiling, for she knew he was only trying to stall the inevitable. But at the boy's cheerful demand, her smile froze.

She'd been amazed at the ease with which the boy called her Mama — amazed at how natural it felt. But this was the first time that Gareth had heard Robbie address her as anything but Gillian.

She could feel the weight of his eyes residing on her profile. She felt suddenly stifled, but dared not show it.

Feigning a lightheartedness, she pressed a kiss on Robbie's lips. Happy now, he skipped away with his nurse.

Collecting all her courage, she ventured a

glance at Gareth. There was an odd expression on his face.

Her heart missed a beat. *Celeste.* He was thinking of Celeste.

"Do you mind that he calls me 'Mama'?" she asked quickly.

"Nay," he said. But neither approval nor disapproval resided in his tone.

Gillian swallowed. "You are not angry? It was while you were gone . . ." She felt compelled to explain. "The children were teasing him. They said that he did not have a mother. He was heartbroken, Gareth. When he asked, I-I could not refuse."

He studied her quietly. "Why would I be angry, Gillian?"

"Because I-I will be the only mother he knows," she blurted. "Me . . . and not Celeste!"

His gaze sharpened. Quietly he said, "And you think that would make me angry?"

She looked away, floundering. "Yes. No." She took a ragged breath. "Oh, heaven help me, I don't know!"

A shadow fell before her, then he was there, his knuckles beneath her chin. "Robbie loves you," he chided gently. "You care for him . . . as only a mother could care for him. And I know that you love him" —

the veriest smile curled his lips — "as only a mother could love him. How on earth could I ever be angry?"

Her eyes filled with tears. "But what about her?" Her lips were tremulous. "Would she have been angry, Gareth? Angry that her child calls another woman 'Mama'?"

Gareth caught his breath. His smile faded. For they both knew, without a word being spoken, who she meant.

Celeste.

And somewhere in his heart, Gareth knew that she was asking another question as well.

"I should like to think," he said softly, "that she would have given thanks — as I do — that her son was loved by a woman such as you."

Carefully he chose his words. Just as carefully, he pulled her into his arms. For somehow, his wife was very fragile right now, and God knew, he would not hurt her . . .

He couldn't tell her of the woman whose hair floated above her shoulders like summer sunshine, whose delicate image spun through his mind in that instant between one breath and the next, whose warmth and caring spun a circle of love around all those she touched.

Someday, perhaps, but not now. For now, it was enough to hold his wife in his arms. To bring her closer and feel the way her small fingers curled trustingly into the front of his tunic. With a sigh, Gareth gathered his precious wife to him, nestling his chin in a cloud of ebony waves. His hand captured hers, bringing it to his lips and pressing a kiss in the palm of her hand.

Gillian, he thought. My heart, my life.

Aye, he thought again. Someday, when the time was right . . .

For now, it was enough simply to remember.

The days of summer drew to a close. The crops were gathered in the fields. The days began to shorten; the nights were cool with a damp chill.

And the babe within her blossomed. He moved so solidly that sometimes he woke her in the dead of night. Many of the women of the castle told her she carried the babe high; indeed she did. Though she was not so ungainly that she was uncomfortable, she could not sit for long, else it was difficult to gain her breath.

She thought often of Brother Baldric and Clifton. She still found it puzzling, the way he had left his deathbed and Father Aidan.

Whatever had been in his mind? She mourned his death, and still missed him greatly — he had been a part of her life for so long! But she had come to accept his passing.

Far more difficult to accept was the possibility that Clifton might be dead. Indeed, she could not. Not yet. Somewhere in this world, she prayed, the summer had seen him enter his thirteenth year. Perhaps he was even a squire somewhere, a knight in training. Indeed, she could think of no finer man to instruct him in that task than her husband. Ah, if only it could have been so! And if only she could have sent word that he would soon be an uncle. . . .

Since his return, Gareth had been busy fortifying the castle defenses. Walls were inspected and mended by the mason. Supplies had been laid in, even before the autumn harvest. Several times Gillian glimpsed a brooding tautness about him as he scanned the horizon. His knights practiced daily, but without quite so much laughter. She knew he worried about the threat from without . . . the king's forces . . . or others.

But he was ever solicitous of the burden she carried, always there to slide a stool beneath her feet, to lend a hand when she needed it.

But Gillian couldn't banish the doubts that took hold and churned within her. Did he regret stepping in to save her from the king? Did he regret this marriage? Would he grow to resent her? He would be forever saddled with a babe he did not want, a wife he did not want.

And now that she was heavy with his child, did he protect her only because the babe she carried was his? What would happen when the babe was born? There would be no reason to withhold her from King John. Would he seek to be rid of her then?

Every look, every touch brought a painful swell of emotion to her breast.

Oh, he made love to her as passionately as ever. She cherished those nights, whether he held her in peace or in passion.

Yet never did he say he loved her.

If she could journey through his mind, what would she find? If it was true what all said, it was a love so great he would never love another . . . never love *her*.

Despair clogged her chest. Ah, but it was so hard to cling to any hope!

Sitting with Robbie one afternoon in the rose garden, she tucked him beneath the folds of her mantle when he shivered.

"I'm glad that Papa is home," he announced suddenly. "I didn't like it when he was gone."

She brushed a kiss across his brow. "Neither did I, Robbie."

For a moment, he stared at her. "I saw Papa kiss you once."

"Did you now?"

"Aye," he said solemnly. "Like this." He mashed his lips against the back of his hand, screwing his face into all manner of contortions.

Gillian smothered a laugh.

"Papa loves you, doesn't he? He must, to kiss you like that."

Her smile withered, along with a little of her heart. She couldn't say a word, but Robbie didn't seem to notice.

"You love him, too, don't you?"

Gillian wasn't prepared for the stark, rending pain that seared through her breast. And now Robbie was gazing at her in that innocent way only a child possessed, awaiting an answer.

"Aye," she whispered past the ache in her throat. "I love him, too. But let this be another secret between us . . . just for a while."

Emerald eyes gleamed. His head bobbed eagerly. Gillian blinked back tears and gathered him close. And it was almost as if she could hear her heart breaking . . .

★ ★ ★

Her time grew near.

Perhaps it was that which kindled a gnawing unease inside her. Or perhaps the way the castle continued preparations for its defenses. Whatever the reason, she was unsettled and uneasy these days.

And she had been dreaming of late. Always it was the same dream. It was the day before the attempt on the king's life, when she had heard another man in the counting room with her father — and seen his shadow. Her father was angry with her, shouting that she should not spy on him.

But that wasn't the way it had happened.

Papa had been angry. *Mention this to no one*, he'd said. And she hadn't, except to Brother Baldric . . .

She saw it again, a shadow high on the wall behind her father. There dwelled in her memory something elusive, something that tugged on the fringes of her mind, something vitally important.

Yet she could never quite place it, either in dreams, or the bright reality of day.

She tossed and turned one night. Gareth was not yet abed. It must have been well after midnight when her mind finally began to blur. But then came the creak of the door.

She woke with a start. Bolting upright, a sharp cry tore from her throat. But it was only Gareth, at last coming to bed.

He was at the bedside in an instant. "What, Gillian? Is it the babe?"

"Nay," she said shakily. "You startled me. And the babe will not come for nearly a month."

Strong arms closed about her.

"Do you think the king will send his hounds sniffing about to see when this babe is delivered?" Indeed, she half-expected Roger Seymour, black, venomous eyes agleam, to appear at the gates that very moment. She shuddered. "If this babe comes on time," she said unsteadily, "John will know that you lied."

Gareth brushed his knuckles across her cheek. "Do not trouble yourself. If that should come to pass, I will deal with it," he told. "But I do believe the king has more important matters to contend with."

She wasn't deceived by his dry tone. She was aware he sought to reassure her. Nonetheless, she prayed this babe would be early, for in his madness, she feared the king's wrath as much as ever.

Gareth pulled off his clothes and stretched out beside her, pulling her loosely into his embrace.

Do not trouble yourself, he said. If only it were so easy!

"Gareth?" she whispered.

"What, sweet?" He dropped a kiss on soft, crimson lips.

"There has been no word from the men you sent in search of Clifton, has there?"

"Nay." It was disclosed with clear reluctance. His tone was quietly troubled.

Gillian took a deep, fortifying breath, willing aside her pain. "The man who conspired with my father. Do you think the king will ever find him?"

"He hasn't yet. He is either very clever, as elusive as smoke. Or already dead."

A shiver went through her. "He was at Westerbrook with my father," she confided, "the day before the attempt on the king."

She'd shocked him. His arms about her grew taut and rigid. "You saw him?"

His sharpness frightened her. "Nay! Not really . . . they were in the counting room. A shadow, perhaps. No more."

"You said you knew nothing!"

"I don't," she cried. "I didn't see him! They were behind the curtain. I heard Papa say something about hunting. When I asked after the other man, he chastened me and said I was not to speak of it. It was only later I realized the man was the other assailant."

"Dammit, Gillian, why did you not tell me this before? Didn't you trust me?" His mouth twisted. "No, I don't suppose you did."

Her eyes cleaved to his. His expression was blackly fierce. Suddenly it was all she could do to hold back a sob.

Her mouth was tremulous. "I'm sorry. I didn't think it mattered. I didn't know him! 'Tis only of late I've begun to feel there is something I should have remembered." She drew a deep, racking breath. Something inside her seemed to crumple and fall. "Gareth, please don't be angry with me!"

Her control was tremulous, her beautiful mouth all atremble. Seeing her thus, he made a muffled exclamation. Strong arms engulfed her. He locked her tight against his side. She wrapped herself around his limbs, burying her mouth against the musky hollow of his throat, breathing in his warm, woodsy scent.

"I'm not angry, Gillian." He tucked her head beneath his chin. With his lips he nuzzled the fine skin at her temple. "But if there is anything else, you must tell me. Do not hide it from me."

She knew then . . . knew he feared for her. Feared for her safety. A shadow slipped over her. All at once she was fast in the grip of an ominous foreboding. She clung to him, and his hold tightened even more. Yet even the heat of his body, the shielding protectiveness of his body around hers, couldn't entirely vanquish the chill inside her breast.

Gareth gave strict orders that she was not to leave the walls of the castle. Gillian chafed at the confinement, but she understood his reasoning. Still, she was restive.

She had taken to walking nightly along the tower walls. The exercise kept her legs from cramping, and the solitude cleared her mind.

Seated at the table with his men, Gareth lifted his head with a frown when she arose. But she inclined her head toward the doorway that led into the courtyard, and up the tower stairs. He gave a nod and returned his attention to his men.

On this late September night, the air was damp with the nip of a recent rain, but the skies had begun to clear. A full moon hovered high in the sky, behind a silvery veil of clouds. A strong breeze billowed her mantle behind her, but she was not cold. There had been a nagging ache in her back throughout the day, and she paused. Her fingers came around to knead the hollow of her spine. Raising her face to the heavens, she took a deep, cleansing breath and allowed the solitude to seep within her bones and wash away the turbulence inside her.

An eerie prickle raised the hairs on her nape, a tingle that warned of a presence beside her own . . . a presence of evil. Her head turned slowly; it skidded through her mind that she was right.

The king had sent his hounds after all. But it was not Roger Seymour who stood behind her.

It was Geoffrey Covington.

22

"I've been expecting you, milady."

Slowly she turned to face him. She could scarcely hear for the pounding of her heart. She'd been right to be wary, she thought numbly. For there was something deadly in his eyes, something that made her go cold to the very tips of her fingers.

"Lord Covington," she said. "What are you doing here?"

Something passed across his handsome features, something she couldn't comprehend. Oddly enough, it was almost as if an air of sadness clung to him . . .

"I think you know, milady."

Ice swirled in her veins. "You mean to kill me," she said numbly.

"I fear I've no other choice."

Gillian's mind was whirling. He sounded bleak — almost resigned.

She wet her lips. "How did you get in?"

she heard herself whisper.

"I hid in a cart brought in by one of the villagers."

Fear began a rising spiral within her. Her nails dug into her palm . . . if she could only keep him talking, perhaps someone would come. Or if she could just dart past him. But she was no longer fleet of foot.

"I've been watching you, you know. You linger here upon the ramparts. You won't be missed for some time to come. The guards in the watchtower will not hear you cry out. The wind is too strong." He shook his head. "I do not relish this, Gillian. Indeed, I regret that I must do this. Truly I do."

Her eyes blazed. "Liar!" she hissed. "How could you harbor any regret when you serve a master who is as vicious as the devil himself!"

"Ah, milady. You do not understand. 'Tis not for the king that I must kill you. 'Tis to save my own neck. I've no desire to hang from the gibbet, as the king would have seen your father hang."

Her lips parted. "What do you mean?"

"Come, Gillian. Surely you know."

Her eyes widened. "Oh, God," she whispered. "It was you with my father . . . you are the other assassin."

"You don't understand, do you?"

Dazed, she stared at him. "Nay," she said faintly. "Nay!"

"I did it for England," Covington said softly. "For the good of the country."

"But that makes no sense! You were — are! — one of his closest advisors."

"Aye. At first I served him out of loyalty to the Crown. I remained because of that loyalty — and because I thought to sway him, to influence his decisions. But he is the monster everyone believes. He listens to no one. He heeds naught but his own interests."

"So you and my father plotted to kill him?"

"Yes. But I am not the callous, heartless man you think, Gillian. I abhor bloodshed. All we sought was to save England from his greed. There was no other way to be rid of John. Your father and I agreed. A single arrow to the heart. We were able to lure John away from his hunting party. And alas, if John's horse had not reared, if that blasted guard had not followed, it would have been done. But nothing went as planned. The guard had glimpsed two figures."

"And you went slinking back to John's side, no doubt pretending outrage, while my father fled for his life. Damn you!" she burst out. "You are a coward!"

431

"Oh, come now. It was I who advised the king that he must leave the forest and the shire at once, thus allowing your father's escape from the woods — and from Westerbrook later that night."

"To save your own hide . . . you didn't trust that if my father was captured, he wouldn't reveal you as his accomplice!"

Covington spread his hands wide. "What else was I to do? Do you think me a fool? John did not suspect me, but he is a sly one. I could not leave then else I'd have aroused suspicion. But later I remembered there was you . . . I didn't worry so much about Clifton. But when I learned your father had sent the two of you away, I wondered if he had told you of our plan to kill John.

"I confess, I've never seen the king so furious as when he discovered your father killed himself without revealing his accomplice. When he dispatched Gareth to do away with you and your brother, I was certain I would never be discovered. I was in a quandary when we returned here to find that Gareth had you in tow."

"So why didn't you kill me then?" she demanded.

He gave a tight little smile. "You are a beautiful woman, Gillian. I had no desire to taint my hands with your blood or the blood of your child. Nor did I wish to make an enemy of your husband. With you under Gareth's wing, John was content to let the matter rest. And I believed you when you told the king you knew naught of your father's attempt on the king's life — naught of his partner."

"Because it was true!" she challenged bitterly. "I heard someone in the counting room with him, but I didn't know it was you!"

"Ah, but now it's too late and you *do* know, dear girl. Only you and I know the truth — and you are the only one who might connect me with the assassination attempt. The king has vowed to find that man and I will not risk being discovered. John's reign is crumbling. His health is waning, but I will not allow myself to be accused of treason! Even if he dies, he still has many supporters who would see that I paid with my life."

"My father paid with his. 'Tis no more than you deserve!"

"And no more than you will get, I'm afraid."

"You bastard! My father died protecting you. He took his own life rather than reveal your name!"

"A brave and admirable man," Covington said smoothly. "A pity he had to die so ignobly. 'Twas an ugly sight, I gather." His smile was both crude and cruel. "But better him than me. Better *you* than me."

"But you'll not escape this time," she cried in heartfelt defiance. "Gareth will know what you did. He'll hunt you down and kill you —"

He laughed outright. "Your husband will never even know I was here," he taunted. His gaze fell on her swollen belly. His lip curled. "All will mourn your tragic plunge from atop the ramparts. A dreadful accident when you chanced to lean out too far. Made clumsy by your condition, you were unable to halt your fall. Ah," he mocked, "but 'tis a long way down, milady."

She lunged at him then, for if she was to die, by God, she would not yield to him so easily. She would fight, and struggle and scream, that Gareth would hear. That Gareth would somehow appear and discover his treachery. Her hands raised, she clawed at his face, feeling his skin rip beneath her nails. Enraged, he gave her a mighty shove, sending her hurtling forward. Gillian twisted slightly to avoid landing on her belly. There was no time to do more; her shoulder rammed into the stone, jarring her from head to toe.

Covington's lips flattened in a vicious

434

snarl. He bellowed like a bull. "By God, you'll pay for that, bitch!"

A hand balled into a massive fist. She braced herself, curling tightly around her middle, determined to protect the life within her, no matter the cost to herself.

"I warned Seymour once that he would pay with his life if he laid a hand on my wife, Covington. But yours, I fear, is already forfeit."

A hundred emotions swept over her in that mind-splitting instant. It was a voice more dear to her than the breath of life itself. Gareth stood in the shadows. He had come after her. Through some miracle, he had heard her prayers and come for her . . .

Gareth's attention was riveted upon Covington. It spun through her mind that Covington was right to fear him. His expression was fierce, his eyes cold as frost yet alight with the very fires of hell.

But Covington spun about. He dragged her onto her feet and began to drag her toward the ramparts — and certain death. Gillian twisted and turned but he was too strong for her. His arms were like a vise around her.

"Release her, Covington!"

Covington was breathing hard. "You can't stop me," he chortled.

They were nearing the edge now. The endless sweep of sky and stars loomed above. Fear clogged her throat. She could hear the lonely keening of the wind, moaning around the tower — like silent fingers of death before her, seeking to grasp at her, clutch at her and pull her into the vastness below. She fought desperately not to give in to it . . . fought the enveloping prison of Covington's hands. But he was so strong, and she could feel herself weakening with every breath.

But Gareth's voice was closer now. "I won't let you do this, Covington."

"Gareth!" she screamed, caring naught that her voice was thick with terror and tears.

Through the night, his eyes found hers. "I love you, sweet." Softly he spoke. So very softly . . . then the sound was carried aloft by the wind.

For the span of a heartbeat, their gazes collided — emerald and sapphire — both rife with a fierce leap of emotion. It was that, as much as the words, that spurred her forth. Her lungs heaving, she gathered everything inside her . . . and wrenched from Covington's hold.

Gareth needed no further opportunity.

Gillian landed hard upon the stone,

scraping her hands and knees. She twisted around in time to see sheer disbelief flit across Covington's features. His eyes reflected his shock. A hand clawed at his neck, seeking to dislodge the bejeweled dagger buried deep in his throat. He lurched almost drunkenly. His shoulder struck the ramparts.

Without a sound, he pitched over the ramparts to the courtyard below. There was a dull thud . . . and then nothing.

A piercing scream suddenly rent the air — her own, she realized numbly. Then all at once she was snug in a warm, familiar embrace. Quivering, trembling with shock and fear and the torrent of emotion that swirled inside her, she choked out his name.

"Gareth!" His name was a half-strangled cry. "Oh, God, I was afraid you would not come. Afraid that I would not live to see you again."

His chest rose and fell as raggedly as hers. With his hand he stroked tumbled skeins of hair.

"For the life of me, I cannot say what brought me here. I felt a flicker of disquiet almost as soon as you left the hall." All at once he crushed her against his chest. "Christ," he muttered, "to think I almost lost you."

Gillian clung to him. "Gareth, it was Covington all along. He was the one who plotted with my father to kill the king . . . he who was with him that day in the forest."

"I know, love. I heard."

Love. Her heart squeezed. She leaned back in the circle of his arms. The gesture speaking for her, she touched his lean cheek.

"Gareth," she said unsteadily. "Did I hear you aright? Do you truly . . . love me?" She was almost afraid to say it, to even breathe, for fear it had been naught but the desperate yearning held deep in her being. That she'd somehow imagined it.

The sound he made was part-laugh, part-groan. He carried her hand to his lips and pressed a kiss in her palm. Trapped in his gaze — as surely as she was trapped in his embrace — she couldn't look away.

"Aye," he said huskily. "I love you, Gillian. I love you quite madly."

"And — I love you. God above, I do!" She couldn't disguise the tiny break in her voice. "But what about Celeste? That day when Robbie called me 'Mama,' you remembered, didn't you? Please, do not spare me," she pleaded. "You remembered how much you loved her?"

She would have ducked her head, but Gareth wouldn't allow it. "Yes, I remem-

438

bered," he said softly. "But as God is my judge, what I felt for Celeste was as nothing compared to the way I love you, Gillian. You share my life, you rule my heart as no woman ever has . . . as no woman ever will. And if it takes the rest of my life to convince you, then so be it."

His confession made her want to weep for the joy that filled her breast. "Truly?" she whispered, her eyes clinging to his.

His eyes darkened. "Truly," he vowed.

A staggering wonder filled her. Like a burst of sunlight, it glimmered, shining, spreading its beacon to lift the shadows suspended within her for so long now.

"Gareth." His name was as shaky as her smile. "Oh, I love you so. I've loved you for so long now. But I was so afraid you could never love me . . ."

"What fools we've been, eh?"

She smiled through her tears. But when Gareth would have claimed the kiss so sweetly tendered by soft, tempting lips that hovered just beneath his own, she suddenly drew back.

One hand came around to the mound of her belly. "Oh, my," she said faintly. Her eyes sought his, her features rather puzzled.

Gareth's eyes flamed. A vile curse exploded. "Bedamned, that bastard hurt you, didn't he?"

His rage would have hurtled him to his feet, but she grabbed his sleeve. " 'Tis not that," she gasped.

"What then? Tell me, sweet." He bent over her. His hand came out to cover hers where it lay on her rounded middle. His eyes widened in slow-growing comprehension, yet there was a dazed, almost blank look in his eyes.

His mouth opened and closed. Not once, but twice, rousing a faint laugh from his wife, who had never before seen him speechless.

"My love?" she murmured.

"What?" he said weakly.

"I do believe I'd like to give birth to our babe in the comfort of our bed" — a barely restrained mirth tugged at her lips — "and not here upon this wretched tower."

So she advised . . . and so it was.

It was not a difficult birth as such things go, though Gillian panted and strained, and swore and sputtered that this might well be the last child she would ever bear. Gareth was there to lend encouragement throughout, wiping the sweat from her brow and gripping her hands when the pains were at their worst. And it was he who first held their daughter in his powerful embrace and placed her tenderly into the eager, outstretched arms of his wife. She cradled the tiny, squalling bundle tight against her heart. She pressed her lips to the babe's scalp — the babe's hair was dark as midnight, for how could it be otherwise? — and he saw the moisture that glazed her eyes and turned them to pure sapphire.

Watching her . . . watching them, Gareth felt an unfamiliar tightness in his chest. He knew why she cried. She'd been so afraid this day would never come to pass. That she might not live to see the birth of their child . . .

Dear God, so had he.

It was Robbie who chose the name Madeleine for the infant. And aye, both mother and father agreed it suited her well indeed.

The third week in October found Gillian sitting on a bench in the hall, nursing Madeleine. It was midafternoon, so the hall was nearly deserted. Gareth came to sit beside her. The babe had fallen asleep at her breast, and he brushed his lips across the crown of her head. Gillian waited expectantly, for she sensed he had something to tell her.

He took his hand in hers. "King John is dead," he said softly.

Gillian's lips parted. "How? Where?" was all she said.

"Illness claimed him. He and his troops were attempting to cross the sands near The Wash, a place where the river empties into the North Sea. John was the first to cross the shallows. 'Tis said he shouted impatiently for the rest of his train to follow; that the sea thundered and roared as the tide began to rise, surging into the river. A great torrent arose, flooding the wagons that followed behind John." A fleeting smile touched Gareth's lips. "He watched in horror as the carts carrying his coveted treasure — his precious gold and jewels, even the royal crown and scepter, were lost. All that he valued above all else was swept away by the fury of the sea and river."

Gillian shook her head. "Perhaps it was justice. The price of his avarice." She could pity him, but she could not mourn him. "What happened then?"

"With nary a word, he turned his horse to Swineshead, to the monastery. There he fell gravely ill with fever. He could ride no longer, but still pressed on to Newark, to the castle of the bishop of Lincoln." He paused. "Some said he was already dying. Some said

442

he knew he'd been beaten, that he could no longer hold his kingdom. Either way, he was never to rise again from his bed, for it was there he died."

She studied him quietly. "What will happen now, Gareth?"

"John's son Henry is now king."

"He is but a boy!"

"Aye. John appointed William Marshal as guardian to the lad. I believe the rebel barons will choose to stand behind Henry — and Marshal, for Marshal is probably the one man strong enough to oust the French. He remained loyal to John throughout his reign, but in the end, I believe only good will come of it. We will prevail, Gillian. I can feel it." His eyes rested warmly on her upturned face. He ran his thumb over the softness of her lips. "You're free, Gillian. *We* are free."

She blinked. "We are, aren't we?" she breathed wonderingly.

Gareth slipped an arm about her. Gladness spilled through her, and she rubbed her cheek against his shoulder in contentment, her heart singing.

But suddenly a pang shot through her. She tried to will it away, telling herself that the time for grieving was past — and she was thankful for so much! Gareth loved her, and she loved him. They had a beautiful daughter, and an equally beautiful son. But one thing dimmed her joy in the moment . . .

If only she knew that Clifton was alive, it would have been perfect.

Three months later, the weather had turned frigid. A chill wind blew, driving gray, billowing clouds to the east and bringing more. Yet within the bedchamber of the lord and lady of Sommerfield was a warmth that shut out even the most bitter cold — for it was lit by the searing passion of their love.

On the seat below the window, Gareth sat holding his wife in his arms, a blanket drawn around them both. Her head was pillowed on his chest, and his chin nested in the billowing cloud of her hair. Robbie played before the fire, while Madeleine slept in her cradle. Together they watched the activity in the courtyard begin to slow, for it would soon be night.

It was then he spied two hooded figures appear from beneath the towering arch of the gatehouse. A guard accompanied them; they stopped, and the guard pointed toward the entrance to the great hall.

The pair advanced.

"It seems we may have visitors tonight, sweet. Oh, but they are hardy souls to brave this blasted cold," he said with a laugh. "I daresay their arrival is most fortuitous" — he pointed out the snowflakes that had begun to drift from the sky — "for I vow we'll see a heavy snowfall by morn."

Never had Gareth turned away anyone who sought shelter on their travels. But it was a comfort to know that Gillian no longer feared the coming of the king and his men.

With a sigh he sat up. "Shall we greet them?" he murmured.

Gillian stretched and yielded her perch with as much reluctance as he. She turned her head and gazed toward the courtyard, eyeing the newcomers.

His wife's reaction was most perplexing.

She gave a stricken cry, then began to sob wildly.

His attention was drawn anew to the pair, who now mounted the stairs which led to the hall. Almost in unison they pushed back the hoods of their mantles. His regard sharpened. An exclamation of disbelief broke from his lips.

For one was Brother Baldric. And the other possessed a profile that was strikingly similar to his wife's. . . .

The reunion of brother and sister was accompanied by unheralded joy and tears. Mostly his wife's, Gareth reflected dryly. Clasped in her brother's arms, Gillian cried for the longest time. Gazing at the two, their dark heads nestled together, it was impossible to remain unmoved. Gareth felt his own throat tighten.

It was Clifton who finally cleared his throat and drew back, a trifle embarrassed, but not too proud to wipe his tears with the sleeve of his tunic. Gillian had already turned to Brother Baldric. Tears wet her cheeks anew.

A short time later, Gillian pressed Madeleine into her brother's arms. "Madeleine," she said to the babe, "I do believe it's time you met your Uncle Clifton."

Clifton stared down at the bundle tucked into his elbow, at the blue eyes and cap of shining dark hair. "Bedamned!" he said in amazement. "She looks like me!"

His sister looked shocked at the utterance. Clifton promptly colored to the roots of his hair, while everyone else laughed, including Brother Baldric. Madeleine yawned, raised a tiny fist and proceeded to drift asleep.

Two hours later they were still gathered round the table in the hall. Gillian listened intently while Clifton relayed all that had happened since the night he and Gillian had departed Westerbrook so long ago. Ellis's man Alwin had taken him to the shores of Ireland in order to escape King John's wrath. But alas, Alwin had fallen victim to illness and expired but a few months thereafter. Clifton had sought sanctuary in a monastery.

He cast a dubious glance at Brother Baldric. "I do believe," he finished, "that I am not given to a religious disposition."

They all laughed, including Brother Baldric.

He looked at Gillian then. "I regret that we could not return sooner and ease your worries, but we had no choice but to wait. When word reached Ireland of the king's death, we decided it would be safe to return to England."

Brother Baldric glanced at Gareth. " 'Tis glad I am to see that you kept your promise and kept Lady Gillian safely away from the king's hand. And somehow I am not surprised that you chose to marry her in order to do it."

Gareth took his wife's hand, his gaze tender as he carried it to his lips. "Ah, but that was not the only reason I married her."

Clifton blushed, while Brother Baldric cleared his throat. "So I see, milord." His gaze encompassed the cradle near the fire where Madeleine slept soundly. Nonetheless, his faded eyes gleamed his approval.

Clifton was thin from his ordeal, but Brother Baldric appeared more frail than ever. Gareth couldn't help but admire him, for it was his loyalty to Ellis of Westerbrook, and Gillian and Clifton, that gave him the strength to go on, a strength that burned from within . . . a strength that few men possessed. Gillian remarked upon it as well.

"Brother Baldric, I still cannot believe you are here. I was convinced we'd lost you, especially when Gareth learned from Father Aidan that you had left your deathbed."

"I thought I would die, too. But I did not," he said simply, "and I can think of only one reason why —"

"Do not tell me," Gillian interrupted with a smile. "'Twas God's will!"

"Indeed." Brother Baldric slipped his hands into his sleeves, his eyes twinkling.

A short time later, they all said their good nights; both Brother Baldric and Clifton were understandably exhausted from their journey.

Gareth and Gillian were soon snug in their bed as well. He slipped a finger beneath her chin.

"Are you happy, sweet?"

Her heart full of joy, she twined about his neck and gave him her answer with her lips. But after a moment, she drew back with a soft laugh.

Gareth cocked a brow aslant. "What do you find so amusing, wife?"

"I was just thinking of that long-ago day we found you on the beach, half-dead and half-drowned."

"Oh, aye. I can see why you would be much amused by that," he observed wryly.

"Brother Baldric wasn't entirely approving when I insisted on taking you back to the cottage. He wasn't certain you were worthy of saving — he thought you might be a scoundrel. But I knew he was wrong. Even then I believed in you."

His eyes incredibly soft, he kissed the corner of her lips. "And what did you believe, sweet?"

"I believed that you were a man of honor and truth. And I was right." Her tone deepened to huskiness. "For you, Gareth of Sommerfield, are a man of true heart . . . the truest heart."